Substance Abuse Assessment, Interventions and Treatment Series

MEN AND ADDICTIONS: NEW RESEARCH

SUBSTANCE ABUSE ASSESSMENT, INTERVENTIONS AND TREATMENT SERIES

Men and Addictions: New Research
Lyman J. Katlin (Editor)
2009 ISBN: 978-1-60692-098-5

Substance Abuse Assessment, Interventions and Treatment Series

MEN AND ADDICTIONS: NEW RESEARCH

LYMAN J. KATLIN
EDITOR

Nova Science Publishers, Inc.
New York

NOTICE TO THE READER

The Publisher has taken reasonable care in the preparation of this book, but makes no expressed or implied warranty of any kind and assumes no responsibility for any errors or omissions. No liability is assumed for incidental or consequential damages in connection with or arising out of information contained in this book. The Publisher shall not be liable for any special, consequential, or exemplary damages resulting, in whole or in part, from the readers' use of, or reliance upon, this material. Any parts of this book based on government reports are so indicated and copyright is claimed for those parts to the extent applicable to compilations of such works.

Independent verification should be sought for any data, advice or recommendations contained in this book. In addition, no responsibility is assumed by the publisher for any injury and/or damage to persons or property arising from any methods, products, instructions, ideas or otherwise contained in this publication.

This publication is designed to provide accurate and authoritative information with regard to the subject matter covered herein. It is sold with the clear understanding that the Publisher is not engaged in rendering legal or any other professional services. If legal or any other expert assistance is required, the services of a competent person should be sought. FROM A DECLARATION OF PARTICIPANTS JOINTLY ADOPTED BY A COMMITTEE OF THE AMERICAN BAR ASSOCIATION AND A COMMITTEE OF PUBLISHERS.

LIBRARY OF CONGRESS CATALOGING-IN-PUBLICATION DATA

Available upon request.

ISBN: 978-1-60692-098-5

HQ1088 .M38 2009

0134111906175

Men and addictions : new
    research
        c2009.

2009 10 19

Published by Nova Science Publishers, Inc. ✛ *New York*

CONTENTS

PREFACE

This new book focuses on men and addictions. Various studies have found that the vast majority of men over 12 years of age (82.6%) had used alcohol at least once in their lifetime. The data indicate that 9% of men reported heavy alcohol use (five or more drinks at one time in the previous month), compared to 2% of women. Approximately 34% of the samples reported using illicit drugs. Studies also indicate that drug use patterns vary significantly by racial and ethnic groupings. Men are more than twice as likely to develop substance use disorders as women. Men begin using substances earlier than women and have more opportunity to try drugs.Men suffer far more adverse consequences of substance abuse than women. Clearly, the social construction of masculinity plays a significant role in these statistics.Men's attitudes toward alcohol and drugs tend to be generally less negative than women's attitudes. expectations.

Co-occurring psychiatric disorders occur commonly among men.

Chapter 1 - Over the past thirty years a great deal of attention has been paid by psychology researchers to the psychological characteristics of athletes in many different sports. In addition, there has also been an increasing research focus on psychological issues relating to exercise activities. This has led to a great improvement in our understanding of sport and exercise psychology, but one activity that has been largely neglected despite it being both a competitive sport and a popular exercise activity is bodybuilding.

Chapter 2 - This chapter highlights clinical and research experience on the use of Seeking Safety therapy with men clients. Seeking Safety is a present-focused, coping skills model that addresses trauma and/or substance abuse, from the start of treatment. Its major goal is to help clients increase safety in their lives. The model was designed for both genders, and all types of traumas and substances. We describe how it has been implemented in various settings with men including mental health and substance abuse programs, veterans' hospitals, correctional settings, and residential treatment. The authors represent a range of clinicians and researchers who have conducted the model with men for many years. We describe key themes, treatment strategies, and research studies on Seeking Safety with men.

Chapter 3 - Personality scales of impulsiveness have been associated with discounting behavior. It has also been shown that nicotine has an effect on the performance of various tasks measuring impulsivity. This study has two main objectives: (1) to determine the relationship between the impulsive personality and the degrees to which delayed and uncertain monetary gains and losses are discounted, and (2) to examine whether the relationship between the impulsive personality and the four types of discounting differ between smokers and never smokers. 31 current smokers and 32 never smokers participated in this experiment. They were required to choose between immediate and delayed monetary gains (and losses), or between guaranteed and probabilistic rewards (or losses). Following completion of this task, they completed two personality questionnaires – Barratte's Impulsiveness Scale (BIS) and the Sensation Seeking Scale (SSS). Several BIS and SSS subscales were positively correlated with the degrees of discounting for delayed monetary gains and losses, but negatively correlated with uncertain monetary gains. Moreover, when dividing participants by smoking status, we found differences between smokers and never smokers in the correlation pattern between impulsive personality and the four types of discounting. Neuro-psychological bases of impulsive behavior, such as discounting behavior, may differ between smokers and never smokers.

Chapter 4 - Research suggests that a high prevalence of men with substance use problems have experienced sexual abuse at one point in their life. Men who have been sexually victimized frequently use substances to cope with unpleasant feelings resulting from the abuse, they experience many psychosocial problems and they tend to report sexual abuse much less than women. They also experience more extreme substance use than women with a history of sexual abuse. The present chapter reviews the prevalence and the significance of this problem, outlines significant gaps in the clinical and research literature, discusses the need for gender sensitive assessment approaches, and relevant treatment strategies specific to men that can enhance both substance use treatment and general functioning of these clients.

Chapter 5 - Conducted in Guadalajara, Mexico, the study focuses on patients' and physicians' beliefs about diabetes causality. The study was conducted in two stages and used cultural consensus model. First, qualitative interviews were conducted with a convenience sample of 28 Type 2 diabetes patients. On the basis of the elicited themes, 21 scenarios on diabetes causes were developed. In the second stage, a convenience sample of 46 Type 2 diabetes patients and 25 physicians working at the primary care level was recruited. Participants were asked to rate each scenario on a three-point scale. Scenario-type interviews were consensus analyzed using ANTHROPAC. Patients and physicians shared very different cultural models of diabetes causality. The patient model included emotional, environmental, some behavioral, and hereditary causes of diabetes. The physician model emphasized heredity as a single most important cause of diabetes. Differences between patient and physician views of diabetes causality may contribute to mistrust and miscommunication in medical interactions. There is a need for clinical practice that would include psychosocial stress and environmental factors in diabetes prevention and care.

Chapter 6 - Cocaine is one of the most widely abused psychoactive substances in the United States, with an estimated 1.3 million Americans using the drug on a regular (at least monthly) basis. Even occasional cocaine use can result in serious medical complications, such as cardiac damage, vascular ischemia, respiratory failure, and persistent alterations in neural function. In this chapter, we will examine the most recent research on impulsivity and decision-making in cocaine use. First, we will present a brief overview of the cognitive processes affected by cocaine use. Next, we will review the relevant literature detailing the status of inhibitory control and decision-making in cocaine users, as well as their proposed neuroanatomical correlates. Finally, we will attempt to integrate these findings with the current view of cocaine addiction and relapse, with an emphasis on the role of impulsivity and decision-making in continued cocaine use despite the elevated risk of negative consequences.

Chapter 7 - This paper addresses controversial topics in the assessment and treatment of heroin addiction. Included in the discussion are issues of dose and outcome, difficulties with toxicology screens, the role of co-occurring Axis I and Axis II disorders, the introduction (and extinction) of newer medications to treat heroin dependence, difficulties of measuring treatment outcome, models of heroin dependence, the role of user personality, and the question of heroin maintenance treatment.

Chapter 8 - Psychostimulants, including amphetamine, cocaine, methylenedioxy-methamphetamine, nicotine, methylphenidate and methamphetamine (MA), represent the most commonly abused drugs *[National Institute on Drug Abuse webpage: Commonly Abused Drugs; http://www.nida.nih.gov/drugpages/drugsofabuse.html]*. In recent years, experimental and clinical studies on MA have experienced resurgence, in part, due to the increased abuse of this psychostimulant and the serious medical and social problems associated with MA abuse. According to the 2004 *National Survey on Drug Use and Health*, nearly 12 million Americans have tried MA *[National Survey on Drug Use and Health - SAMHSA web site; http://oas.samhsa.gov/nsduh.htm]*.

Short Commentary A - *Introduction:* Social norms and personality play important roles in the initiation and maintenance of addictive behaviors. The aim of this preliminary study was to explore how social norms and personality influence areca quid chewing in adolescents. *Materials and Methods:* A total of 179 students from a junior high school in Chia-Yi city (Taiwan) participated in the study in 2003. Areca quid-chewing behavior and intention scales were used to determine attitude to, and usage of, areca quid. Social norm and conscientiousness scales were denoted as factors for perceived social environment and personality factors. *Results:* Forty of the sample (22.5%) has been areca-quid users. The mean scores for the subjective and behavioral social norms were 7.7 ± 3.75 (range 4-20) and 11.8 ± 3.26 (range 4-19). Statistical significance was demonstrated for the relationships between behavioral and subjective social-norm scores and intention to chew for the high-conscientiousness group ($r=.27$, $p=.008$; $r=.416$, $p<.001$), but not for the low-conscientiousness analog. *Conclusions:* The intention to chew areca quid was enhanced by the perceived social norms in highly conscientious Taiwanese adolescents.

Short Commentary B - Substance abuse disorders and consequent infections are among the most significant problems in the world today. This chapter will briefly review the health problems of substance abuse and co-occurring infections such as those caused by the human immunodeficiency virus (HIV) and the hepatitis C virus (HCV) and related issues of clinical management.

In: Men and Addictions: New Research
Author: Lyman J. Katlin

ISBN 978-1-60692-098-5
© 2009 Nova Science Publishers, Inc.

Chapter 1

BIG, BUFF AND DEPENDENT: EXERCISE DEPENDENCE, MUSCLE DYSMORPHIA AND ANABOLIC STEROID USE IN BODYBUILDERS

Dave Smith[1], Bruce Hale[2], Deborah Rhea[3], Tracy Olrich[4] and Kevan Collier[5]

1. Manchester Metropolitan University, Manchester, UK
2. Pennsylvania State University –Berks, Reading PA, USA
3. Texas Christian University, Fort Worth, TX, USA
4. Central Michigan University, Mount Pleasant, MI, USA
5. University of Chester, Chester, UK

INTRODUCTION

Over the past thirty years a great deal of attention has been paid by psychology researchers to the psychological characteristics of athletes in many different sports. In addition, there has also been an increasing research focus on psychological issues relating to exercise activities. This has led to a great improvement in our understanding of sport and exercise psychology, but one activity that has been largely neglected despite it being both a competitive sport and a popular exercise activity is bodybuilding.

However, the existing bodybuilding research shows a number of interesting psychological issues that are prevalent in the sport. For example, researchers have investigated issues such as exercise dependence, muscle dysmorphia, and rampant drug use in bodybuilding. A common theme linking all these issues is that of addiction. Bodybuilding appears to have an addictive quality in several different ways: bodybuilders can be addicted to the actual activity of lifting weights, the social aspects of being involved in the bodybuilding scene (the so-called 'bodybuilding lifestyle'), and simply being big and muscular. In addition, even the most casual of observers will notice that the use of various muscle-enhancing drugs, such as anabolic steroids and human growth hormone, is the rule rather than the exception in the 'hardcore' bodybuilding scene. The aim of this chapter is to examine issues of addiction in bodybuilding, reviewing past research, presenting some new findings and making suggestions for future research. First, Dave Smith of Manchester Metropolitan University and Bruce Hale of The Pennsylvania State University will review and synthesise their findings on exercise dependence in bodybuilders, focusing on the psychological antecedents, correlates and consequences, and charting the development and validation of their Bodybuilding Dependence Scale. Deborah Rhea of Texas Christian University will then critically examine the extant literature on muscle dysmorphia, and present a new, empirically-validated model of this phenomenon. The remainder of the chapter will focus on anabolic steroid use by bodybuilders. Tracy Olrich of Central Michigan University will examine the current literature on motivations for, and psychological effects of, anabolic steroid use in bodybuilders. Finally, Kevan Collier of Rathbone and Dave Smith will report new findings from a UK-based qualitative study examining the psychosocial context of steroid use in recreational bodybuilders and the motives of these individuals for steroid use. Conclusions will then be drawn from these studies and recommendations made for future research on addictive behaviour in bodybuilders.

EXERCISE DEPENDENCE IN BODYBUILDERS

In recent years, increasing attention has been paid to the fact that exercise can become addictive. This phenomenon has been termed 'exercise dependence', a condition where moderate to vigorous exercise becomes compulsive (Hausenblas and Symons Downs, 2002). Exercise dependence can be defined as "a process that compels an individual to exercise in spite of obstacles, and results in physical and psychological symptoms when exercise is withdrawn" (Pierce, 1994 p.149). Anecdotal and research evidence strongly suggests that exercise dependence can be damaging to physical and psychological health. For example, such individuals almost always grossly overtrain, even training when suffering from injuries or 'flu'. Also, they often place such an inordinate emphasis on their training that other important areas of their life, such as work or family, suffer (Chan and Grossman, 1988; Sachs and Pargman, 1979; Morgan, 1979; Thaxton, 1982; Veale, 1995).

The possibility that individuals could become dependent upon exercise was first noted by Baekeland (1970). As part of his sleep deprivation research, Baekeland wanted to explore the effects of exercise deprivation. He had to abandon this part of his research, however, as he found participants impossible to recruit. Despite offering large sums of money, he could not persuade enough participants to forego regular exercise for several weeks. His observations led him to conclude that many of these individuals were obsessed with their exercising.

Since this time, psychologists have paid exercise dependence a great deal of attention. However, most of this research has focused on aerobic activities, particularly long-distance running. As we noted in our original paper on this topic (Smith, Hale and Collins, 1998), this is unfortunate as there is a great deal of anecdotal evidence (Fussell, 1991; Klein, 1993) that exercise dependence is common in bodybuilding. For this reason, over the last few years we have been performing research aimed at increasing our understanding of bodybuilding dependence. In that 1998 paper, we noted the fact that many scientific studies have shown that weight training can significantly enhance the individual's self-esteem (see, for example, Tucker 1983a, 1983b, 1987). This is not surprising for males, as a muscular physique is the most socially desirable aspect of body image in our culture. People tend to view the muscular male as possessing more favourable skills and personality traits, and to be more physically adept and athletically capable, than less muscular males (Berscheid and Walster, 1972). Therefore, it makes sense that as an individual increases the size of his muscles through weight training, he will begin to view himself more favourably.

As individuals successfully use weight training to improve their self-esteem and body image, some may begin to rely exclusively on their training to feel good about themselves. This is most likely to occur in those who have low self-esteem in most or all of the areas of their lives that they feel are important to them. For such individuals, the time they spend in the gym may be the only time they feel a high degree of self-worth. Because of this, they try to spend as much time in there as possible. In this way, they become compulsive about their training, placing a higher priority on it than on other activities, and neglecting other responsibilities in order to train. Given the effects of weight training on body image, this is a particularly powerful. Anyone who trains in a bodybuilding gym probably knows a number of people who display symptoms of an exercise dependence disorder. Some examples may serve to illustrate just how serious this problem can be. For example, in his autobiography, former bodybuilding champion Sam Fussell (1991) chronicled a lifestyle which was entirely geared around the sport. After losing his job (indirectly due to his obsession with bodybuilding), he devoted every hour of the day to the gym. Time which was not spent lifting was spent preparing for it. This behaviour was clearly detrimental to his health. For example, he noted that when preparing for an important competition,

> "Thanks to the rigors of my training, my hands were more ragged, callused and cut than any longshoreman's. Thanks to the drugs and my diet, I couldn't run more than 20 yards without pulling up and gasping for air. My ass cheeks ached from innumerable steroid injections, my stomach whined for sustenance, my whole body throbbed from gym activities and enforced weight loss. Thanks to the competition tan, my skin was breaking out everywhere".

Fussell noted that bodybuilding was the only thing which he felt gave his life any meaning, thus providing some support for the above hypothesis as to how and why individuals become dependent upon weight training. He makes it clear that the lifestyle he describes was relatively common amongst the Southern Californian bodybuilding community.

In the BBC radio documentary Iron Maidens (Thompson and Mares, 1993) several top British female bodybuilders discussed their lifestyles and their attitudes towards the sport. One woman, a former British champion, stated that bodybuilding was her whole life; her commitment to her training even led to the breaking off of her engagement to her fiance. Another woman's daily training programme involved such long weight training and aerobic workouts that it left virtually no time for her to do anything else. When faced with injuries which forced her to withdraw from an important competition and temporarily cease training, she suffered from psychologically debilitating symptoms:

> "I was dead depressed and really down about the whole thing. All this year I've been training for this competition and now I'm not doing it everything has just totally stopped. My life has just fell apart really because I have been training non-stop and I just don't know what to do with myself now. I'm lost".

This example supports the suggestion made by some psychologists and psychiatrists that individuals whose identities are strongly bound to their sport will be vulnerable to emotional difficulties when unable to perform that activity, particularly when other sources of self-worth are lacking.

Due to the obsessive attitude which many bodybuilders have towards their training, they may be at a high risk of developing such problems. As bodybuilding journalist TC Luoma notes, many bodybuilders have a total lack of balance in their lives: "Many bodybuilders do nothing else. They spend every living hour, every minute of the day building their muscles, to the exclusion of any kind of life" (Luoma and Mentzer, 1995).

Of course, it could be argued that these may just be isolated examples. However, to determine how common this phenomenon is, as well as to determine its psychological antecedents, correlates and consequences, it is necessary to be able to accurately measure it. Therefore, we developed the 9-item Likert-scored Bodybuilding Dependence Scale (Smith et al., 1998). This was based on the symptoms of exercise dependence noted in the previous literature and exploratory factor analysis indicated that it comprised three subscales. One subscale (social dependence) appeared to reflect the need to be in the bodybuilding social environment. Another subscale (training dependence) seemed to reflect the need to engage in regular weight training. The third subscale (mastery dependence) appeared to measure the need to exert control over training schedules. Results (Smith et al., 1998) appeared to strongly support the internal reliability of all three subscales and construct validity of the social dependence subscale, but were less supportive of the validity of the other two subscales. We concluded that it appears to be the social nature of bodybuilding training that individuals can become dependent upon, rather than the actual activity of lifting weights.

A follow-up study (Hurst, Hale, Smith and Collins, 2000) examined differences between experienced and inexperienced bodybuilders in BDS scores, and examined the construct and concurrent validity of the scale. The findings supported the concurrent and construct validity of all three BDS subscales with experienced bodybuilders scoring significantly higher than inexperienced bodybuilders and weightlifters on these subscales and on the Social Support Survey - Clinical Form (Richman, Rosenfeld and Hardy, 1993). In addition, significant correlations were found between all three BDS subscales and the Social Physique Anxiety Scale (Hart, Leary and Rejeski, 1989) and a bodybuilding-specific version of the Athletic Identity Measurement Scale (Brewer et al., 1993).

Therefore, these early findings were supportive of the validity and reliability of the BDS. Possibly more importantly, they shed light upon some of the psychosocial and motivational antecedents of exercise dependence in bodybuilders. For example, Smith et al. and Hurst et al. supported the idea that many bodybuilders begin training to reduce feelings of low self-esteem and poor body image, and as their self-esteem and body image improve through their training they can apparently become dependent upon it to feel positive about themselves. Hurst et al. also found that social support was an important antecedent of bodybuilding dependence.

More recently, Smith and Hale (2004) performed a confirmatory factor analysis to re-examine the factor structure of the BDS more thoroughly, and also examined the effects of competitive status and gender on bodybuilding dependence. The findings strongly supported the three-factor model of bodybuilding dependence described by Smith et al. (1998). In terms of between-group differences, competitive bodybuilders scored higher on all three BDS subscales than non-competitive bodybuilders, but there were no significant gender differences. This study also found a relationship between bodybuilding dependence and muscle dysmorphia, a body image disorder where individuals see themselves as thin and puny even though they are actually large and muscular (Lantz, Rhea and Mayhew, 2001). Thus, this finding supports the notion that exercise-dependence is an important part of the pattern of behaviour that characterizes the muscle dysmorphic individual.

The most recently-published paper from this group was a 2005 study by Smith and Hale that examined social and psychological antecedents of bodybuilding dependence (life satisfaction, socio-economic status, marital status and parental status) and also examined the test-retest reliability of the BDS, using a sample of 181 male bodybuilders. Pearson correlations revealed high test-retest reliability for all three subscales (r = .94, .96 and .94 for social dependence, training dependence and mastery dependence respectively). Pearson correlations also revealed significant negative correlations between all three BDS subscales and scores on the Satisfaction With Life Scale (Diener, Emmons, Larsen and Griffin, 1985). For the analysis of socio-economic status participants were classified into managerial and professional class (for example lawyers, accountants), intermediate class (for example nurses) and working class (for example production line workers, shop assistants) according to the UK Government's National Statistics Socio-Economic Classification (NS-SEC; Office for National Statistics, 2001). Working class participants scored higher on all three BDS subscales than intermediate class participants who, in turn, scored higher than professional class participants. Participants who were not currently involved in a romantic relationship scored significantly higher on all BDS subscales than those who were romantically involved. Parents scored significantly higher than non-parents on social and mastery dependence, but not on training dependence. Thus, these results demonstrate that life satisfaction, socio-economic status, marital status and parental status can successfully predict BDS scores. More specifically, the 'typical' male bodybuilder in the UK who displays symptoms of dependence will be single, childless, of intermediate or low socio-economic status, and will have a relatively low level of subjective well-being. Therefore, clinical attention should be paid to the possibility of bodybuilding dependence if a bodybuilder with such a demographic profile presents to a physician or psychologist with apparent symptoms of overtraining and/or obsessive/compulsive behaviour.

So far, therefore, this line of research has yielded a simple, quick, valid and reliable measurement tool and lots of interesting and potentially useful information regarding the psychological and psycho-social issues surrounding exercise dependence in bodybuilders. However, there are still many related issues that remain to be explored by researchers. For example, cut-off scores for the diagnosis of bodybuilding dependence need to be developed to make the BDS a useful tool for use by physicians, psychologists, coaches and others who may wish to use the BDS to diagnose bodybuilding dependence. Also, research has not yet been performed to examine the effectiveness of strategies aimed at treating bodybuilding dependence. Such research would be very useful, helping sport and exercise psychologists and others to understand and deal with this problem. The interaction of steroid use with the development of exercise dependence and muscle dysmorphia should also be examined.

Finally, it is important to note that we are not arguing that bodybuilding is pathological *per se*, or that all bodybuilders are dependent upon the activity. Bodybuilding is a perfectly healthy pursuit, both physically and psychologically, and can fit well into a well-balanced, healthy lifestyle. For some, though, it can become an unhealthy obsession, and it is these individuals that this line of research is ultimately aimed at helping. Other researchers have noted that exercise dependence in bodybuilders appears to be part of an overall pattern of behaviour that has been termed 'muscle dysmorphia', and the following section will examine this issue.

MUSCLE DYSMORPHIA

American culture is saturated with images depicting the ideal physique. The pursuit of and preoccupation with obtaining this image are common themes for both women (Fallon and Hausenblas, 2005; Strahan, Lafrance, Wilson, Ethier, Spencer, and Zanna, 2008) and men (Frederick, Buchanan, et al., 2007; Harrison, Taylor, and Marske, 2006; Neighbors and Sobal, 2007), with perception of our own physiques often heavily influenced by the "normative" images portrayed in the popular media (Baird and Grieve, 2006; Frederick, Fessler, and Haselton, 2005; and Lorenzen, Grieve, and Thomas, 2004). Although these normative images often define only the current cultural ideals of beauty, health, and fitness, many people desire and are motivated to obtain the physiques of these extreme subgroups (e.g., fashion models, athletes, entertainers), often to the exclusion of more realistic or healthy physiques. The pursuit of this culturally desired physique may result in the development of a distorted image of one's own body.

Current cultural trends promote the concept of a lean, heavily-muscled, more mesomorphic male body as ideal (Andersen, 2002; Grieve, 2007). Mesomorphic males are viewed as more socially desirable and possessing greater physical and athletic prowess than ectomorphic males (Pope, Phillips, and Olivardia, 2000). As society continues to endorse this specific body type, an increasing number of males report body dissatisfaction (Phillips and Drummond, 2001) and an increased desire for a lean, heavily muscled physique (Leone, Sedory, and Gray, 2005). This emphasis has resulted in males beginning to evidence "bodily concerns" similar to women (Grieve, 2007; Leone et al., 2005) with some males engaging in pathological behaviors in an effort to achieve the cultural ideal.

Body Dysmorphic Disorder (BDD) is a growing line of research that addresses pathological attitudes and behaviors of females and males. The DSM-IV describes BDD as a distressing or impairing preoccupation with an imagined or slight defect in appearance (American Psychiatric Association, 2000). In addition, the preoccupation must not be better accounted for by another mental disorder (e.g., body dissatisfaction associated with anorexia nervosa). Concerns about appearance can involve specific body parts such as hair loss, skin, and nose as well as the shape and size of the whole body. While a 1991 review of BDD indicated a trend toward equal incidences with males and females (1.0 to 1.25 ratio, respectively) (Phillips, 1991), it should be noted that males and females focus their concerns on different issues. The BDD research has indicated that females are abnormally concerned with individual body parts (i.e., thighs and waist) while men are more likely to be abnormally concerned with the shape and size of the whole body. Pope, Gruber, Choi, Olivardia, and Phillips (1997) introduced a novel form of BDD termed "Muscle Dysmorphia (MD)." Since then, MD has been more completely explored with the development of a psycho-behavioral model with precipitating factors and consequences that may result from the development of MD (Lantz, Rhea, and Mahew, 2001; Lantz, Rhea, and Cornelius, 2002) as well as different scales to measure the factors associated with MD such as the Muscle Dysmorphia Inventory (MDI) (Rhea, Lantz, and Cornelius, 2004).

While Muscle Dysmorphia is a new topic to the sport psychology research community, it has long been recognized as a way of life in the body building community. Historically, body builders have termed, what researchers now consider Muscle Dysmorphia, simply as "the disease" (Fussell, 1991, p. 19). Through his experiences with the body building subculture, Fussell described "the disease" in anecdotal terms:

> Its symptoms pertain to iron...the kind used to create bulges and muscle mounds in their bodies. You overhear them in vitamin stores discussing the merits of branch-chain amino acids and protein powders. You scan them on the subway, their hypertrophied bodies a silent, raging scream of dissent. And, walking to work in the morning, you can see them through the windows in their gyms, hoisting and heaving weights in a lifting frenzy (Fussell, 1991, p. 19).

According to many researchers, people with muscle dysmorphia view themselves as too thin and may feel pressure to gain muscle size and/or strength even though they may actually be quite large and muscular (Lantz et al., 2001; Lantz et al., 2002; Olivardia, 2001; Olivardia, Pope, Borowiecki, and Cohane, 2004). These researchers also suggest their lives become consumed by weightlifting, dieting, and associated activities. In addition to preoccupation with muscle size, these individuals are obsessed with leanness. For example, Fussell (1991) eludes to body builders examining their physiques in the mirror expecting to see large muscles that are striated or "ripped" and symmetrically presented over the whole body. Thus, it may be that some people with muscle dysmorphia are confronted with the paradoxical obsession of gaining muscular size and strength while maintaining a lean muscle build with little or no body fat. Much of the recent research has focused on developing a conceptual framework to identify the factors contributing to Muscle Dysmorphia (see Figure 1). The following section discusses the different variables that may influence this disorder within a conceptual framework (Lantz et al., 2001).

Conceptual Framework for Muscle Dysmorphia

Precipitating Factors. Several authors, generalizing from case studies and ethnographic research, have suggested a variety of predisposing factors commonly associated with BDD and AN are also associated with MD: body dissatisfaction (Cafri, vandenBerg, and Thompson, 2006; Lantz et al., 2001; Olivardia et al., 2004; Pope et al., 2001; Ridgeway and Tylka, 2005), perfectionism, specifically concern over mistakes (Grievc, 2007; Henson, 2004; Kuennen and Waldron, 2007), appearance related social pressures (Olivardia, 2001), self-esteem (Grieve, 2007; Lantz et al., 2001; Olivardia et al., 2004), and media influences (Baird and Grieve, 2006; Lorenzen et al., 2004).

As a result of the identification of these variables, three MD models have been proposed over the past decade to illicit effective variables which precipitate MD or identify variables which actually represent MD. The only conceptual model that has tested specific precipitating variables to MD is the conceptual framework model presented by Rhea, Lantz, and Trail (2000). They have shown that self-esteem and body dissatisfaction serve as precipitating variables which influence a person's motivation to engage in anaerobic exercise for the purpose of physique development. Their thoughts are that positive reinforcement based on muscular development facilitates self-esteem and body satisfaction. In turn, individuals will more fully invest themselves in activities that lead to increased self-esteem and body satisfaction. In this fashion, a cyclical pattern is established. The behavior only becomes pathological when the individual becomes so dependent on the connection between precipitating and psycho-behavioral factors that it requires the individual to engage in more pathological behaviors in order to continue the enhancement of self-esteem. These two precipitating variables are included in the other proposed models (Grieve, 2007; Olivardia, 2001).

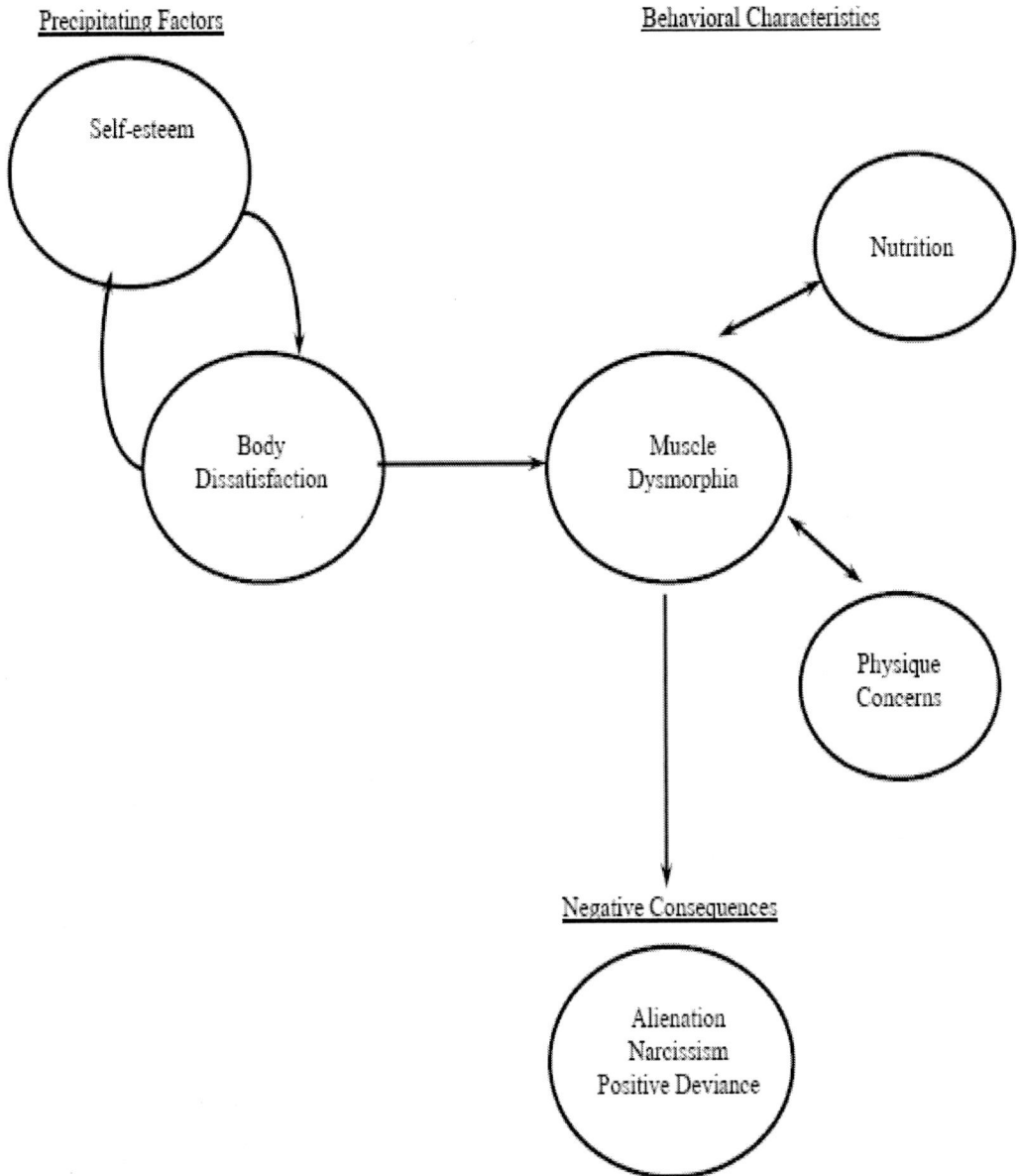

Figure 1. Conceptual Framework for Muscle Dysmorphia.

The other two models that have been proposed to explain MD suggest that there are categories of variables that can influence the development of MD. Grieve's biopsychosocial model (2007) suggests that there are four types of variables that interact with each other in a complex manner which contribute to the etiology of MD. They are socioenvironmental factors (media influences, sport participation), emotional factors (negative affect), psychological factors (body dissatisfaction, ideal body internalization, self-esteem, body distortion, perfectionism), and physiological factors (body mass). Olivardia (2001) presents a brief biopsychosocial model that includes genetic contributions, a drive for muscularity, low self-esteem, appearance related social pressures, and body image consciousness. At this juncture, Kuennen and Waldron (2007) are the only researchers to have tested some of the other variables, such as perfectionism and narcissism with known characteristics of MD to evaluate the functionality of the three models. They found that perfectionism may be another precipitating variable. Much more research is needed to develop a better understanding of the precipitating variables linked with muscle dysmorphia.

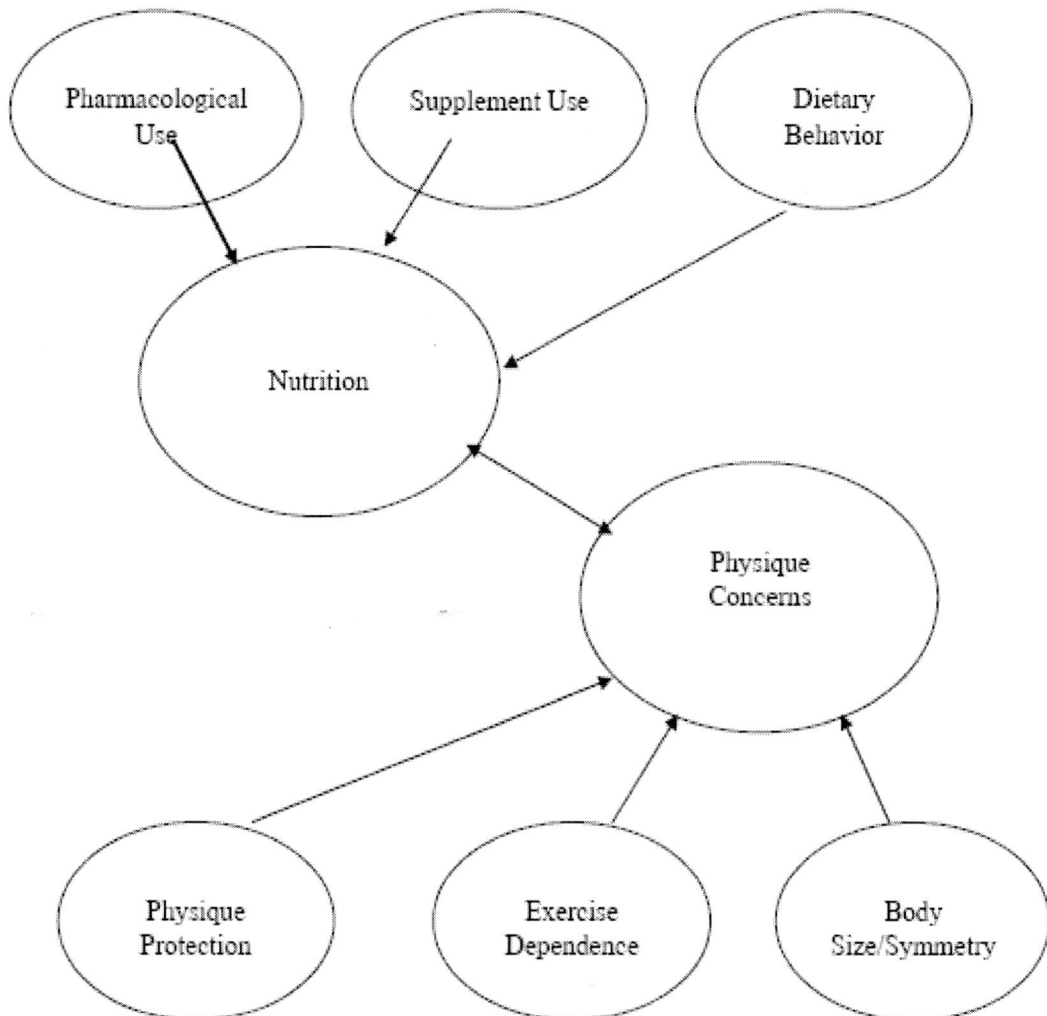

Figure 2. Psychobehavioral model of Muscle Dysmorphia.

Psychobehaviorial Model of MD. Lantz and Rhea have developed a six factor psychobehavioral model of MD which functions within the framework of the suggested precipitating variables and the suggested negative consequences that are derived as a result of the six factor psychobehavioral model (see Figure 2; Lantz et al., 2001, 2002; Rhea et al., 2000, 2004). Their research indicates that people with MD exhibit specific behavioral and psychological characteristics that can be divided into two categories: nutrition and physique concerns. Nutrition is comprised of behaviors concerned with pharmacological use, supplement use, and dietary behavior. Pharmacological use involves the use of steroids and other illegal synthetic hormones in order to increase muscular size and definition. Supplement use is associated with the use of legal substances designed to enhance the quality of a workout (e.g., energy drinks) or aid in post-workout recuperation (e.g., creatine monohydrate). Dietary behavior involves the close monitoring of proteins, carbohydrates, and fats in order to achieve maximum muscle size and striation. The common thread among these three behaviors is that the individual ingests specific foods and supplements in order to enhance muscle size and definition. The model suggests that muscle dysmorphic persons are more likely to engage in these nutritional behaviors in pursuit of enhancing muscular, well-defined physiques than are non-dysmorphic individuals. Pope and associates (2000) provide support for this component of the model. They have reported that dysmorphic weightlifters were significantly different from non-dysmorphic weightlifters in a number of areas including eating attitudes and anabolic steroid use.

Physique Concerns, the second category associated with the psychobehavioral model of MD, is characterized by concerns surrounding body size/symmetry, physique protection, and exercise dependence. Body size/symmetry focuses on the degree of satisfaction one has with muscle size, shape, and definition. Physique protection includes behaviors designed to avoid having the body viewed by others. According to Klein (1993), these behaviors can include wearing baggy or bulky clothing, altering workout times to avoid scrutiny by other weightlifters, and avoiding situations where the physique may be exposed (e.g., going to the beach). Exercise dependence involves preoccupation with exercise, maintaining a rigid schedule of intense exercise, resisting temptations to lapse into nonexercising, feeling guilty when the exercise schedule is violated, and exercising even when ill, tired, or injured. The conceptual model argues that muscle dysmorphic persons are more likely to experience dissatisfaction with their physiques, use bulky clothing, alter training times to hide their physiques, and exercise compulsively to develop a hypermesomorphic physique. This component of the model is also supported by other researchers (Olivardia et al., 2000), who found that dysmorphic weightlifters expressed significantly greater body dissatisfaction than did non-dysmorphic weightlifters. These six factors have been supported by other research (Kuennen and Waldron; Smith and Hale, 2004, 2005), however most of the research has examined these behaviors with non clinical subjects. Any of these factors alone would not constitute a diagnosis of MD, but several behaviors considered in concert would appear to be symptomatic of what is termed as Muscle Dysmorphia.

Negative Consequences of MD. Continued involvement in the pathological characteristics associated with the six factors of the psychobehaviorial model will result in negative consequences (see Figure 1). Thus far, three negative consequences have been identified in the literature that result from the pathological behaviors of Muscle Dysmorphia: alienation, narcissism, and positive deviance (Lantz, Rhea, and Mayhew, 2001). In the bodybuilding subculture, where much of the information on Muscle Dysmorphia has been derived, alienation is defined as a psychological and social malaise that furthers separation between self and extensions of the self. For the bodybuilder, this becomes a separation between the psychological self and one's body (the object); Klein, 1992). Researchers are concerned about bodybuilders' negative feelings associated with engagement in work and social activities until sufficient weight lifting activities have been completed. In Lantz and Rhea's research on developing the complete model of precipitating factors and negative consequences associated with MD, found that bodybuilders spend an inordinate amount of time in physical development activities. As a result, these individuals who invest a considerable amount of time in both physical and mental resources typically develop the characteristics associated with muscle dysmorphia. Hypothetically, these individuals can be completely consumed by the need to increase his or her muscular size or shape. Such a restricted existence may serve to alienate the individual from even his or her closest friends. They become compulsive about their training, placing a higher priority on it than on other activities and neglecting other responsibilities in order to train (Fussell, 1991; Smith et al., 1998). This process can become cyclical as friendships are based in gyms and acceptance of outsiders is unlikely. Although the present research concentrates on bodybuilders and weight lifters, other types of athletes may be at risk as well.

Lantz and associates have argued that someone with characteristics of Muscle Dysmorphia often possesses low levels of self-esteem. After engaging in physical development in an effort to compensate for feelings of inadequacies, one affirms his or her existence through the negative or positive attention from others. This attention creates a narcissistic attitude that has been defined as a person who is preoccupied with oneself to the exclusion of everyone else (Klein, 1993; Lowen, 1983). Due to the over investment in physique development, individuals identified with muscle dysmorphia may develop narcissistic tendencies characterized by preoccupation with inspecting their own physiques. These tendencies may be best illustrated by the wall to wall mirrors which adorn the gyms where these individuals train.

Positive deviance has been defined as the over conformity to a particular role (Hughes and Coakley, 1991). Hughes and Coakley (1991) suggest that the "no pain, no gain" philosophy often adopted by athletes represents one example of a negative consequence associated with Muscle Dysmorphia. This potential negative outcome is seen in the tendency to train through pain and injury. Persons practicing these behaviors, viewed as deviant, are often so preoccupied with gaining size and strength that they are likely to overlook, minimize or simply disregard the messages of pain and injury. For many athletes, training through pain or playing injured is a sign of commitment and strength. The bodybuilding subculture has its share of individuals who feel this way. Persons of this subculture viewed with "the disease" are likely to disregard pain and injury because they associate the inactivity accompanying recovery with muscle atrophy. These individuals will often train while injured, rationalizing their behavior as aiding in the recuperative process. Further, when these individuals do experience an injury, they often refuse to be seen without baggy clothing, and look at themselves in the mirror or weigh themselves, fearing weight loss associated with muscle atrophy.

Presently, the conceptual framework for the inner workings of Muscle Dysmorphia from precipitating factors to negative consequences has only been tested in its entirety in one study (Lantz et al., 2001). The findings thus far have linked the precipitating factors of self-esteem and body dissatisfaction to the two categories of MD (physique concerns and nutrition) in the form of six psychobehavioral characteristics (i.e., body size/symmetry, exercise dependence, physique presentation and pharmacological use, supplement use, and dietary behaviors) which then maintain a cyclical influence of more pathological behaviors, thus creating negative consequences as a result of the pathological behaviors. For example, as the pathological attitude increases, the individual perceives a greater need to manipulate their diet (behavior) in order to further the development of physique. As the body increases in size and/or shape, as a result of this dietary manipulation, the individual gains additional reinforcement (consequences), thus further solidifying the connection between the precipitating factors and the pathological attitudes related to physical development. Simply engaging in a single behavior is most likely not characteristic of a pathological disorder.

Development of the Muscle Dysmorphia Inventory (MDI)

Using the comprehensive description and classification of muscle dysmorphia factors provided by Lantz et al. (2001) as the foundation, the goal was to develop an instrument that measured characteristics associated with muscle dysmorphia. The qualitative and quantitative processes employed resulted in a 27-item, six-subscale measure that demonstrates a psychometrically sound scale. The Muscle Dysmorphia Inventory (MDI) has shown that it can empirically distinguish between the various known factors associated with muscle dysmorphia, it is reliable across several non-clinical settings or populations (i.e., variety of exercise types), and is understandable, short, and easily answered.

The six subscales of the MDI address the most salient aspects of muscle dysmorphia as known at this juncture: nutritional aspects and physique concerns. The nutritional component includes questions related to aspects of one's eating habits, nutritional supplements to enhance one's performance, and illegal synthetic hormones to increase muscular size and strength. The physique concerns component includes questions related to preoccupation with the size of one's body, exercise dependence, and hiding defects of one's body.

Much of the energy of scale validation was focused on construct validity. The MDI's construct validity was verified through item-to-total correlations and the more rigorous confirmatory factor analysis to confirm whether the subscale structure was supported by different data sets. Convergent validity was also found for the MDI through significant correlations among the six subscales of the MDI and training dependency, and drive for thinness.

Utility of the MDI

The MDI was designed for use with non-clinical adult samples to measure at-risk behaviors associated with muscle dysmorphia as developed from Lantz et al.'s conceptual framework (2001). At this time, norm-referenced standards of a clinical population are not available from which to compare scores of individuals that might be considered at higher risk of muscle dysmorphia. This scale was derived from a variety of weight lifting populations, hence this scale can be generalized to those types (i.e., bodybuilders, recreational weightlifters, male cheerleaders, and football players). The scale should be useful in any population where body image and exercise are key components of success. This scale has not been tested on children or young adult populations, so the impact with these populations is not known. Subscale scores are computed by simply summing all item scores for that particular subscale. The higher the score per subscale translates into a higher risk of characteristics associated with muscle dysmorphia (Lantz et al., 2002). However, caution should be given when extracting any one of these subscales individually to explain MD. It should be noted that the MDI is not intended to serve as a diagnostic instrument; however, it does provide valuable information regarding symptomatology and psychological themes that may be relevant in some sport subcultures.

One of the debated issues raised in the MD literature is the concern about the degree a person must possess specific characteristics associated with MD to be diagnosed as muscle dysmorphic. Lantz and Rhea (2002) have made an attempt at this through setting cut-off scores for each of the measured characteristics associated with MD. Although one cannot diagnose individuals with muscle dysmorphia, they do represent an initial attempt to identify individuals with at-risk levels associated with MD. While the authors feel that identifying someone exhibiting concerns with only one of the factors is not sufficient to diagnose a muscle dysmorphic, they feel that using cut-off scores examines the seriousness of these initial characteristics associated with MD. Based on cut-off scores, some studies have identified as many as 13% of bodybuilding subgroups having extreme concerns with dietary behavior, 8% with size, and 7% with exercise dependence (Lantz et al., 2002). These percentages give us initial insight into the disorder, although much more research is needed in order to determine the severity of these concerns and the number of factors needed in order to identify someone as muscle dysmorphic.

Susceptibility of MD

A growing concern in the MD literature is the identification of persons who are most susceptible to developing MD. Clinical studies of MD (Lantz et al., 2002; Olivardia et al., 2000, Pope et al., 1997; Rhea et al., 2004) suggest that this proposed disorder is most likely found in persons who are dissatisfied with their bodies and are heavily involved in weight lifting and other muscle-development activities. Several studies have examined a range of people to identify who is more at risk for muscle dysmorphia than others. In doing so, most of the research has found that bodybuilders seem to be more at risk of characteristics associated with MD than any other subgroup. One of the key distinctions that has been made with different types of weightlifters is in separating those individuals who are motivated primarily with developing muscle size and definition (body builders) and those who pursue primarily muscle strength (Power lifters/Olympic weightlifters; Fussell, 1991; Lantz et al., 2002). Power lifters or Olympic weightlifters train to lift as much weight as possible in a single repetition in three distinct lifts (squat, bench press, and deadlift) or in the case of the Olympic lifter, two lifts (clean and jerk, and the snatch). Rarely are these persons concerned with muscle development or body size/symmetry, except as it relates to body weight restrictions that may force them to participate in a higher weight class (Veale et al., 1996). Conversely, competitive body builders are rarely concerned with one-repetition maximums but rather use weight training to develop hyper-mesomorphic physiques that show tremendous muscular shape, striation, and symmetry. Given the divergent goals of power lifters and body builders, it is erroneous to classify them into a single group assuming that they both manifest characteristics associated with MD to similar extents. Much of the research thus far has shown that body builders of all competitive levels engage in greater levels of behaviors characteristic of MD than do competitive power lifters, recreational weightlifters, male cheerleaders, or football players (Lantz et al., 2002; Rhea et al., 2004). Specifically, body builders report greater dissatisfaction with their physiques, greater engagement in physique protection, greater dietary manipulation, and greater likelihood to use pharmacological aids to improve physique development than power lifters or any of the other aforementioned groups (Lantz et al., 2002; Rhea et al., 2004). For some, though, the unhealthy obsession of MD may be driven most directly from the use of anabolic steroids in order to look and feel better about themselves. The following section will examine the current literature on motivations for, and psychological effects of, anabolic steroid use in bodybuilders.

MOTIVATIONS FOR ANABOLIC STEROID USE IN BODYBUILDING AND SPORT

The psychological effects of AAS use has garnered significant attention from a vast array of concerned individuals and groups including psychologists, educators, coaches, law enforcement, politicians and parents. Topics receiving greatest interest within the literature include issues of increased aggression, changes in mood states including euphoria and depression, body image distortion and concerns over psychological dependence and motivational bases for use. This section of the chapter addresses the latter two topics, motivational bases for AAS use and psychological dependence to AAS.

Much has been written regarding the motives surrounding the initiation of AAS use. The National Institute on Drug Abuse (NIDA) estimates that as many as 3 million Americans may have used AAS for non-medical purposes (NIDA, 2000). Speculation as to the reason why so many have chosen to use this type of drug has revolved around primarily around efforts to improve athletic performance, gain muscle size and strength, improve appearance, and to positively impact self-perceptions (Kutcher, Lund and Perry, 2002). Of particular concern has been the use of AAS by athletes attempting to gain an unfair advantage over opponents and secondarily, use by minors.

Recently, two large studies have been completed which gained access to participants through the internet (Cohen, Collins, Darkes and Gwartney, 2007; Hildebrandt, Langenbucher, Carr, Sanjuan and Park, 2006). Both studies asked questions regarding motivations for steroid use.

Cohen et al.'s (2007) study of 1955 AAS users gave an interesting portrait of the "average" AAS user and their motivations for use. The average AAS user in their study was 31.1 years of age, Caucasian (88.5%) well-educated (74% had post-secondary degree), considered themselves goal-oriented, were employed as professionals. They had median household incomes ($60,000-79,999) well above the general U.S. population ($44,684). Slightly under 6% began use as minors. Most were not involved in sport (89%) and had not been involved in sport in the past, even at the high school level (81.8%). Obviously the motivation for AAS use of these men was not sport. The reasons receiving the highest rating for motivations of use were increased muscle mass, increased strength and to look good. Sport was of little importance to these men.

While the study above indicates that the adolescent is not the primary AAS user, the question remains as to the prevalence of use among the adolescent population. Local and national survey studies conducted in the U.S. generally shows 3-12% of high school students have used AAS in their lifetime (Yesalis, Barhke, Kopstein and Barsukiewicz, 2000). Findings by Johnston, Bachman, O'Malley, Schulenberg and Wallace (2007), however, in their longitudinal work investigating drug use among adolescents have found usage rates to be substantially lower and declining from a peak in 2000. In 2007, annual usage rate among 12th grade boys was 2.3%, 10th grade boys was 1.7% and 8th grade boys 1.1%. Usage rates among girls was significantly lower (8th grade , 0.4%; 10th grade, 0.4%; 12th grade, 0.6%). Unfortunately, their work does not attempt to elicit motivating factors leading to use.

We have been conducting qualitative research concerning AAS use with both athletic and non-athletic populations (Olrich and Vassallo, 2006; Olrich and Ewing, 1999). The research has consisted of conducting in-depth, structured interviews with male AAS users (current and former) about their AAS use experience. A total of 49 men were interviewed in the two studies. Of these men, 33 were former Division I scholarship athletes, 11 were non-competitive bodybuilders, and 5 were competitive bodybuilders. Questions ranged from prior and current sport involvement, motivations for beginning AAS use, perceptions of positive and negative consequences due to AAS use to perceived psychological dependency.

Consistent with the studies described above our research found very few (N=4) of the men had began using AAS while in high school. Of those four, three began after their high school sport experience had ended. All three had committed to an athletic scholarship at a Division I university. After making a campus visit and realizing the size and strength of the athletes the men would soon be playing with and against, the three men made a decision to begin AAS use. The fourth individual who began using in high school was not a high school athlete, but a non-competitive bodybuilder wanting to increase muscular size and strength. The remaining men began using AAS while in college or later in life.

Concerning motivations to begin AAS use, we found distinct differences concerning motivations to begin using AAS between athletic and non-athletic users. The motivation to begin using AAS among the athletic user was to enhance athletic performance to keep up with teammates and opponents. The men expressed a concern that if they did not do something immediately to get bigger and stronger, they would no longer be competitive and perceived a danger of losing their scholarship. As one of the men stated, "After my red-shirt year I decided in the spring that I could compete with everyone else if I had little more size to my body. That is the only reason that I decided to take steroids."

At times coaches reinforced those concerns. As one participant said,

> "I was told after about three weeks that I was going to be red-shirted and that I needed to get a little quicker and lose some body fat...I chose roids and it is a decision that I never regret even till this day."

Also of great importance was the fact that each of the men realized that there was a significant number of AAS using individuals on the team. When the men decided to begin use they were able to develop relationships with the AAS using individuals. Such relationships were important as the men were able to discuss the intricacies of AAS use, including how to use, what types of AAS to use, how to cycle AAS, and often where to obtain AAS.

The motivational basis for beginning AAS use among the bodybuilding and non-athletic population was significantly different. For this group the initiation of AAS use occurred as a result of three main occurrences. First, the men reported feeling they were at a plateau in their training. They believed they had made nearly all the gains they could make without AAS. Second, frustration then occurred as they saw others pass them with the aid of AAS. Third, a certain amount of curiosity concerning the efficacy of AAS arose as they viewed others experiencing the seeming benefits of AAS use. The following quote captures this sentiment well:

> "I felt I had reached a peak, a plateau. I did them partly to see what it was like, partly because of my friends (who) had tried them and said that there was something magical about them. And, I guess, partly because I just wanted to be bigger like everyone else."

A point of further importance, as with the athletic AAS users, these men had found themselves a part of an environment where AAS use was occurring and perceived as an accepted practice. The men belonged to gyms which were considered "hard core" gyms with a significant number of bodybuilders and/or powerlifters and a prevalent AAS using population.

While the men's motivation to begin AAS use varied by their participation athletics or bodybuilding, their experiences once use began were strikingly similar. Forty-six of the 49 men described the steroid use period as very positive. As one former athlete stated:

> "I would have to say that it was definitively a positive experience. I wish that everyone could experience this stuff so people could get away from the media's stereotype...I loved it every time that I did the stuff and would do it again if I was ever to train for a team again."

Another had the following to say:

> "I definitely felt stronger physically, but as I mentioned earlier I was amazed with the way I felt mentally. I was just on top of the f-----g world man. I just never realized that those things would make me feel like that. That is the best f-----g feeling in the entire world."!

As the men described their experiences, it became increasingly clear that such reinforcing experiences from the AAS use could lead to a strong motivation to continue use. The possibility that such reinforcement could lead to a state of dependency, seemed significant. Below the topic of psychological dependency to AAS is discussed.

Psychological Dependency on Anabolic Steroids

The suggestion that AAS use may lead to dependency was first hypothesized in the literature by Wright (1980). Over the next decade three anecdotal accounts of AAS dependency were reported (Taylor, 1985; Goldman, 1987; Whitehead, 1987 [cited in Brower, 2000]). Due to the anecdotal nature of the reports, and because these cases were not placed within a theoretical context, the validity of a dependency to AAS came into question (Dreyfuss, 1990; Cicero and O'Connor, 1990[cited in Brower, 2000]).

Yesalis et al.'s (1990) study was the first evidence of psychological dependence to AAS among users. They surveyed over three thousand high school students (N=3,403), and found 6.6% of the population to be AAS users (N=226). Yesalis and colleagues' elucidation of survey responses led them to judge that up to ¼ of the AAS using students had a potential psychological dependency to AAS.

Brower (2000), found at least 4 reports in literature of psychological dependence (Tennant, Black and Voy, 1988; Blow, Beresford, and Fuelling, 1989; Hays, Littleton and Stillner, 1990; Copeland, Peters and Dillon, 1998). Brower (2000) has presented a theoretical model detailing mechanisms impacting dependence on AAS. Brower hypothesized that when a person begins using AAS he/she receives positive reinforcement through primary reward systems (physiological reinforcers, especially brain reward systems) and secondary reward systems (psychological and sociological reinforcers, including increased muscle mass, increased self-esteem and increased recognition from others). Additionally, within Brower's model, the avoidance of negative reinforcement mechanisms were of equally important. Negative reinforcement mechanisms included the loss of primary physiological rewards, possibly leading to a physiological withdrawal and the loss of secondary rewards, including the psychological response to the loss of muscle mass and a psychological response to the loss of reinforcement within one's environment.

The importance of what Brower identified as secondary reinforcement mechanisms, Sharp and Collins (1998) highlighted as being vital in understanding psychological and behavioral effects of AAS. In a strong critique of previous research emphasizing physiological explanations for user behaviour, both Sharp and Collins and Keane (2003; 2006) emphasized the importance of the secondary reinforcers within the environmental context. They argue that the distinctive patterns of AAS use which include pyramiding, stacking, tapering, and periods of non-use contradict the conception of a physiological dependence to AAS. They do not disregard the possibility of a psychological dependency to AAS. However, they propose that attention needs to be placed upon secondary reinforcers users find within the environmental context in order to accurately understand the nature of a dependency to AAS.

The findings from our research seem to provide strong support for Sharp and Collins' (1998) and Keane's (2006; 2003) viewpoint. As a part of our research the men were asked whether they believed there was a psychological dependency on AAS that could develop. All the men felt there could be a strong psychological dependency on AAS, even if they had not experienced it themselves. Their responses colourfully described their perceptions concerning the nature of the dependency. One of the bodybuilders stated the following when asked whether a dependency to AAS was possible:

> "Sure, I know there is (a psychological dependence). There's definitely. I know that. I know for a fact that, because I have troubles when I do a cycle, coming off. Because you see, you like how they make you feel, okay? Mentally, they just do something to you. You feel great. And then you get so much stronger. And you blow right up. And you puff up, you know. And you look good. And you put on the weight. And that's what bodybuilders want to do the most, is you want to get that weight."

Within this quote, the participant's responses seem to give support for both primary and secondary reward systems. As primary reward systems are those reinforcers resulting from physiological reinforcers, the participant talked of how the AAS made him feel: "Mentally, they just do something to you. You feel great." This would seemingly lend support for the role played by primary reinforcers in the development of a dependency to AAS. But he also described positive benefits from the secondary reward systems such as the positive feelings ensuing from increases in muscle mass, including receiving reinforcement from one's immediate environment. Obviously, the quote spoke compellingly to the role of such secondary reward systems and reinforcement mechanisms.

Another one of the bodybuilders spoke of reinforcement from the secondary reward system. In the quote below, he emphasized the recognition from others in the environment, and his belief that the dependency on AAS was actually a dependency on recognition. He stated:

> "I've never been on the drugs where, 'Oh my God, I have to have a shot, or I have to have a pill.' I've never met anybody that's that way. But, they definitely want the effects of being big, because of the side effects of that. The side effects that they are getting, peer recognition or personal recognition of some sort. 'God, you're really growing.' 'God, you look great.' 'God, you're stronger than shit.' People thrive off that, and you can't tell me in our society that people don't thrive off recognition."

Several of the men gave a different interpretation concerning psychological dependency on AAS. They related how the AAS gave them extreme confidence. They perceived the psychological dependency to be tied to the feeling of confidence experienced when on a cycle of AAS. The confidence as described by the men was a result of a combination of perceived benefits from both primary and secondary reinforcers. First, the use of AAS seemed to increase positive mood states. Second the AAS gave the men feelings of invincibility. And third, the men indicated that confidence was tied to the increase in muscle mass and the attendant benefits. Below two quotes are provided. The first is from an athlete who had tried several recreational drugs including cocaine and begins with a comparison to those chemicals.

> "I know this sounds crazy, but I really think that they are more addictive than any recreational drug I have tried in my life. I mean once you have that feeling of invincibility you never want it to go away. And it was something that I needed more and more the older I got. I mean the last four cycles that I did was due only to the fact that I missed the mental edge that I had over my opponent."

Another athlete stated the following:

> "There definitely is an addiction there that affects your mind. I think it is because the stuff gives you a mental edge that you will never experience in your life unless you do the stuff. I know it is not easy for someone to believe, but I promise you that the stuff gives you such a mental boost in everything you do. It is f---g awesome. I hope people realize that this is why a majority of people decide to do the stuff more and more. It just seems to give you an edge that is far more than the physical aspect that everyone thinks about. Physical strength that you get from this stuff is great. But I promise you the stuff that you miss when you are done with your cycle is the edge that the stuff gives you in your head."

The men perceived AAS as having the capability to cause a strong psychological dependency. Therefore, we were surprised when the participants were questioned concerning current usage. Of the 49 participants, only 11 were still using AAS. Thirty-eight had discontinued using AAS. If there was a true dependency to AAS, then why would over three-fourths of the men no longer use?

The men were asked to share their reasons for ending use. The main motivation given for no longer using AAS was that the men were no longer involved in competitive athletics. The men had either finished their career as a Division I athlete, or as a competitive bodybuilding. Below one of the athletes comments regarding cessation of use.

> "I really don't have the time for the dedication and devotion it takes to do a cycle. I have a real job now and I have a little baby so I really don't get to the gym that often."

The quote above highlights how athletics and exercising were no longer the central focus of this man's life. The man was now a father, and had a "real job."

Another man explained how athletics were no longer seen with the level of importance. This person's eligibility was now done.

> "I don't have the desire anymore and I find there is no need for me to do them now. I am not training for any sport and I really don't have the time to put all the energy I would need to have success with using the juice again."

The findings of our research lend support for the model of dependency to AAS as proposed by Brower (2000). Repeatedly the men spoke of how AAS impacted them mentally, making them feel "invincible," "confident," "having the edge" and "feeling on top of the world." Descriptors such as these seem to indicate reinforcement of the brain reward systems. However, with equal emphasis the men spoke of the benefits resulting from increased muscle mass and the changes in physique and increased peer recognition. Such reinforcers are identified as secondary reinforcers in the model provided by Brower. Therefore, the results of this research also lend support to that aspect of the model of dependency.

The impact of having significant amounts of muscle mass and a muscular physique on a male cannot be understated. Mishkind, Rodin, Silberstein, and Streigel-Moore (1987) have stated that the male mesomorphic physique is the "embodiment of masculinity" in western culture and those individuals possessing a mesomorphic physique will experience much privilege. For instance, mesomorphic males are judged as being more confident, successful, sexually attractive, and intelligent than males with any other type of physique. One could assume the privilege then given to those possessing a hyper-mesomorphic physique would tend to be magnified further.

Therefore the mechanisms by which AAS lead to dependency seem very powerful and clear. Rewards come from a variety of reinforcers. Brain reinforcement mechanisms, increased muscle mass, increased feelings of confidence, recognition from peers and larger society all contribute to make AAS very addictive.

Further research must be pursued, as the generalizability of this research to the greater population is problematic. This work does, however, lend insight to the nature of the AAS use phenomena and can provide a basis for further investigation into this important phenomenon.

MOTIVES FOR ANABOLIC STEROID USE AMONGST RECREATIONAL BODYBUILDERS: A CASE STUDY

Introduction

This section of the chapter will report a study examining the motivations for bodybuilders engaging in AAS use in the UK, particularly how 'hardcore' gym and bodybuilding subculture may contribute to recreational bodybuilders engaging in AAS use. Indeed, in the UK, steroid use is becoming a major part of the recreational drug scene, and they are used increasingly amongst recreational bodybuilders (Monaghan, 2001, 2002).

Patterns of steroid use in the UK, where steroids are legal to possess for personal use, are fairly well-documented. For example, Korkia (1994) discovered that prevalence of AAS use ranged between 24% and 46% of members within four gyms, and Korkia and Stimons (1996) found that 11.4% of gym members used steroids. In contrast, Lenehan, Bellis and McVeigh (1996) found that 80% of respondents from 'hardcore' gyms had used or were currently using AAS, but the figure was significantly lower for mixed gyms and fitness gyms. This difference in prevalence of use in 'hardcore' versus fitness gyms may explain the large differences in the usage figures in the studies cited above. Most of the steroid users purchased the drugs from friends who were also users, and the drugs were easy to obtain in most of these gyms. Similar findings were reported by Grace, Baker and Davis (2001) and Wright, Grogan and Hunter (2000, 2001).

The prevalence of AAS use needs to be seen in the light of the use of illicit drugs in the UK. The 1996 British Crime Survey (cited in Ramsay and Spiller, 1997) found that steroid use was more common than heroin use in the UK. Clarke (1999) found that AAS were the third most offered drug to school aged children in the North-West of England, behind cannabis and amphetamines. AAS are also the second most commonly- injected drug reported to needle-exchange clinics within the North-West of England (Lenehan et al., 1996). Despite this, relatively little attention has been paid by researchers and policy makers to this group. In a study of 64 gym owners, McVeigh (2000) found that gym owners expressed concerns about the lack of credible information relating to AAS use; a lack of health provisions and access to doctors with specific knowledge of AAS; the increasing number of counterfeit AAS, and the growing numbers of adolescent males using AAS. Indeed, Best and Henderson (1995) and other studies have commented on how AAS using bodybuilders are a relatively inaccessible group, making it difficult for health professionals, such as those involved in exercise psychology, and policy makers to devise and implement effective provisions for this group.

Although these studies provide us with an insight into the patterns and trends associated with AAS use, and give some idea of the prevalence of AAS use in the UK, the figures given can only be viewed as estimates (British Medical Association, 2002). We argue that AAS use is probably more prevalent than existing studies suggest, as due to the relative inaccessibility of AAS users it may not be possible to gain the large scale and sustained access to this group needed to conduct large, long-term studies. Lenehan (2003) also argues that many of the issues related to AAS use remain unexamined and somewhat misunderstood.

Interestingly, most steroid-using bodybuilders do not consider themselves drug users because they claim not to 'abuse' steroids, as they often obtain medical and ethnopharmacological advice regarding their use. Pates and Temple (1992) also found that

AAS using bodybuilders did not associate themselves with other drug users, claiming that others were 'junkies'. This is despite them engaging in potentially risky behaviours. For example, Wright et al. (2000) found that 92% of the steroid users in their sample reported 'stacking' (taking two or more types of steroid simultaneously) on average four AAS. The maximum number of AAS stacked was 15. Grace et al. (2001) reported that 20% of their sample admitted sharing needles. Given the prevalence of such behaviours, and the well-documented health risks from steroid use, such as increased low density lipids (LDLs) and left ventricular hypertrophy (British Medical Association, 2002), it is important for us to understand the motivations of steroid users. However, surprisingly little research has been performed on this topic.

In one of very few such studies to be conducted in the UK, Wright et al. (2000) found, perhaps not surprisingly, that the main motive for steroid use amongst both recreational and competitive bodybuilders was to increase muscular size and definition. However, users were also motivated to use AAS by potential increases in confidence and self-esteem. Indeed, Pope et al (1999) suggests that an increasing objectification of the male body within media and culture has contributed to a greater focus on masculinity, whilst Leit et al, found that some male models depicted in the media displayed physiques that may only be attainable with the use of AAS. Another motive suggested by Lenehan (2005) and Atha (2004) is that individuals may use AAS for occupational reasons. Specifically, security personnel may use steroids to make them more imposing and increase their credibility in that role. This also suggests that the social environment may be an important influence on individuals' steroid use. The social environment in which bodybuilders operate has been written about in various academic (Klein, 1993) and non-academic (Fussell, 1991; Hotten, 2004) texts, and more recent studies (Collier, Smith and Liston, 2006; Collier and Smith, 2007 and Grogan, Shepherd, Evans, Wright and Hunter, 2006) suggest that the social network within bodybuilding subculture does contribute to AAS use. This issue was the focus of the present study, which used observation sessions and semi-structured interviews to examine the motivations for recreational bodybuilders' steroid use, and how social influences within the bodybuilding subculture may shape this use. Due to the exploratory nature of this work we did not formulate hypotheses, but were particularly interested in exploring several factors that popular authors (Fussell, 1991; Hotten, 2004) and academics (Atha, 2004) have suggested to be important influences on bodybuilders' steroid use. Specifically, we sought to examine whether becoming a steroid user was necessary to become an accepted member of the bodybuilding subculture, whether such use was motivated by improved recognition and social status both within and outside the bodybuilding world, and whether occupational motivations for steroid use were prevalent.

Method

This study adopted a qualitative approach using semi-structured interviews and a mixture of covert and overt field observation as research methods. Once ethical approval was granted by the relevant ethics committee, in depth interviews were conducted with 11 male recreational bodybuilders who identified as AAS users at the time of interview, and observation sessions were conducted in four 'hardcore' bodybuilding gyms over a twelve-month period. The two data sets complemented and supported one another. The interviews provided insights into the experiences of respondents, whilst the observation sessions allowed the researchers to witness first-hand the behaviours of this group. These data sets were then crosschecked to highlight any similarities and/or differences between them, in an attempt to check the reliability of the data generated.

Participants

Participants ranged in age from 19 to 27, with the average age being 24. All respondents were white working-class males from the North West region of England, and were employed within semi or unskilled occupations. These occupations included manual labour, nightclub security, factory work, janitor and work within leisure centres. All but two of the respondents were educated to secondary school level, and those who were not reported 'dropping out' of school early. Participants described themselves as recreational bodybuilders, that is, although they did adhere to ritualistic training and dieting, they had not participated in any formal bodybuilding contests, and did not intend to do so in the future. Despite this, the participants were considered to be 'serious' trainers, as they trained 4 to 6 times a week, and in some cases, twice daily. Their exercise programmes centred on heavy weight training and low levels of cardiovascular exercise. They also consumed a high protein/low carbohydrate diet, and avoided eating foods that were high in saturated fats. They also used supplements such as amino acid capsules, creatine phosphate and protein powders.

Participants were accessed via the first author. This was possible as he was employed within the fitness industry, and regularly worked and trained within bodybuilding gyms. Due to this, the researcher was familiar to this environment and acquainted with many AAS using bodybuilders. Those who met the criteria of a recreational bodybuilder and identified as an AAS user, were provided with a synopsis of the research and asked if they would participate in the study. This level of familiarity between participants and the first author was believed to be useful, as it provided a level of 'insider status'. It was also thought to facilitate participants when discussing questions that related to personal and sometimes sensitive subjects. In an attempt to assure anonymity and confidentiality to participants, the research location, participants and gyms were given pseudonyms.

Interviews

All interviews were conducted on a one-to-one basis between the lead researcher and individual respondents. To minimise interference from others, interviews were conducted in a private and secure location. This location was either the work office of the lead researcher, or the office of a participating gym. Interviews were designed to elicit information relating to three main areas: (1) the nature of bodybuilders' training and drug use, (2) motivations for AAS use, and (3) the influence of social aspects of the bodybuilding subculture on their motivations for AAS use. Although interviews were semi-structured, an interview schedule was compiled using the findings of existing studies, in order to devise questions that related specifically to these three areas. All questions were open, allowing respondents to provide detailed accounts relating to bodybuilding and AAS use. The interviewer would then use additional questioning when necessary, to probe into areas of importance. Interviews lasted between 45 minutes and 1 hour 30 minutes, and were tape recorded via Dictaphone.

Observations

It was essential that observation sessions were conducted within 'hardcore' bodybuilding gyms, i.e. gyms characterised by heavy-duty free-weights/equipment, little or no cardiovascular equipment and frequented by bodybuilders. These gyms were also sparse in appearance and lacked the well-kept furnishings of large corporate health clubs. Indeed, they were mostly independently owned businesses and subscription was on a 'pay as you use' basis. Thus, the gyms generally comprised of fewer members than larger health clubs; however, due to this, there was an extremely close-knit relationship between members. White working-class males predominantly used these gyms, and there was little gender or ethnic diversity. The few females who did use the gyms did so to increase strength for martial arts training, rather than to increase muscle mass for bodybuilding. Existing studies support this choice of research location, as they have shown there are greater incidences of AAS use within 'hardcore' gyms (Lenehan, Bellis and McVeigh, 1996).

Access to four 'hardcore' gyms was gained via the first author. Managers and gym owners were contacted, provided with a synopsis of the study and asked if they would allow research to be conducted within their facility. As with interviewees, all gym managers/owners were assured confidentiality and anonymity throughout the research process, and informed a pseudonym would be provided.

Covert observations were used during puliminary observations as it was believed that this method would provided a more valid insight into the behaviour exhibited by AAS users within 'hardcore' gyms. However, we felt that the first author's perceived 'insider status' would help facilitate the research process and minimise observer effects in the use of overt observation during later observation sessions. It was also believed that this would help to minimize the potential ethical issues around participants not being unaware of observation taking place.

Observation time was divided equally between research locations, allowing three sessions lasting between 1 and 2 hours to be conducted each week, within all four gyms. As a participant observer, the first author engaged in bodybuilding training (lifting weights and performing various other exercises) whilst in the gyms. However, during this time, all aspects of the environment and relevant information were being recorded. Notes were immediately recorded in a field diary in an attempt to reduce selective recall. This was thought to pose no problem by way of observer effects, as many bodybuilders in the gyms also kept training diaries. Thus, the taking of notes would not look out of place within this environment. Discussions relating to bodybuilding and/or AAS use were recorded in detail, whilst the sale and use of AAS were recorded in a tally format.

Data Analysis

Once all empirical research had been completed data sets were content analysed and crosschecked. Firstly, interviews were transcribed and colour coded according to themes; for example, red for information relating to AAS use and blue for information concerning motivations for AAS use. These data were then subject to more a detailed analysis, whereby themes within the above categories were identified. This allowed first and second-order themes to be highlighted, and patterns to be identified within these data. In addition, the data provided us with a descriptive account or 'narrative' of bodybuilding and AAS use. This information was then crosschecked against observation notes, which had also been content analysed, in an attempt to support or contradict the accounts of respondents.

Results

All respondents reported specific factors and processes that impacted on their view of masculinity and what a male should look like within society. Table 1 illustrates that two prominent first order themes emerged within this 'masculinity' aspect. Respondents reported becoming involved in bodybuilding during their mid-to-late teens. Contemporary forms of media, particularly those that depict fit, muscular males, were fundamental to respondents' perceptions of masculinity and their motivations to engage in bodybuilding. Moreover, they felt that the depiction of desirable male bodies within the media had increased, placing men under increased pressure to prescribe to socially desirable body types. In particular, TV, movies and magazines were cited in relation to this, with specific individuals (Arnold Schwarzenegger and Sylvester Stallone) being said to epitomise the 'masculine male':

"You know in the action films you don't get some thin lad or thin fella playing the action hero. You tend to get someone who's well built. I mean, look at Arnold Schwarzenegger, he's been in loads of action films and is an icon of masculinity. He's huge!" (Participant #1)

"You see it on TV and you see it in magazines. Every time you turn over a paper you see a picture of the bronzed body of one of the super stars. You just want to look good. You get the impression this is what you should look like. You don't ever flip over the TV channels and see Calvin Klein with some fat hairy person. It's always some bloke who's well toned and looking good". (Participant #4)

Two respondents were particularly keen to improve their aesthetic appearance, and consequently, elevate their social status. They commented:

"I want to look good in the summer, you know, wear a tight T-shirt, and in the local community I don't want to be seen as the usual me". (Participant # 7)

"You get more attention from the girls when you are using the gear (steroids), and you're looking good". (Participant # 1)

Table 1. Factors that impacted on participants' view of masculinity and motivated them to engage in bodybuilding

Theme	Number of respondents
Body media influence	n= 11
Significant others Father/teacher and other male role models	n= 9
To elevate social status	n = 7
Become more physically attractive to the opposite sex	n = 11

Strong male role models (father and teachers) and institutionalised periods of life (school) also appeared to be fundamental in motivating respondents to develop a muscular physique. For example, respondents discussed how their father's strong physical appearance and physically demanding occupation impacted upon their views of manliness.

"My dad has always worked with his hands, he is a strong man. I always looked at him like, and thought that is what dads and men are like. All my mates' dads were physical men as well, so you just assume that is what all men are like". (Participant # 8)

Thus, expectations of masculinity centred on physical strength and being capable of providing for and defending loved ones. The strong labour divisions within working-class communities further solidified these views, as they helped to build images of men being providers, and females performing roles within the home.

"My mum and dad are dead old fashioned. My dad went out to work and my mum stays in and does the washing, cleaning and cooking. When he came home he did nothing. That's just the way it is, isn't it?" (Participant # 11)

School was also found to impact on the formation of masculine identities, as teachers were said to show greater respect to, and give additional privileges to, more physically capable male students. Physical strength and 'hardness' (the ability to fight well) were also reported to be necessary during school years, in order to avoid bullying and gain sexual attention from females.

"In school the bigger lads were always respected. The ones who were bigger, stronger got the respect, got the attention off the girls. In sports they got the attention of the P.E. teachers because they were bigger and stronger… they got the attention they wanted". (Participant # 3)

Connell (1987) and Mac an Ghaill (1994, 1997) have also discussed working-class masculinity in a rather homogenous sense within this context. However, we found variations in working-class masculinities with some men adhering to the 'metrosexual' image (a heterosexual male who places great emphasis on well-groomed aesthetic appearance) whilst others aspire to the 'hard man' image. Despite these variations in masculinity, physical strength and a muscularly-developed body underpinned them both. For this reason, adolescent males who are entering into adulthood may see bodybuilding as a means of developing such a body, and therefore, being perceived as a 'real' man within their community.

Table 2. Factors that motivated participants to engage in AAS use

Theme	Number of respondents
Plateau in training	n = 11
Elevate social status amongst bodybuilding peers	n = 11
To engage in informal competition with bodybuilding peers	n = 6
To gain employment in security occupations	n = 5

As with motivations for engaging in bodybuilding, respondents also had specific motivations for using AAS. Table 2 indicates the themes, which emerged in relation to respondents use of AAS.

All interviewees and those consulted during observation sessions reported beginning training naturally before using AAS. However, they did report experimenting with ergogenic aids early on in their training. The prospect of using AAS only occurred after experiencing 'sticking points', and becoming frustrated with slow progress.

"You get so far and your gains stop. When you're on a cycle you put on two stone (authors' note: 28 pounds) it's great, you feel great. But when you come off you lose weight and feel crap". (Participant # 1)

"Yeah, I use gear. It's a case of having to when you want to get this size, it's impossible without the gear. I've taken all sorts of stuff: Sust, deca, primobolin, Winstrol: Loads of stuff." (Participant # 6)

Peers within the gym were said to have suggested AAS use to respondents after discussing slow progress, and ways to 'move past' their sticking point. Bodybuilders within this study reported beginning AAS use progressively; firstly, using small dosages of oral tablets, and then progressing to intra-muscular injections. The most commonly used AAS were Anadrol, Dianabol, Deca-Durabolin, Primobolin-Depot, Sustanon and Winstrol. Observation sessions revealed that many AAS users come to use injectable AAS more frequently as they believe that they are less harmful than oral tablets. Further to this, bodybuilders were also observed performing peer administration of injectable AAS, in order to administer the drugs into the buttocks. Respondents would stack between four and eight AAS during a cycle lasting between eight and twelve weeks. However, drug use was not limited to AAS, as three respondents reported using Human Growth Hormone (HgH), and two stated that they used amphetamines in order to reduce body fat.

AAS use was also viewed as means of gaining greater social standing amongst peers within the bodybuilding subculture, as high levels of ego/social enhancement were attached to those who use AAS, whilst natural bodybuilders were mostly excluded from this subculture. This supports the findings of existing studies (Collier, Smith and Liston, 2006; Monaghan, 2002; Olrich and Ewing, 1999), which also found that bodybuilders reported gaining more acceptances from peers after commencing AAS use.

"When you go into a gym like that you either go one-way or the other; you go totally on your own and don't get involved in the loop [social group], or you get in the loop and get involved in the steroids. There is no two ways about it, the more you get involved the more you get accepted. It is an accepted factor so you decide to get involved and take it. [steroids]" (Participant # 4)

This fits with anecdotes from observations in which AAS users discussed how they disliked what they preserved to be the 'pretty trainers' who 'play' at being bodybuilders in health clubs. Indeed, when such a person was seen to enter the gym they were isolated and mocked by the gym's established members.

Although the bodybuilders within this study trained on a recreational basis, and therefore, did not use AAS to prepare for bodybuilding contests, some did use AAS to compete in informal competition against peers within the gym. These contests included posing and making physical comparisons between physiques, and lifting weights to determine who were the strongest bodybuilders. Bodybuilders discussed how they used AAS because they wanted to be one of the biggest and strongest in the gym. Bodybuilders who displayed less physical strength and muscular development were subjected to mocking by peers and referred to as 'faggots' and 'tarts'. There was also a level of competition attached to how fully one adhered to a 'bodybuilding lifestyle'. For example, comparisons were made between cycle time and the number of drugs used when stacking; those who used a greater number of AAS for a longer time were considered to be 'better' bodybuilders. One respondent commented on how a peer was a 'real' bodybuilder because he trained and dieted religiously, used large amounts of AAS and woke every three hours during the night to take nutritional supplements.

Similar to Pates and Temple (1992), we found that AAS-using bodybuilders did not consider themselves to be drug users. All respondents presented negative images of other drug users, claiming that they were 'dirty', 'smack heads' and 'thieves'. They also felt that other drug users simply used drugs to elicit a high, whereas they claimed to use, rather than abuse, AAS to improve their bodies and health. Anecdotal evidence provided by staff at a needle exchange clinic also suggested that there are regular altercations between AAS users and other drug users. Although respondents did not report engaging in physical altercations with other drug users they did refer to them as 'dirty, thieving bag-heads' and 'scum'. There was also a general consensus amongst bodybuilders that the medical claims concerning the health implications of AAS use were exaggerated, and that only the negative side effects of AAS were presented. Further to this, bodybuilders felt that there were a number of benefits to using AAS and felt that the 'pros outweighed the cons' with regards to AAS.

We also discovered that many recreational bodybuilders were employed within nightclub and other security occupations. Those who were believed increased size and strength to be essential to this role, and used AAS to meet these occupational requirements:

"Yeah, putting the size on got me the job on the doors [nightclub door security staff] in the first place". (Participant # 10)

"You need to be the biggest, or any little pipsqueak will knock you back!" (Participant # 7)

As with 'hardcore' gym subcultures the 'doorman' culture was also underpinned by working-class perceptions of masculinity and 'hardness', with respondents reporting that the ability to fight and 'look after yourself' were necessary attributes to be accepted by peers within this culture. Thus, respondents felt it necessary to exhibit muscular development in order to firstly gain employment within these security occupations, and also to gain acceptance and elevate their social status within this culture. Again, observation sessions supported the accounts of interviewees as those who did work as 'doormen' often discussed having altercations with customers, seemingly acquiring kudos and enhanced status due to their physical capacity when fighting.

The 'hardcore' gym environment was also found to contribute further to AAS use, as it also provides easy access to these drugs. For instance, peers, staff and illegitimate dealers were found to be the main source of AAS within 'hardcore' gyms. Bodybuilders also discussed how the relatively 'lax' laws regulating AAS use in the UK make it easy to purchase and use AAS.

> "I get them from the gym. A few of the fellas deal them there; it is dead easy to get them anywhere from any gym. You just need to know who to go to. You can get whatever you want, gear [steroids], growth [human growth hormone], wiz [amphetamines]'. (Participant # 6)
>
> "It is legal to use them [AAS] for your own use, so what can they [police] do? No one can do anything about it because they can't prove that they aren't for personal use". (Participant # 5)

Several sources of information relating to the use of AAS were also available within 'hardcore' gyms. These sources included informal advice from peers, and underground texts such as the *Anabolic Review*. Local needle exchange clinics were also used to obtain clean needles/syringes and other paraphernalia, in return for used sharps. Thus, in addition to promoting the use of AAS, the bodybuilding subculture also provides networks through which bodybuilders can more easily engage in AAS use.

Discussion

Our findings suggest that there is no single factor that can explain why men become involved in bodybuilding and AAS use. For example, although many men become involved in bodybuilding to aspire to dominant views of masculinity depicted in the media and their community, in many cases they use AAS to compete for employment and to gain social recognition within the bodybuilding subculture. It also became apparent that this issue warrants examination on two levels; firstly, the formation of masculine identities in relation to wider social processes, and how this may lead to some men gravitating towards bodybuilding in an attempt to adhere to contemporary forms of masculinity, and secondly, how engaging within bodybuilding subcultures may contribute to AAS use.

Given this, we would argue that there is a developmental process that many bodybuilders go through before becoming AAS users. This process begins during childhood when individuals engage with and are influenced by their social/cultural environment. For example, respondents reported that significant others such as their fathers and school teachers helped to shape their view of what men ought to be like. In many cases, these images centred on men being physically strong, robust and dominant within their home and community. The notion of male dominance and patriarchy was further solidified by the strong gender-based labour divisions that existed in respondents' working class communities. Therefore, wider social and cultural processes appear to be fundamental in shaping mens' masculine identity.

The increasing emphasis on muscular body images within society also has a great impact on the formation of masculine identities. In particular, media that depict images of lean, muscular males had a fundamental impact on respondents' perceptions of a socially desirable physique. Mens' magazines that associate success, virility and social dominance with those who do adhere to such body types motivated men to engage in bodybuilding in order to develop such a physique, and attain these social qualities through their improved appearance. This is in accord with research that has found that, for males, the mesomorphic (muscular) body type is the most preferred and socially desired in Western culture (Tucker, 1982). The mesomorphic male is generally viewed as possessing more favourable skills and personality traits, and to be more physically adept and athletically capable, then his less mesomorphic counterparts (Berscheid and Walster, 1972). Given that AAS use appears to produce muscle-building results impossible through natural means, it is not difficult to understand their attraction to individuals such as the participants in this study.

Given these findings we argue that when examining this issue, it is necessary to avoid a 'present centred' investigation, and to acknowledge the developmental nature of identity formation and motivations for engaging in bodybuilding. For instance, although media sources may impact upon one's view of masculinity and heighten awareness of the social benefits of adhering to a muscular body type during adolescence, in many cases their masculine identity has already been shaped via the processes outlined.

Our findings suggest that AAS use amongst recreational bodybuilders could be viewed as a consequence of engaging within bodybuilding subcultures, as motivations to use these drugs only develop once an individual has engaged within the bodybuilding subculture for some time. The easy access of these drugs within 'hardcore' gyms, made it easy for bodybuilders to access and use AAS, whilst the pro-drug views amongst AAS using bodybuilders made it easier for respondents to legitimise and justify drug use. These justifications also helped AAS users to rationalise engaging in sustained AAS use despite potential health implications. Therefore, it would appear that the bodybuilding subculture not only promotes, normalize and legitimise AAS use amongst its members, but also provides sources through which bodybuilders can access AAS.

The fact that AAS were viewed as a means through which one could develop the muscular size necessary in order to gain employment in the security industry, in which may bodybuilders are employed, also suggests that occupational factors may contribute to some bodybuilders' motivations to use AAS. Many of the ideologies present within the bodybuilding subculture also appeared to be present within the 'doorman' culture, and may have motivated bodybuilders to develop a muscular physique and present a veneer of 'hardness'. Thus, motivations for AAS encapsulate much more than aesthetic improvement, as social and occupational factors are also significant contributors. Given this, we would argue that AAS is a product of the environment in which recreational bodybuilders operate, and whilst wider social processes contribute to men becoming involved in bodybuilding, AAS use is more likely to be a product of the social environment within 'hardcore' bodybuilding gyms and security occupations.

To conclude, we do not claim that this small-scale study is representative of AAS-using recreational bodybuilders as a whole. The findings of this exploratory investigation relate to a relatively small sample of AAS using recreational bodybuilders; therefore, our findings should be interpreted as such. However, this study has added to the current body of literature within this under-researched area of study, and provided a unique insight into the processual development of bodybuilders' motivations for engaging in bodybuilding and using AAS. Moreover, this study suggests that recreational AAS-using bodybuilders' motivations for engaging in bodybuilding and AAS use develop throughout the course of their life, and have been shaped by wider social and cultural processes.

As suggested, it would also appear that this issue warrants examination on two levels, as motivations for engaging in bodybuilding, and motivations for using AAS, appear to develop through different processes, and at different stages in one's life. For instance, our findings would suggest that whilst adolescent males become involved in bodybuilding and physique enhancing behaviours to adhere to what they believe to be socially desirable physiques and a favourable masculine identity, motivations for using AAS emerge once one becomes increasingly immersed within the bodybuilding subculture. It is also apparent that, whilst the 'hardcore' gym environment does contribute to AAS use, the occupational requirements of some security occupations also influence AAS use amongst recreational bodybuilder. Thus, there is no sole factor that can explain AAS use amongst this group of recreational athletes. Therefore, to gain a more informed understanding of recreational bodybuilders' motivations for using AAS it is necessary to view this issue in a developmental sense, and to pay particular attention to the subcultural dimensions present within 'hardcore' gyms. By doing so it will be possible avoid limiting investigations to the present-centred examination of aesthetic and cosmetic factors.

It would also appear that bodybuilders and indeed other drug users should not be viewed as a homogenous group, as clear distinctions are present between natural and AAS using bodybuilders, and between the latter and recreational drug users. Many of these distinctions centre on attitudes towards drug use or what is perceived as drug 'abuse', the kinds of drugs used and for what purpose, and ethnographic environments within which drug users operate. Therefore, it is quite feasible that the cultural significance, motivations and views towards drug use may differ considerably between groups of athletes, and groups within the wider society.

AAS-using bodybuilders are a hard group to access and more information relating to AAS use is required by health professionals and policy makers, in order to provide this group with better information and interventions to minimize the risks posed to themselves and to the wider society by their drug use. In light of our findings, we suggest that it is necessary to firstly acknowledge the cultural and social processes that contribute to adolescent males becoming involved in physique enhancing behaviours; and secondly, to acknowledge how ethnographic and occupational factors further contribute to AAS use. By doing so, it may be possible to build a more accurate picture of AAS use by bodybuilders, and to devise more appropriate and effective resources and interventions for this group. We also suggest that exercise psychologists and other health professionals must understand the strong motivations driving such behaviour, and realise that simple messages that AAS use is morally wrong or physically unhealthy are unlikely to have any impact on these individuals' behaviour given the positive reinforcement they receive within the AAS users' subculture. The most fruitful line of enquiry as regards to effective anti-AAS interventions may be to understand the motivations of those who have ceased AAS use, a line of research that we are currently pursuing.

CONCLUSION

In this chapter we have presented evidence from several lines of research that shows addictive behaviour in bodybuilders. This addiction can manifest itself in compulsive exercising, psychologically addictive steroid use, and muscle dysmorphia. Such research has provided a valuable window into psychological issues in bodybuilding and is beginning to provide tangible benefits: Such findings will aid those working with bodybuilders, whether sport psychologists, drug workers or medical professionals. Also, those involved in drug education will find our results very interesting when trying to produce interventions to combat steroid use. Of course, much research remains to be done, and we have made various suggestions in this regard throughout the chapter. However, the research reported and reviewed has, we believe, made at least a very good start to a greater understanding of some of the darker psychological issues involved in this fascinating sport and physical activity.

REFERENCES

American Psychiatric Association (2000). *Diagnostic and Statistical Manual of Mental Disorders (DSM IV-TR.. 4*[th] *ed.* Washington, DC: American Psychiatric Associaton.

Andersen, A.E. (2002). Eating disorders in males. In K.D. Brownell and C.G. Fairburn (Eds.), *Eating disorders and obesity: A comprehensive handbook* (2nd ed., pp. 188-192). New York: Guiford.

Atha, J. M. (2004). *Anabolic steroid usage, prices and effects*. Liverpool: Independent Drugs Monitoring Unit.

Baekeland, F. (1970). Exercise deprivation; sleep and psychological reactions. *Archives of General Psychiatry, 22*, 365-369.

Baines, J. (2004). *Anabolic steroids hardcore info*. Manchester: Lifeline Publishing.

Baird, A.L., and Grieve, F.G. (2006). Exposure to male models in advertisements leads to a decrease in men's body satisfaction. *North American Journal of Psychology, 8,* 115-121.

Berscheid, E., and Walster, E. (1972). Beauty and the best. *Psychology Today, 5,* 42-46.

Best, W., and Henderson, D. (1995). Anabolic Steroids and The Mass Media. *Relay, 1* (3), 20-23.

British Medical Association, (2002). *Drugs in sport: The pressure to perform*. London: BMJ Publishing Group.

Brewer, B.W., Van Raalte, J.L., and Linder, D.E. (1993). Athletic identity: Hercules' muscles or Achilles' heel? *International Journal of Sport Psychology, 25*, 237-54.

Brower, K. (2000). Anabolic steroids: Potential for physical and psychological dependence. In C.E. Yesalis (Ed.), *Anabolic steroids in sport and exercise* (2nd ed.). Champaign, Ill: Human Kinetics.

Brower, K., Blow, F., Beresford, T., and Fuelling, C. (1989). Anabolic-androgenic steroid dependence. *Journal of Clinical Psychiatry, 50*, 31-33.

Cafri, G., van den Berg, P., and Thompson, J.K. (2006). Pursuit of muscularity in adolescent boys: Relations among biopsychosocial variables and clinical outcomes. *Journal of Clinical Child and Adolescent Psychology, 35,* 283-291.

Chan, C.S., and Grossman, H.Y. (1988). Psychological effects of running loss on consistent runners. *Perceptual and Motor Skills, 66,* 875-883.

Clarke, J. (1999). Anabolic Steroids-a growing problem. Network Northwest: *Healthwise Liverpool,* edition no 10.

Cohen, J., Collins, R., Darkes, J. and Gwartney, D. (2007). A league of their own: demographics, motivations and patterns of use of 1,995 male adult non-medical steroid users in the United States. *Journal of the International Society of Sports Nutrition,* http://www.jissn.com/content/4/1/12.

Collier, K. and Smith, D (2007). Steroids in the weight room. Paper presented at the Anti-doping in Sport Congress, Louisville, Kentucky.

Collier, K., Smith, D., and Liston, K. (2006). Motives for anabolic steroid use amongst recreational bodybuilders: A case study. *Proceedings of the annual meeting of the Association for the Advancement of Applied Sport Psychology.* Middleton, WI: Association for the Advancement of Applied Sport Psychology.

Connell, R.W. (1987). *Gender and power.* Cambridge: Politry.

Copeland, J., Peters, R., and Dillon, P. (1998). Anabolic-androgenic steroid dependence in a woman. *Australian and New Zealand Journal of Psychiatry, 32,* 589.

Diener E., and Lucas, R. E. (1991). In M Lewis and J. M. Haviland (Eds). *Handbook of emotions* (2nd Ed.), pp. 325-327. New York: Guilford.

Fallon, E.A., and Hausenblas, H.A. (2005). Media images of the 'ideal' female body: Can acute exercise moderate their psychological impact? *Body Image, 2(1),* 62-73.

Frederick, D.A., Buchanan, G.M., Sadehgi-Azar, L., Peplau, L.A., Haselton, M.G., Berezovskaya, A., and Lipinski, R.E. (2007). Desiring the muscular ideal: Men's body satisfaction in the United States, Ukraine, and Ghana. *Psychology of Men and Muscularity, 8,* 103-117.

Frederick, D.A., Fessler, D.M., and Haselton, M.G. (2005). Do representations of male muscularity differ in men's and women's magazines? *Body Image, 2,* 81-86.

Furnham, A., and Calnan, A. (1998). Eating disturbance, self-esteem, reasons for exercising and body weight dissatisfaction in adolescent males. *European Eating Disorder Review, 6,* 58-72.

Fussell, S. (1991). *Muscle: confessions of an unlikely bodybuilder.* London: Abacus.

Goldman, R. (1984). *Death in the locker room: Steroids, cocaine and sports.* Tucson, AZ: Body Press.

Grace, F., Baker. J., and Davies, B. (2004). Anabolic androgenic steroids use in recreational gym users: A regional sample of the Mid-Glamorgan area. *Journal of Substance Abuse, 6,* (3), 189-195.

Grieve, F.G. (2007). A conceptual model of factors contributing to the development of muscle dysmorphia. *Eating Disorders, 15,* 63-80.

Grogan, S., Shepherd, S., Evans, R., Wright, S., and Hunter, G. (2006). Experiences of Anabolic Steroid Use: In-Depth Interviews With Men and Women Bodybuilders. *Journal of Health Psychology,* 11, (6), 845-856.

Harrison, K., Taylor, L.D., and Marske, A.L. (2006). Women's and men's eating behavior following exposure to ideal-body images and texts. *Communication Research, 33,* 507-529.

Hart, E. A., Leary, M. R., and Rejeski, W. J. (1989). The measurement of social physique anxiety. *Journal of Sport and Exercise Psychology, 11,* 94-104.

Hausenblas, H. A., and Symons Downs, D. (2002). How much is too much? The development and validation of the Exercise Dependence Scale. *Psychology and Health, 17*, 387-404.

Hays, L., Littleton, S., and Stillner, V. (1990). Anabolic-androgenic steroid dependence [Letter to the editor]. *American Journal of Psychiatry, 147*, 122.

Henson, C.T. (2004). Potential antecedents of muscle dysmorphia. Unpublished master's thesis, Western Kentucky University, Bowling Green, KY.

Hildebrandt, T., Langenbucher, J., Carr, S., Sanjuan, P., and Park, S. (2006). Predicting Intentions for Long Term Anabolic-Androgenic Steroid Use Among Men: A Covariance Structure Model. *Psychology of Addictive Behaviors, 20*, 234-240.

Hotten, J. (2004). *Muscle: A writer's trip through a sport with no boundaries.* London: Yellow Jersey Press.

Hughes, R., and Coakley, J. (1991). Positive deviance among athletes: The implications of overconformity to the sport ethic. *Sociology of Sport Journal, 8*, 307-325.

Hurst, R., Hale, B., and Smith, D. (2000). Exercise dependence, social physique anxiety and social support in experienced and inexperienced bodybuilders and weightlifters. *British Journal of Sports Medicine, 34*, 431-435.

Johnston, L., Bachman, J., O'Malley, P., Schulenberg, J., and Wallace, J. (2007). Monitoring the Future: National results on adolescent drug use. http://www.monitoringthefuture.org.

Klein, A. (1993). *Little big men: Bodybuilding subculture and gender construction.* New York: Albany.

Klein, A. (1992). Man makes himself: Alienation and self-objectification in bodybuilding. *Play and Culture, 5*, 326-337.

Korkia, P.(1994). Anabolic steroid use in Britain. *The International Journal of Drug Policy, 5* (1), 1-6.

Korkia, A., and Stimons, G. V. (1996). *Anabolic steroid use in Great Britain: An exploratory investigation.* Report For the Centre Research on Drugs Health and Behaviour. London.

Korkia, A. (1996). Use of anabolic steroids has been reported by 9% of men attending gymnasiums. *British Medical Journal, 3*, (13), 1009-1010.

Kuennen, M.R., and Waldron, J.J. (2007). Relationships between specific personality traits, fat free mass indices, and the muscle dysmorphia inventory. *Journal of Sport Behavior, 30*, 453-470.

Kutscher, E., Lund, B. and Perry, P. (2002). Anabolic steroids: A review for the clinician. *Sports Medicine*, 32, 285-296

Lambert, C.P., Frank, L.L., and Evans, W.J. (2004). Macronutrient considerations for the sport of bodybuilding. *Sports Medicine, 34,* 317-327.

Lantz, C.D., Rhea, D.J., and Cornelius, A.E. (2002). Muscle dysmorphia in elite level power lifters and body builders: A test of differences within a conceptual model. *Journal of Strength and Conditioning Research, 16,* 649-655.

Lantz C. D., Rhea, D. J., and Mayhew, J. L. (2001,Winter). The drive for size: a psycho-behavioral model of muscle dysmorphia. *International Sports Journal,* 71-86.

Leit, R.A., Pope. H. G., and Grey. J. J. (2001). Cultural Expectations of Muscularity in Men: The Evolution of Playgirl Centrefolds. *International Journal of Eating Disorders*, 29, 90-92.

Lenehan, P., Bellis, M., and McVeigh, J. (1996). A study of anabolic steroid use in the north west of England. *The Journal of Performance Enhancing Drugs, 1*, 57-70.

Lenehan, P. (2003). *Anabolic steroids and other performance enhancing drugs*. London: Taylor Frances.

Lenehan, P. (2005). *Anabolic steroids: A hidden public health issue or Why athletes give drugs a bad name*. Paper presented at University College Chester's Annual Conference on Sport and Social Issues, Chester, UK.

Leone, J.E., Sedory, E.J., and Gray, K.A. (2005). Recognition and treatment of muscle dysmorphia and related body image disorders. *Journal of Athletic Training, 40,* 352-359.

Lorenzen, L.A., Grieve, F.G., and Thomas, A. (2004). Exposure to muscular male models decreases men's body satisfaction. *Sex Roles, 51,* 743-748.

Luoma, T.C. (interviewer) and Mentzer, M. (interviewee). (1995). *Muscle Media 2000 Audio Tape Interview Series: Mike Mentzer Part 3.* Golden, CO: Muscle Media 2000.

Mac An Ghaill, M. (1994). *The making of men: Masculinities, sexualities and schooling.* Buckingham: Open University Press.

Mac An Ghaill, M. (1997). *Understanding masculinities.* Buckingham: Open University Press.

Messner, M. and Sabo, D. (1990). *Sport, Men and the Gender Order.* Champaign, Ill: Human Kinetics.

Mishkind, M., Rodin, J., Silberstein, L., and Streigel-Moore. (1987). The embodiment of masculinity: Cultural, psychological and behavioral dimensions. In M. Kimmel (ed.), *Changing men: New dimensions in research on men and masculinity.* Newbury Park, CA: Sage Publications.

Monaghan, L. F. (1999). Creating 'the perfect body': A variable project. *Body and Society, 5,* 267-290.

Monaghan, L. F. (2001). *Bodybuilding drugs and risk.* Routledge: London.

Monaghan, L. F. (2002a). Regulating 'unruly' bodies: Work tasks, conflict and violence in Britain's night-time economy. *The British Journal of Sociology, 31,* 440-77.

Monaghan, L. F. (2002b). Vocabularies of motivation for illicit steroid use amongst bodybuilders. *Social Science and Medicine, 55,* 695-708.

Morgan, W.P. (1979). Negative addiction in runners. *The Physician and Sportsmedicine, 7*(2), 57-70.

Neighbors, L.A., and Sobal, J. (2007). Prevalence and magnitude of body weight and shape dissatisfaction among university students. *Eating Behaviors,8(4),* 429-439.

Office for National Statistics (2001). The ESRC review of government social classifications. London: Office for National Statistics.

Olivardia, R. (2001). Mirror, mirror on the wall, who's the largest of them all? The features and phenomenology of muscle dysmorphia. *Harvard Review of Psychiatry, 9,* 254-259.

Olivardia, R., Pope, H.G., Borowiecki, J.J., and Cohane, G.H. (2004). Biceps and body image: The relationship between muscularity and self-esteem, depression, and eating disorder symptoms. *Psychology of Men and Masculinity, 5,* 112-120.

Olivardia, R., Pope, H.G., and Hudson, J. (2000). Muscle dysmorphia in male weightlifters: A case control study. *American Journal of Psychiatry, 157,*1291-1296.

Olrich, T.W. and Ewing, M.E. (1999). Life on steroids: Bodybuilders describe their perceptions of the anabolic-androgenic steroid use period. *The Sport Psychologist, 13,* 299-312.

Olrich, T.W. and Vassallo, M. (2006). Psychological dependency to anabolic-androgenic steroids: exploring the role of social mediation. *New England Law Review, 40,* 735-46.

Pates, R., and Temple, D. (1992). The use of anabolic steroids in Wales: A report by the Welsh Committee on Drug Misuse. Cardiff: Welsh Office.

Perry, M. H., Wright, D., and Littlepage, N. C. (1992). Dying to be big: A review of anabolic steroid use. *British Journal of Sports Medicine, 26*, 259-261.

Phillips, K. (1991). Body Dysmorphic Disorder: The distress of imagined ugliness. *American Journal of Psychiatry, 148,* 1138-1149.

Phillips, J.M., and Drummond, M.J. (2001). An investigation into body image perception, body satisfaction and exercise expectation of male fitness leaders: Implications for professional practice. *Leisure Studies, 20,* 95-105.

Pierce, E.F. (1994). Exercise dependence syndrome in runners. *Sports Medicine, 18,* 149-155.

Plewis, I., and Mason, P. (2002) What works and why? Combining quantatative and qualitative approaches in large scale evaluations. *International Journal of Social Research Methods, 8,* 185-194.

Pope, H.G., Gruber, A.J., Mangweth, B., Bureau, B., deCol, C., Jouvent, R., and Hudson, J.I. (2001). Body image perception among men in three countries. *American Journal of Psychiatry, 157,* 1297-1301.

Pope, H.G., Phillips, K.A., and Olivardia, R. (2000). *The Adonis complex: The secret crisis of male body obsession.* New York: Free Press.

Pope, H., Olivardia, R., Gruber, A., and Borowiecki, J. (1999). Evolving Ideals of Male Body Image as Seen Through Action Toys. *International Journal of Eating Disorder*, 26, 65-72.

Pope, H.G., Gruber, A.J., Choi, P.L., Olivardia, R., and Phillips, K.A. (1997). Muscle dysmorphia: An underrecognized form of body dysmorphic disorder. *Psychosomatics, 38,* 548-557.

Ramsey, M., and Spiller, J. (1997). *Drug Misuse Declared in 1996: Latest Results from the British Crime Survey.* London: Home Office.

Rhea, D.J., Lantz, C.D., and Cornelius, A.E. (2004). Development of the Muscle Dysmorphia Inventory (MDI). *Journal of Sports Medicine and Physical Fitness, 44,* 428-435.

Rhea, D.J., Lantz, C.D., and Trail, G.T. (2000). Muscle dysmorphia: A confirmatory test of a new model. *Research Quarterly for Exercise and Sport, S71,* A-94.

Richman, J. M., Rosenfeld, L. B., and Hardy, C. J. (1993). The Social Support Survey: An initial evaluation of a clinical measure and practice model of the social support process. *Research in Social Work Practice, 3,* 288-311.

Ridgeway, R.T., and Tylka, T.L. (2005). College men's perceptions of ideal body composition and shape. *Psychology of Men and Masculinity, 6,* 209-220.

Sachs, M.L., and Pargman, D. (1979). Running addiction: a depth interview examination. *Journal of Sport Behaviour, 2,* 143-155.

Sharp, M., and Collins, D. (1998). Exploring the "inevitability" of the relationship between anabolic-androgenic steroid use and aggression in males. *Journal of Sport and Exercise Psychology, 20,* 379-394.

Smith, D., and Hale, B. (2004). Validity and factor structure of the Bodybuilding Dependence Scale. *British Journal of Sports Medicine, 38,* 177-181

Smith, D., and Hale, B. (2005). Exercise dependence in bodybuilders: antecedents and reliability of measurement. *Journal of Sports Medicine and Physical Fitness, 45,* 401-408.

Smith, D., Hale, B.D., and Collins, D. (1998). Measurement of exercise dependence in bodybuilders. *Journal of Sports Medicine and Physical Fitness, 38*, 66-74.

Smith, D. (2005). Psychology and bodybuilding. In J. Dosil (Ed) *Sports psychology: Working with athletes in different sports.* Chichester: Wiley.

Stanford, J. N. and McCabe, M. P. (2002). Body image ideal among males and females: Sociocultural influences and focus on different body parts. *Journal of Health Psychology, 7*, 675-684.

Strahan, E.J., Lafrance, A., Wilson, A.E., Ethier, N., Spencer, S.J., Zanna, M.P. (2008). Victoria's dirty secret: How sociocultural norms influence adolescent girls and women. *Personality and Social Psychology Bulleting, 34*, 288-301.

Tennant, F., Black, D., and Voy, R. (1988). Anabolic-androgenic steroid dependence with opioid-type features [Letter to the editor]. *New England Journal of Medicine, 319*, 578.

Thaxton, L. (1982). Physiological and psychological effects of short-term exercise addiction on habitual runners. *Journal of Sport Psychology, 4*, 73-80.

Thompson, H. (Writer and Presenter), and Mares, A. (Producer). (1993). *Iron Maidens.* Manchester: BBC Radio 4.

Tucker, L. A. (1982). Effects of a weight-training program on the self-concepts of college males. *Perceptual and Motor Skills, 54*, 1055-1061.

Tucker, L.A. (1983a). Effect of weight training on self-concept: a profile of those influenced most. *Research Quarterly for Exercise and Sport, 54*, 389-397.

Tucker, L.A. (1983b). Weight training: a tool for the improvement of self and body concepts of males. *Journal of Human Movement Studies, 9*, 31-37.

Tucker, L.A. (1987). Effect of weight training on body attitudes: who benefits most? *Journal of Sports Medicine and Physical Fitness, 27*, 70-78.

Veale, D. (1995). Does exercise dependence really exist? In J. Annett, B. Cripps and H. Steinberg (Eds.), *Exercise addiction: motivation for participation in sport and exercise.* Leicester, UK: British Psychological Society.

Wright, J. (1980). Anabolic steroids and athletics. *Exercise and Sport Science Reviews, 8*, 149-202.

Wright, S., Grogan. S., and Hunter. G. (2000). Motivation for anabolic steroid use among bodybuilders. *Journal of Health Psychology, 5*, 566-571.

Wright, S., Grogan. S., and Hunter. G. (2001). Bodybuilders' attitude towards steroid use. *Drugs Education Prevention and Policy, 8*, 2001.

Yesalis, C., Barhke, M., Kopstein, A. and Barsukiewicz, C. (2000). Incidence of Anabolic Steroid Use: A discussion of Methodological Issues: In C.E. Yesalis (Ed.), *Anabolic steroids in sport and exercise* (2nd ed.). Champaign, Ill: Human Kinetics.

Yesalis, C., Vicary, J., Buckley, W., Streit, A., Katz, D., and Wright, J. (1990). Indications of psychological dependence among anabolic-androgenic steroid abusers. *National Institute on Drug Abuse Research Monograph Series, 102,* 196-214.

All authors contributed equally to production of this chapter

In: Men and Addictions: New Research
Author: Lyman J. Katlin

ISBN 978-1-60692-098-5
© 2009 Nova Science Publishers, Inc.

Chapter 2

SEEKING SAFETY THERAPY FOR MEN: CLINICAL AND RESEARCH EXPERIENCES

Lisa M. Najavits[1], Martha Schmitz[2], Kay M. Johnson[3], Cary Smith[4], Terry North[5], Nancy Hamilton[6], Robyn Walser[7], Kevin Reeder[8], Sonya Norman[9] and Kendall Wilkins[10]

1. Harvard Medical School / McLean Hospital, Boston MA, USA
2. San Francisco VA Medical Center, CA, USA
3. St. Luke's-Roosevelt Hospital,
Crime Victims Treatment Center, New York, NY, USA
4. Vet Centers, Readjustment Counseling Service,
Department of Veteran Affairs. Washington DC, USA
5. VA Omaha, NE, USA
6. Operation PAR, St. Petersburg, FL, USA
7. VA Palo Alto, CA, USA
8. Central Arkansas Veterans Healthcare System, AR, USA
9. VA San Diego Healthcare System and University of California, San Diego, CA, USA
10. San Diego State University and University of California, San Diego, CA, USA

ABSTRACT

This chapter highlights clinical and research experience on the use of Seeking Safety therapy with men clients. Seeking Safety is a present-focused, coping skills model that addresses trauma and/or substance abuse, from the start of treatment. Its major goal is to help clients increase safety in their lives. The model was designed for both genders, and all types of traumas and substances. We describe how it has been implemented in various settings with men including mental health and substance abuse programs, veterans' hospitals, correctional settings, and residential treatment. The authors represent a range of clinicians and researchers who have conducted the model with men for many years. We describe key themes, treatment strategies, and research studies on Seeking Safety with men.

INTRODUCTION

Seeking Safety is an evidence-based therapy for trauma and/or substance abuse (Najavits, 2002). The manual was designed for both genders, and thus includes examples from both men and women as well as gender-neutral language where appropriate. Because many of the studies on Seeking Safety were conducted on women, it is sometimes assumed that the model was intended for woman rather than men. This also derives from an early paper on the model (Najavits *et al.*, 1996), which focused on women in group treatment. However, by the time the model was finalized and published in book form, it explicitly targeted both genders and both group and individual modalities (Najavits, 2002). The idea was for the model to be as inclusive as possible—in addition to both genders, it is intended for use across trauma and substance abuse types; across modalities; across treatment settings (e.g., outpatient, inpatient, residential); and for any clinician within those settings who treats this population.

It is worth commenting on why so many studies of the model were on women (for a summary of research see Najavits, 2007). This was largely due to growing recognition of the importance of trauma and substance abuse in the lives of women. Earlier, both of these areas were largely understood as men's problems. Substance abuse has historically been much higher in men, and trauma was associated with men and combat (Najavits et al., 1996). Studies on women with trauma and substance abuse became an important area of work in the 1990's and early 2000s. There was increased recognition of traumas typical in women (child abuse, domestic violence); and greater focus on making substance abuse treatment more gender-sensitive. Thus, Seeking Safety studies addressed what was considered a new need: treatment for women with trauma and substance abuse.

The model is characterized by the following key features:

- Integrated treatment of trauma and substance abuse (although it can also be used for either alone);
- Early-stage treatment (can be used from the start of treatment, as it is designed for stabilization);
- Coping-skills oriented (to help increase safety from trauma and substance abuse)
- Present-focused (no exploration of trauma details, although it can be used in conjunction with any other treatment)
- Idealistic (to restore hope)
- Evidence-based (the only model thus far established as effective for the dual diagnosis of PTSD and substance use disorder; Najavits et al., in press)
- Designed to be engaging (use of quotations, humanistic language, creative exercises)
- Flexible (it offers 25 topics that are each independent of the others; the clinician can do as few or many topics as there is time for, for any treatment length)
- Clinician-sensitive (addressing countertransference, clinician self-care, and secondary traumatization)

A variety of male subgroups have been treated with the model including veterans, adolescents, men abused in childhood, and men in various settings (e.g., community treatment, criminal justice, substance abuse treatment, mental health treatment, inpatient, outpatient, residential, and private practice). Across these settings, a wide variety of traumas and addictions have been addressed. The model has been conducted in group and individual format, and in single and mixed-gender format.

In this paper, we explore themes related to its use with males. We also summarize existing studies of Seeking Safety with men.

The experiences of men with trauma and/or substance abuse are deeply important to validate and understand. For anyone interested in reading more about male gender-based themes, some helpful books include Shay (1994) on combat PTSD; Lew (1988) on sexual abuse of males; and Sonkin (1998) on male child abuse of all types.

BASIS FOR THIS CHAPTER

This chapter is based on the following clinical and research experiences. These diverse sources also highlight the many ways in which men seek help for trauma and substance abuse.

I. Clinical Experience

Lisa M. Najavits, PhD. Nine years experience conducting Seeking Safety with men in the Boston area in hospital and community settings; primarily clients with severe addictions and PTSD from child abuse and neglect; also treatment of women using the model, and teaching and research on it.

Martha Schmitz, PhD. Six years experience conducting Seeking Safety with men in Boston and San Francisco, including veterans (Vietnam and Iraq/Afghanistan eras), in private practice, and as the lead clinician on a pilot study of Seeking Safety with men (Najavits et al., 2005); worked with men who experienced child abuse, combat, and other traumas; also provided supervision, consultation, and training for over five years on the use of Seeking Safety with various populations (prisoners, immigrants, survivors of gangs/street violence, homeless, drug court, and mental health and substance abuse treatment).

Kay Johnson, LICSW. Six years conducting Seeking Safety with men in a community-based program in Harlem, New York, most of whom had experienced multiple violent traumas; ran both group and individual modality Seeking Safety in residential and outpatient programs; provided training and ongoing supervision for community-based programs and research projects involving men in alternatives-to-incarceration and crime victims' programs; also, conducted Seeking Safety with women for ten years.

Cary Smith, LMSW. Nine years conducting Seeking Safety in Washington DC for with men combat veterans with dual diagnosis (various wars), in an outpatient community veterans clinic; both group and individual Seeking Safety.

Terry North, PhD. Eight years conducting Seeking Safety as Director of the PTSD Clinic at the Omaha VA. Seeking Safety was conducted in group or individual modality with veterans who experienced trauma in the military (combat, line of duty, and military sexual trauma, from all war eras); many had a dual diagnosis. Seeking Safety groups were single- and mixed-gender.

Nancy Hamilton, MPA, CAP, CCJAP. Three years as principal investigator on a Substance Abuse Mental Health Services Administration (SAMHSA) grant to provide

Seeking Safety and other services to young African-American men mandated to residential substance abuse treatment in St. Petersburg, Florida.

Robyn Walser, PhD. Seven years experience conducting Seeking Safety in inpatient and outpatient VA settings serving as clinician and supervisor of trainees learning Seeking Safety. Five years conducting training in use of Seeking Safety in VA facilities. Currently involved in randomized controlled trial investigating Seeking Safety in outpatient VA substance abuse clinic.

Kevin Reeder, PhD. Four years conducting Seeking Safety groups with men and women veterans in group format in both residential PTSD programs and outpatient mental health clinic settings at VAs in Kansas City, Missouri and Little Rock, Arkansas; also trained interns and colleagues to conduct Seeking Safety.

Sonya Norman, PhD. Three years' conducting Seeking Safety in San Diego with veterans from Iraq and Afghanistan and with dually diagnosed women in a community outpatient psychiatric clinic; also conducting research on Seeking Safety in both domestic violence and veterans' settings.

Kendall Wilkins, BA. Six months conducting Seeking Safety with dually diagnosed women in a community outpatient psychiatric clinic in San Diego; also part of research team evaluating Seeking Safety with new veterans (Iraq/Afghanistan) in the VA.

II. Research Experience

Four different investigator groups have conducted research on Seeking Safety with men. They are as follows and are described in more detail in the section Research later in the chapter:

- − -A qualitative evaluation study that addressed the feasibility of Seeking Safety with men veterans (Weaver, Trafton, Walser and Kimerling, 2007).
- − -A pilot study of five men with chronic, severe PTSD and substance dependence, based on childhood trauma (largely physical and sexual violence) (Najavits et al., 2005).
- − -A pilot evaluation of Seeking Safety with 76 young African-American males referred by drug courts into residential treatment (Hamilton, 2006).
- − -A pilot study of Seeking Safety with older veterans, primarily male (Cook *et al.*, 2006).

CLINICAL THEMES

Several major themes emerged based on our clinical experiences conducting Seeking Safety with men. It is important to emphasize, however, that factors other than gender may play a role, such as trauma type and setting. Thus, where possible, we try to distinguish between these. Further, any of the patterns below can occur with women too, but appear more prominent with men, in our experience.

Bonding in male ways (like warriors, teams). It has been emphasized in developmental psychology that males tend to bond in different ways than females. Part of this is the tendency to form teams, often represented by sports or war units going into battle. In the use of Seeking Safety with men veterans, for example, it has been observed that when it goes well, they "bond like a symbolic combat unit; they are supportive of each other, and connect almost like a fire team [a group on a military mission]. The recovery of these men is like a different version of combat; it's a real love for their comrades and they get to re-live it here. A lot of Seeking Safety groups directly express that notion of being combat veterans on a mission to recover." These sorts of bonds also have been observed in civilian men, and there has been a sense when doing Seeking Safety that there is less of the scapegoating and intense interpersonal dynamics that can occur with groups of women (particularly those severe in PTSD and substance abuse). One clinician commented that after a few weeks with the men, "it feels as if they almost don't even need me in there—in the beginning I'm doing a lot of the work and then toward the end, they're doing it." Women too, of course, bond in positive ways when doing Seeking Safety or other treatments, but the "feel" of the bond may be different.

Difficulty with feelings. Another theme observed in Seeking Safety and generally in the treatment of men is they have more difficulty with feelings. They may believe that it is not masculine to express feelings, especially vulnerable ones such as sadness, weakness, and shame. They may not even be aware of what they are feeling or may be prone to alexythymia. They may appear more guarded and hypervigilant than women initially; for some, "everything is a threat". Several Seeking Safety topics may help men address their feelings. The topic *Grounding* can increase awareness, for example. One clinician said, "Many experience feelings in an all-or-none way, from 'I don't feel angry' to exploding in anger. What has worked is to help them identify levels of feeling (what is a level 1, 4, 6, 8 and 10 on the 0-10 scale) and what triggers the feelings. Then they have used grounding successfully in anticipating situations where they will be triggered and in bringing themselves down if triggered suddenly. They become less surprised by their own feelings." Other Seeking Safety topics that emphasize feelings include *Healing from Anger; PTSD: Taking Back Your Power; Coping with Triggers;* and *Integrating the Split Self.* In the topic *When Substances Control You*, they also learn why they may have turned to addiction as a way to keep painful feelings at bay. Focusing on feelings may also be a way to engage them in the substance abuse work. One clinician said, "Clients have a lot of minimization and denial about substance use. Some would refuse to go to the substance abuse clinic. We have found that the PTSD piece really brings them in. The trauma piece engages them and then we are able to motivate them to do work on substance use."

Anger. Anger problems are also a common issue when conducting Seeking Safety with men. Sometimes the men are aware of their anger problems, barely able to keep a "lid" on it and feeling great remorse over anger outbursts. Other times, the anger feels so familiar that they are not even clear that it's a problem—they may need additional work just to motivate them to reduce anger. Anger may feel like part of their identity or like a power they do not want to give up. Topics in Seeking Safety that are especially relevant for anger issues are *Healing from Anger, Integrating the Split Self* (to observe their angry and non-angry sides), *Recovery Thinking* (to shift out of angry cognitions), *Case Management* (to refer the client to additional anger management treatment if needed). Anger problems may be especially visible in veterans, as the military trained them to channel anger into aggression for combat. They may need to unlearn such anger patterns once back in civilian life. Indeed, some older veterans have commented that if there is one major Seeking Safety skill they wished they had learned when younger, it is *Healing from Anger*. Similar issues may apply to men in the community who have been involved in gangs, street violence, or domestic violence. For men who suffered child abuse, anger may be directed more toward themselves (self-harm, suicidality) than toward others.

Perpetration of violence. A small but important subset of men will raise issues of perpetration of violence. Some have revealed legal charges against them a few sessions into the therapy. Others have a history of perpetration and there remains a question of whether they will act on violent impulses again. One client told his individual Seeking Safety therapist that he felt protective of her and would assault anyone who hurt her. A common observation is that many of the men were not violent prior to trauma, and indeed appear to be quite unaware of their impulses until triggered or startled. They may appear overwhelmed or perplexed by their own behavior, and feel sadness and remorse when talking of perpetration incidents. If they have severe antisocial personality disorder, however, they may not show remorse. In Seeking Safety, clients are guided to view violence as unsafe both for others and themselves, and learn better coping skills to manage such thoughts and impulses.

Sexuality issues. Men have expressed a variety of concerns related to sexuality in the course of Seeking Safety. These include sexual addiction; pornography addiction; hooking up with strangers for unsafe sex; lack of condom use; having affairs; fears or ambivalence about being gay related to sexual abuse by a male; reenactments of sexual abuse (one client, when high on drugs, would torture himself with various objects sexually in repetition of what had occurred to him as a child); and sometimes a feeling of being used for sex. Most of these issues were reported for community-based men who were sexually abused as children or adolescents; indeed, veterans rarely focused on sexuality except for an occasional mention of pornography addiction. Women who had been sexually abused also expressed sexual problems during Seeking Safety, but these were typically about staying with partners who hurt them, anxiety or dissociation during sex, fear of engaging in sex, difficulty setting boundaries on sex, and lack of pleasure. As part of Seeking Safety with men, we have encouraged them to understand that sexuality problems may relate to trauma; this can help reduce their sense of shame. Also, several of us have found sexual-based addictions can improve with Seeking Safety by using the same principles as apply toward substance use. Psychoeducation about sexuality sometimes becomes part of the work, including having clients read about healthy male sexuality. Referral to a sex therapist may be part of case management for clients who need more intensive treatment.

Hard to engage in treatment / hard to end treatment. There is a paradox that males appear harder to engage in treatment initially but also appear not to want to end treatment once engaged. Strategies for initial engagement include letting the men sit in on a few sessions of Seeking Safety after which they can decide if they want to join; calling the treatment "training" rather than "treatment" (especially for men in military settings who may be resistant to the idea of treatment); and conducting the therapy in shorter blocks of 6 or 12 sessions. One program conducted an orientation group of a few key topics (*Safety; PTSD: Taking Back Your Power; Asking for Help*), conducted in lecture format, and then let the men decide whether to join the actual therapy. Also, it is strongly advised not to insist on any specific attendance requirement on the front end; and, if a client wants to leave, take a "no harm, no foul" approach by letting them end easily without judgment or blame.

Observations on men's difficulty *ending* Seeking Safety have occurred primarily in group modality. Some men want to end a few days early to avoid having to say goodbye. It helps to teach them that saying goodbye is part of healthy relationships (e.g., using a topic such as *Healthy Relationships, Creating Meaning,* or *Honesty*). One program ran an alumni group in which men could return on a drop-in basis to check in and focus on their safe and unsafe coping; this helped prevent a feeling of an abrupt ending. Another program let men go through Seeking Safety a second time if desired.

Isolation. The men we have worked with appear to struggle more with isolation than the women do, and initially appear more quiet. With women it often takes effort to keep them on task and limit their talking if they "spill" too much. With men it is the opposite: overly quiet, withdrawn, needing to encourage them to open up more. In Seeking Safety, they often come to feel a strong positive bond with men who have similar trauma, addiction, and life problems, and can ultimately feel less alone. For veterans, it helps to identify how military life may have reinforced isolation (sharing feelings was discouraged; making "contact" with the enemy was dangerous). When they return to civilian life they may need to stop "hiding in the bunker," such as sitting alone in front of the TV for hours. One clinician encouraged a client to buy an answering machine to help him stay connected to others. Another prompted her clients to interact with various people, not just veterans, to help build commonality and identity outside of war experience. Some found the topic *Discovery* especially helpful for moving out of "stuck" beliefs and patterns.

Caretaking problems. This emerges in two ways. First, men may carry the societal role of caretakers for their family (financially and otherwise) and feel strong guilt and failure when they let their partner or children down due to addiction or trauma. They may feel "not man enough". Also some have experienced trauma related to their children. One man chose to go to prison instead of treatment and his child was killed by the abusive man who was then living with the child's mother. He felt unable to forgive himself, but was able to use *Grounding* and *Asking for Help* when triggered by this situation. Other men use Seeking Safety as a forum for planning how to first establish safety (e.g., sobriety and stability on medication) and then reconnecting with children or other important people in their lives. A second area of caretaking difficulty is self-care. Like the classic "guy who won't go to the doctor," many men we have worked with appear unable to take basic steps toward healthy living (nutrition, exercise, routine medical and dental care). These are especially pronounced in men with chronic addiction problems. The topic *Taking Good Care of Yourself* is especially relevant for such issues.

Issues with authority and control. Clients with trauma and substance abuse often present with problems of control, such as taking too little control of their lives (overly passive) or too much control (power struggles) (Najavits, 2002). The men we have worked with exhibit a wide range along this continuum. Some want the therapist or other authority figure to tell them what to do, showing difficulty making healthy decisions for themselves. Others resist influence, refusing to go to the hospital or additional treatment, rejecting therapeutic suggestions, and in some cases, struggling with authority figures or work settings (e.g., police, social services, or bosses). In Seeking Safety clients can benefit from hearing how other men handle such problems. They can also use the skill *Grounding* as an immediate way to calm down. One client, for example, reported that he was pulled over by a police officer while driving. His first instinct was to run, but he was able to use grounding to talk calmly with the officer and handle the situation without negative consequences. In one of the pilot studies on Seeking Safety with men (Najavits et al., 2005), at each session they were given control over whether to focus on the past or present (see below for more details). Allowing them to choose appeared to be an important element in the success of that project. In general, the Seeking Safety emphasis on empowerment-- "no one right way, but many", choice of coping strategies, and support for trying new ways of coping-- all seem to enhance healthy control while lessening unhealthy control. One clinician said, "They like idea of 'choice' and noticing what works for them because they have often have been in programs which give them 'one right way.'"

Identity ("Who are you?"). More than many other issues, trauma and addiction tend to become "who the person is", as perceived by both themselves and others. Thus, there is a strong emphasis in these fields on the centrality of identity. In conducting Seeking Safety with men, several identity themes were observed. First, both trauma and substance abuse violate the traditional male role of being strong and in control. As one clinician noted, "Men may have to fight these images to accept where they are and to be able to work on achieving genuine strength and control." Second, when the work goes well, one sees a "recovery identity" emerge—speaking the language of recovery, making more active efforts toward it, and understanding the need for it. As Seeking Safety is a first-stage stabilization treatment, a large part of the work is helping co-create this recovery identity with the client (in conjunction with other treatments the client attends). As one male client said (quoted in {Najavits, in press}, "Am I the guy who is homeless, living in the woods, using drugs (the way I used to be), or am I the guy who is able to work, taking care of my family, able to stay clean (the way I am now)? I can't tell which is the real me." The topic *Integrating the Split Self* can be very helpful to the client who is trying to integrate conflicting aspects of his identity.

Another key area of identity is how much clients "own" their trauma. Men who were physically or sexually traumatized as children, for example, seem to disown their traumas much more than veterans. They try to forget their traumas and "just get on with their lives." It is as if they want to pretend that trauma never happened. For such clients, the treatment encourages them to become aware of the impact of trauma; to face it so they can move on. In contrast, veteran men seemed to hold a strong attachment to their trauma identity. One clinician said, "When I conduct the topic *PTSD: Taking Back your Power*, the Vietnam veterans have a much stronger reaction to the idea that people can recover from PTSD than do community-based clients. They are adamant that healing isn't possible, even though they made significant treatment gains. Many acknowledged that their symptoms of nightmares, angry outbursts, and panic were much better than before. But they viewed it as managing symptoms rather than recovery. The idea that people could recover from PTSD seemed to undermine their sense of self-- they would 'disappear' if their traumas healed. Their identity was based on being a combat veteran: 'If I heal my PTSD, no one will believe that my combat experiences were as bad as they were. If I heal my PTSD, I am no longer a combat veteran. If I heal my PTSD, I will lose my benefits.'" With addiction too, the client may either accept or deny it, and an important part of recovery to accept it more. In addiction, however, others (family, treaters, systems) are often working to help the client recognize it whereas in trauma this is less common; in fact others may not acknowledge trauma as part of the client's problems. When exploring identity issues, the topics *Creating Meaning* and *Recovery Thinking* may be especially useful. For example, in Creating Meaning, veterans seem to identify with: "I am my trauma"; "The past is the present"; "Dangerous permission";

"Actions speak louder than words"; "Focusing on the negative"; and the "Uniqueness fallacy" (only combat veterans can understand). The cognitive topics can also help shift the clients out of all-or-none beliefs ("This is my last time to enter treatment"; "Nothing will help me with my disorders"; "I never feel like using.")

Self-hatred (feeling "like a monster"). Some men we have worked with feel that they are bad, which they sometimes describe as being "like a monster" or a "mean person". This is prominent in veterans who as part of military work had to kill or maim others, but also occurs among community-based men who perhaps fought in prison or gangs. Men and women traumatized as children tend to turn hatred against themselves (feeling like damaged goods, unworthy, or used). However, they too sometimes identify with the perpetrator and believe they are bad because they have scary thoughts or impulses to hurt others, even if they never act on them. In Seeking Safety, clients can explore the connection between trauma, addiction and such internal feelings. The topic *Compassion* is especially useful for this. As one VA clinician said, "A lot of guys don't understand compassion. We talk about how when you first go into the service, compassion is something you unlearn. You go to basic training, and then combat, and the only way to survive is to lose compassion for all others, even for yourself. Once you're home you have to relearn it. When we use Seeking Safety and the language of compassion, they can put it into context instead of seeing themselves as bad people. They can see themselves as courageous warriors again, but now toward healing and regaining intimacy and the love of their families. It gives them hope." Another clinician said, "They sometimes have a strong reaction to the topic *Compassion*-- difficulty understanding what compassion means, difficulty believing that changing harsh self-talk is an appropriate goal. It has become a powerful change tool when there is at least one group member who relates to the material and connects it to the way he was treated as a child and notices the benefits of changing self-talk. Once this happens, compassion often becomes a theme or identified way of coping during the check-in questions." The topic *Honesty* can also bring out a lot in this area— helping clients explore more of what they feel inside. One clinician said, "Sometimes they may have an initial resistance to the topic of *Honesty*, feeling like they're being accused of lying, or having different definitions of what honesty is. But it is still a really good session, one of the best, because they work on it. We never know what we will get but it typically goes really well." Finally, the topic *Integrating the Split Self* was also identified as important. "They can look at the combat side and the caring side and the work they have to do to integrate those; the purpose of them; how the two sides interact. The guys get it. It's fantastic stuff to see that change."

Intimacy. Men with trauma and addiction often have difficulty with intimacy. They may engage in relationships without being fully present, or may enact relationship styles that alienate others. After everything they have endured others' concerns may seem trivial ("Oh come on-- is this a life or death issue? Why are you bothering me?"). They may find it hard to be open and genuine. One VA clinician said, "They have trouble going to the store for a pack of cigarettes—the wife thinks they're running around, but it really is just cigarettes. They do it so stealthily; everything is a big secret; because in the military that was an important way to stay alive." Some men have repeated superficial romantic relationships, unable to become close to anyone. "They've done such a good job keeping people away; they seem to be saying, 'I don't want to be known right now; if people knew me they wouldn't like me.'" In Seeking Safety, the concept of secrecy is explored in relation to trauma and addiction; this can help explain where such behavior originates. According to one clinician, "Clients said the

Seeking Safety material felt 'personal, as if the writer was talking about me.' They found the material engaging and noted that they were sharing it with their spouses. This was viewed as positive and helpful, and offered one way of helping them become more known to people in their lives." Other emphasized the topic *Setting Boundaries in Relationships*: "That really takes off as a topic. We spend more time on that and provide extra materials on it because it really seems to be an important topic. The men really do get into it. They are pretty perplexed by the boundary issues but they are interested in sorting them out."

Multiple problem areas. Uniformly, all of the clinicians emphasized that the men they saw in Seeking Safety had numerous problem areas, beyond just trauma and addiction. They applied it as a general coping skills model and did not require clients to meet formal PTSD or substance use disorder criteria (consistent with prior implementation efforts (Najavits, 2004). The men presented with many different issues, including other Axis I and II disorders (e.g., eating disorders, pathological gambling, bipolar disorder, psychotic disorders); addictions not defined in the DSM-IV (e.g., sex or pornography); medical issues (especially those associated with substance abuse such as HIV and hepatitis C; but also diabetes, high blood pressure, and other health problems); suicidality; dissociative symptoms; poverty; discrimination; and homelessness. The *Case Management* and *Community Resources* topics in Seeking Safety guide clients toward needed treatments of all kinds. The topic *Commitment* teaches clients how to follow through on goals to help improve their lives.

RESEARCH

Four formal research efforts have evaluated the use of Seeking Safety with men; each is described below. All addressed samples of men who were typically severe and chronic in both trauma symptoms and substance abuse, along with numerous other life problems.

Qualitative study on use of Seeking Safety with men veterans. Weaver et al. (2007) report as follows. "In 2006, we conducted a 12-week pilot test of Seeking Safety with male veterans in methadone maintenance treatment at a Department of Veterans Affairs (VA) mental health clinic before the initiation of a five-year randomized controlled trial. We then conducted a semiformal focus group of volunteer participants to ask about general concerns, such as what we could improve, and specific concerns, such as whether the examples of sexual trauma were a problem. We also asked a male researcher and a male veteran who was also a counselor to review the protocol for gender-biased language. In addition, we consulted extensively with the therapist who ran the pilot therapy sessions and the therapist's clinical supervisor, the latter of whom has extensive experience training and supervising clinicians to conduct Seeking Safety.

Without exception, the consensus was that the protocol did not need substantive gender-related changes to work well with our population of male veterans with substance use disorders and PTSD. For instance, despite specific concerns, sexual trauma examples helped our participants who had a relevant history discuss this more 'taboo' form of trauma, perhaps for the first time. In contrast, those with primarily combat trauma readily brought the general concepts to bear on their experience. In our view, this phenomenon actually increased the need for sexual trauma examples, while decreasing the need for additional explicit combat examples. No protocol modification could have kept combat trauma from being a prominent focus in our groups. Modifying the focus away from sexual trauma could actually have exacerbated inequality in our group and reinforced avoidance of sexual trauma issues.

Careful wording in the Seeking Safety protocol also appears to avoid appreciable gender bias…[Thus] although concerns that Seeking Safety would need significant adaptation for use with men made excellent clinical sense, the consensus of our experts and consumers indicates that this does not appear to be the case. The careful construction of the manual appears to allow for adaptation as a natural part of the group process" (pg. 1012).

Pilot study on men with PTSD (based on childhood trauma) and substance use disorder (SUD). This study by Najavits et al. (2005) evaluated "a novel combination: Seeking Safety plus Exposure-Therapy Revised…The latter is an adaptation of Foa's exposure therapy, modified for PTSD and SUD. In this small sample (n=5) outpatient pilot trial, patients with current PTSD and SUD were offered 30 sessions over five months, with the option to select how much of each type of treatment they preferred. Outcome results showed significant improvements in drug use; family/social functioning; trauma symptoms; anxiety; dissociation; sexuality; hostility; overall functioning; meaningfulness; and feelings and thoughts related to safety…. Treatment attendance, satisfaction, and alliance were extremely high. The need for further evaluation using more rigorous metholodogy is discussed" (pg. 425). Also notable was that the clients chose an average of 21 Seeking Safety sessions and 9 exposure sessions; the study did not rule out patients for active suicidality (unlike prior trials which typically did); and significant results were obtained despite the very small sample size.

Pilot study on veterans (72% men). Cook et al. (2006) report that, "…four Seeking Safety groups were initiated and completed at the Philadelphia VA Medical Center (PVAMC). Twenty-five outpatient veterans with clinician-diagnosed comorbid SUD-PTSD voluntarily began participating in the groups. Of those, 18 completed a series of 25 group treatment sessions (had attended at least 14 sessions and were still coming at the end of therapy). Of the completers, 72% were male…with a mean age of 50. Primary substance use disorders included alcohol abuse/dependence (78%; n=14), cocaine abuse (61%; n=11) and heroin dependence (33%; n=6). The majority were receiving services in the SUD treatment program but were not receiving PTSD care at the time.

The veterans who completed Seeking Safety evidenced statistically significant improvements from pre- to post-treatment in self-report PTSD symptoms and quality of life. PTSD symptoms decreased as measured by the PTSD Checklist-Military (Weathers et al.; pre M=65.54, SD=8.80, post M=51.15, SD=14.38, t (12)=6.60, p<.001). Quality of Life increased, as measured by the Quality of Life Inventory; Frisch et al., 1992; pre M=-15.43, SD=20.82, very low; post M=.29, SD=18.38, low; t (6)=-2.46,p<.05). Qualitatively, the veterans reported increased ability to identity and manage PTSD and substance use triggers. They also endorsed improvements in their communication and problem solving skills. Regarding substance use, the veterans did demonstrate continued abstinence from substances confirmed by urine testing. The veterans spoke of the value of having their own manual to refer to when they felt distressed (i.e., experiencing triggers or cravings) or were having difficulty employing a particular coping skill. Finally, the veterans indicated that the treatment made them feel valued and hopeful for the first time in years. This was an uncontrolled pilot study and thus there was no control group, no followup on dropouts, and no followup months after completion to see if there were lasting effects of treatment." (pgs. 90-91).

Evaluation project on young African-American men. Hamilton (2006) conducted a SAMHSA project titled the African-American Center of Excellence (AACE). It served two Florida county drug courts, offering residential treatment at Operation PAR in Florida. All participants in AACE (n=76) were African-American males between the ages of 18 and 25, all with lifetime criminal justice involvement. During the six-month residential program, all clients completed all of the assigned modules of Seeking Safety.

Overall, clients were high severity with significant substance abuse and mental health problems. In the year prior, 55% had drug-related charges; 29% interpersonal crimes; and 24% property crimes. A total of 80% met current criteria for substance abuse or dependence (marijuana and cocaine were the most common), with the remaining 20% reporting substance use. Other current diagnoses included 20% ADHD, and 17% each for major depression, PTSD, and conduct disorder. Also, 12% had current suicidal or homicidal thoughts; 76% had been victimized during their lifetime (60% prior to age 19); and 20% had been homeless during their lifetime.

Results indicated a notable drop in substance use, based on self-report. At baseline, the mean days clients reported using substances was 25.3 days; at six months (the ending of the residential program) there was 100% abstinence from substances; at 12 months post-intake, the mean numerous of substance use days was 2 days (twelve-month follow-up $n=55$). Significant reductions were also found from baseline to six months on various scales: the Anxiety subscale of the SCL-90 ($p<.05$); all five subscales of the Cognitive Distortions Scale at $p<.05$ (self-criticism; self-blame; helplessness; hopelessness; and preoccupation with danger); and seven subscales of the Trauma Symptom Inventory at $p<.05$ (anxious arousal; depression; anger/irritability; intrusive experiences; dysfunctional behavior; impaired self-reference; and tension reduction behavior). No data are available for those measures at 12 months, however. Finally, the rate of self-reported unprotected sex decreased from 22% at baseline to 5.9% at 6-month followup, but returned to baseline levels at 12-month followup.

Several conclusions were drawn from this project. First, the implementation of Seeking Safety made significant progress with AACE clients and their understanding of trauma and its relationship with substance abuse. Based on anecdotal information, the use of Seeking Safety provided a structured and safe environment where clients were enabled to express and address their behaviors and emotions without fear of reprisal or judgment. Second, the findings from the AACE data seem to indicate that clients do very well while they are in the residential phase of treatment. However, when they enter the aftercare phase after the six months of residential treatment, recidivism begins to increase and treatment compliance begins to decrease. Thus, it is suggested that future efforts should target the post-residential phase more intensively.

Overall research conclusions. In sum, these research projects reveal high acceptability of the model among several subsets of men: veterans, men traumatized in childhood, and young African-American men referred by drug courts. Moreover, all three projects that reported on quantitative outcomes found statistically significant positive results on various domains. Yet research thus far is at an early stage, and no randomized controlled trial on Seeking Safety with men has been conducted. Future research is needed to verify and extend the positive results of existing studies.

ADDITIONAL SUGGESTIONS FOR CONDUCTING SEEKING SAFETY WITH MEN

In the section *Clinical Themes* earlier in this chapter, various ideas were offered that may help when implementing Seeking Safety with men. The following are additional suggestions.

Use language and examples relevant to men. The Seeking Safety manual encourages language and examples relevant to any subpopulation, whether based on gender, ethnicity, age, setting, or other factors. Below are examples that may be helpful for men clients.

- *"Seeking Safety"* or *"Seeking Strength"*. For military settings, Najavits [2005] suggested the title *Seeking Strength* as soldiers cannot always seek safety-- they must pursue dangerous situations as part of their work. With other men, some clinicians use *Seeking Safety;* others use *Seeking Strength.* One program used *Strength Through Safety* (Stillson, personal communication, 2006).
- *Asking For Help*
  - Men seem to respond well to the idea of asking for help if it is described as a collaboration. Men actually help each other all the time with tasks and activities. They have the experiences of working together to achieve a common goal in battle, the work place, and sports. These examples help men to focus on the reciprocity rather than the vulnerability of asking for help.
- Grounding
  - When conducting the grounding exercise with men, incorporate a phrase about feeling "strong in your body, empowered, more focused."
  - Highlight that there is a middle ground between hypervigilance and being completely vulnerable (especially for men in situations that may be currently dangerous, such as prison or the military). "Staying grounded will help you to make safer choices when you have to go back into battle or the prison yard."
- *Compassion*
  - "Using compassionate self-talk is like being a good sports coach."
  - "It's found that Olympic athletes perform the best when coaches give them balanced feedback. A coach may say: 'When you cleared the hurdle, you did well, but your right leg was a bit too low.' This is more helpful than just praise or criticism.'"
- *Safety/Safe Coping Skills*
  - In general, men seem to think in terms of degrees of safety (what is *safer)* rather than safe versus unsafe. When you think about this from the perspective of a trauma survivor, this seems more adaptive than a more all-or-nothing view.
  - Men seem to respond especially well to the following coping skills (in the topic *Safety*): take responsibility; leave a bad scene; notice the source; notice what you can control; solve the problem; examine the evidence; plan it out; find rules to live by; work the material; focus on now; rethink; notice the cost; set an action plan; notice the choice point; if one way doesn't work, try another; get organized; list your options; when in doubt, do what's hardest.
- *PTSD: Taking Back Your Power*

- Some men are so used to trauma that they view it as normal. Many are surprised to find their experiences qualify as traumatic events. Talking about "violence" may be helpful for some men to understand the word trauma.
- "Think of it as a purple heart winner getting ammunition to use in the real world."
- One VA clinician said, "I even use Lisa's preface which helps the guys see her as the warrior that she is and that she understands it's about restoration of ideals and that kind of thing; it's not about not being strong enough or that it's for women."
- Get them to visualize a young person they care about (son or daughter, etc) coming to them with a problem such as combat or abuse. Ask, "How would you respond to that person?" and then ask if they themselves are worthy of this same response.

- *Creating Meaning*
  - The term "beliefs" rather than "meanings" can be used.
- *Life Choices Game (Review)*
  - Have men create their own scenarios for this topic so relevant issues will emerge.

Know that men like the treatment format. Men have consistently reported that they like the Seeking Safety format. As one clinician said, "I can't say enough about how important the session structure is. It is very comforting to them. Over and over they tell me: I know what I'm getting into; it's not a horribly unknown situation, I know what I'm getting into." Some men have also commented on liking the check-in question, "How are you feeling?" because they often are not asked this question.

Gently encourage homework ("commitments"). Those who do the commitments "take the work to a whole other level. It's also one of the best ways of getting to know the clients." But getting them to do commitments can be challenging. "A lot of them are 'high school holdovers'—they don't like the idea of homework." It helps to remember that commitments are optional, not required, in Seeking Safety. Gentle encouragement is thus the best strategy. In groups, subtle peer pressure sometimes exerts an influence on those who are not doing commitments. One program made the commitments more formally part of the session by holding a 2 hour meeting, with a half-hour of that peer-led and set aside for completing commitments. The half hour can be added to the front or end of the clinician-led session. They also allowed clients to try a buddy system in which they paired up with another client to do the commitment during that half hour or outside of it.

Consider mixed-gender groups. Because Seeking Safety focuses on the present and coping skills, it can be done in mixed-gender format. Sometimes this is necessary in settings where there are only a few of one gender and they would otherwise not have access to group treatment. Suggestions include making sure the minority gender clients (whether male or female) know there will be many more of the other gender in the group, and that they can choose whether or not to join. Also, encourage them to try it for a few sessions to see if they feel comfortable, before they decide. One clinician spoke of the positive value of a mixed gender group: "A female veteran who had experienced military sexual trauma, was in our mostly male group. She got some excellent, very compassionate feedback and pointers regarding boundary issues with males. Another female military sexual trauma victim reported that this group experience helped her develop a more balanced view of men--no longer seeing them all as predators-- because for the first time in her life she received emotional support and positive feedback from males."

Address men's issues as part of supervision. One clinician emphasized the importance of good supervision for clinicians who have concerns about conducting Seeking Safety with men. She stated, "The questions about the Seeking Safety materials seem to come more from clinicians who aren't sure how to respond to men, rather than the men rejecting the materials. The clinician is taken off guard by men's questions, and then buys into the idea that the materials are for women, rather than seeing the client's questions as stemming from curiosity or viewing it as a growth opportunity for the men. In my experience supervising clinicians who work with men, they occasionally bring up questions, such as: 'Can we use a different word, other than safety?' The men will just say: 'There's no way to feel safe in prison!' Can we ask a different question, other than 'How are you feeling?' The men think this is a women's question!" Or, "*Compassion* isn't for men – it suggests taking a warm bath." These are clinical dilemmas for supervision, not a sign that the materials need to be adapted. In supervision, we discuss how to personalize the materials to use relevant examples from clients' lives."

Learn from the clients. One program director reported that her staff initially had a lot of concerns about using Seeking Safety with men. "It will be too long." "They won't like the topics." "The case management will not work." "The structure of the sessions will be hard to do." She said that in fact, the men clients "were open to the Seeking Safety treatment explanation and rationale. They agreed that the disorders should be treated simultaneously and noted that they were thankful that such a treatment had 'finally' been developed. They recognized that the disorders were interrelated." She said her staff eventually realized that it is important not to make up-front assumptions about what they will or will not like, but instead to try the model as is and obtain clients' feedback. In the Seeking Safety book, two main ways of obtaining their feedback are emphasized: the End of Session Questionnaire (in chapter 2) and the End of Treatment Questionnaire (in the final chapter). Occasionally there may even be humorous moments. One clinician said the men in her group had "interesting responses to the part about saying 'no' to continuing prostitution when doing the topic *Setting Boundaries in Relationships."*

Strive to respond to men's different needs. Recognize that there are many variations in how men will respond to the material. For example, VA clinicians have observed that the topic *Respecting Your Time* goes differently with older veterans than younger ones. Older veterans may need to increase activities in their available time whereas younger veterans may be overwhelmed by too many demands (trying to get a job, find a partner, raise children, attend treatment). Also, do not assume that all reactions are based on gender. Men and women who experienced the same type of trauma (such as early child abuse) may appear more alike than men with different trauma types. Also, many other factors may play a role beyond gender: poverty, legal problems, length of substance abuse, treatment setting, resiliency factors, and relationship with the clinician.

Adapt Seeking Safety to your setting. Clinicians reported different ways of conducting the model, such as the following:

- − -An orientation group to present a few key Seeking Safety topics in psychoeducational format (allowing the clinician and clients to see if it feels like a good fit).
- − -An alumni group conducted on a drop-in basis so that men can return for support as needed.
- − -Letting clients go through Seeking Safety a second time, if desired.
- − -Conducting the treatment in blocks (4, 6, 8, or 12 sessions).
- − -Encouraging clients sit in on up to three sessions to see if they like it, before joining.
- − -Adding additional materials as may be helpful (additional anger management tools; information on the biology of trauma and substance abuse, etc.).
- − -Allowing a client to do individual Seeking Safety if the group modality does not work for him.
- − -Bringing in treatment-relevant videos.
- − -Adding creative exercises or games.

Rehearse the skills. Frequent rehearsal of the Seeking Safety skills helps clients use them when new situations arise. One clinician said, "The structure, coping skills format, and cohesiveness of the groups have helped many participants cope constructively with very difficult situations in the present as well as in the past. For example, the child of a combat veteran disclosed sexual abuse by a neighbor. Naturally this news put the veteran in fighting mode and he was struggling with intense rage and homicidal thoughts. The group gave him a safe place to process very charged emotions and his reports of effectively controlling his rage by using grounding and cognitive strategies was very reinforcing in demonstrating that these techniques can work well when one is motivated to apply them. Also, I believe the broad focus on a range of traumas offered by the materials helped the veteran respond in a very understanding, compassionate manner to his child's disclosure and emotional distress. Another veteran received some serious threats from a co-worker. He initially had thoughts of a pre-emptive strike, but the group helped him safely work through this (did some problem solving to help him identify reasonable steps he could take to feel safer and to consider the potential negative consequences of making a pre-emptive strike)."

If needed, shorten the check-in. Some programs that treat men have very limited resources, such as in prisons and community settings. Seeking Safety may therefore be conducted in large groups and it may be necessary to reduce the check-in to one or two questions (e.g., "What good coping have you done?" and "Any substance use or other unsafe behavior?"). If conducting the model with extremely large groups (20 or more), consider having just a few clients answer the questions (ask for volunteers, or have different clients answer at each session). One program modeled the check-in for clients so they could see that it was designed to be short.

CLINICAL EXAMPLES

Below are two types of clinical materials that may help illustrate the use of Seeking Safety with men: quotations from clients and clinicians; and two case examples.

I. Quotations

- An email from a male clinician treating men at a veterans' center:

"Thank you for bringing your expertise to the men and women who served our country. Thank you also for making my practice here so overwhelmingly successful with such a hard to reach population of combat veterans. You've allowed me to reach the unreachable. It never ceases to amaze me how such a bunch of nice guys, with a high body count, 'get it', immediately. Your program gives them the recovery of intimacy and helps them to see the transcendent in the everyday intimacies of love, work, and play. As they recover through the epiphany of your treatment program I see them move from distrust to trust, from fear to faith, from self-enclosure to mutual disclosure. We old combat vets thank you for your knowledge that shows how it is never too late to recover the intimacy to change things, and inviting us to experience more epiphanies like this through your sessions focusing on the ideals lost in combat."

- A male Vietnam veteran: "I wish I would have learned these skills 30 years ago; it would have changed my life."
- A female clinician treating men in the community: "Seeking Safety provided a missing component on trauma that the 12-Step program did not address. I find Seeking Safety a valuable tool to address both issues and have seen enormous benefits in the lives of clients."

II. Case Examples

Case example #1. Joe is a 37 year-old Italian Catholic man who was molested during childhood by both his parish priest and by his swim coach. When Father Dominic started taking a special interest in him, such as inviting him to the movies or out to ice cream, he initially felt flattered. He grew up in a large family (one of 7 children), so was pleased to feel "special". The first molestation occurred on an outing for the altar boys. Afterwards, he tried to forget about it and to convince himself that he had "imagined the whole thing." After he was molested several more times, he told his parents. However, they never took action; in their traditional Catholic family, one never questioned the authority of a priest.

At age 14, Joe was also molested by his soccer coach. He had learned from his previous molestations that "spacing out" and just "getting it over with" was the best way to deal with these events. He started drinking and using marijuana in high school. Soon, it became a daily habit.

At age 20, Joe met and married his wife who was also a traditional Catholic. They had 4 children. He worked as a civil servant for the county. Although he "felt ok," he found that he could not attend or even pass by a Catholic church without having a panic attack. Eventually, he became more and more depressed. He and his wife were estranged, though they continued to live in the same house. He felt a tremendous void from the loss of his spirituality, as well as estrangement from his family of origin (who continued to actively participate in church events). His daily marijuana use began to impact his work. He found himself contemplating suicide. One day, shortly before beginning the Seeking Safety treatment, he tried to hang himself.

Joe immediately felt comfortable with Seeking Safety and began carrying around the safe coping skills sheet. The connection between trauma and substance abuse made sense to him, and he felt motivated to stop his marijuana use. Later in the treatment, he was even able to confide in his father about his marijuana use. His father, a recovering alcoholic, strongly supported Joe in becoming substance-free.

The PTSD symptoms were another matter. As soon as Joe stopped smoking marijuana regularly, his flashbacks and nightmares increased with a vengeance. He and his wife began arguing more. She was concerned that treatment might be making him worse, rather than better. After an exposure therapy session, Joe became dissociative, and later, suicidal. He was hospitalized on the inpatient unit for several days. He stated that one of the interventions that "helped things turn around" for him was discussing the "Getting Others to Support Your Recovery" handout. The therapist had conducted the session with Joe and his wife on the inpatient unit.

Once he was discharged from the hospital, Joe made a firm commitment to practice the safe coping skills on a daily basis. He used grounding whenever his anxiety started to creep up. He practiced driving to his old neighborhood, past his childhood church, and using grounding. He noticed that over time, his anxiety started to decrease. Towards the end of treatment, he was able to attend his niece's baptism at a Catholic church, though "I had to practice grounding the whole time." As his anxiety decreased and his sleep began to improve, Joe started to believe that "I can get past the trauma." He and his wife also began couples therapy.

Case example #2. D is a tall, 50-something, Hispanic man. Upon meeting him, his gentleness and humor are quickly apparent. D has survived a lot. While growing up, he was sexually abused for many years by his uncle. He began using drugs (primarily heroin) at an early age and quickly became involved in the criminal justice system. He had many different sexual relationships with both men and women. His long-term partner committed suicide while in prison, and this was the beginning of D's road to recovery. He became suicidal and was hospitalized for several months, which allowed him to engage in treatment for the first time. He established sobriety. He began to receive regular medical evaluations; although he learned he was HIV positive he received treatment for it. Recently, however, the gains he made were threatened. During a sexual encounter, he contracted a sexually transmitted disease which worsened his medical conditions. He felt betrayed and this triggered a flooding of memories and feelings related to the sexual abuse. He felt like getting high again. After "spilling" his story to his primary care doctor, he agreed to a referral to receive help for the trauma and substance abuse problems.

Even though D's HIV-related problems make it difficult for him to remember appointments, he has worked to find ways to remember them and attends consistently. He readily engaged with the present-focused approach. He has embraced the overall goal of increasing safety in his life. He has started to use the skills he is learning, to address trauma-related symptoms as well as substance cravings. The grounding skill helped him to "detach from painful feelings and memories related to the sexual abuse" he experienced and he no longer "spills" his story to anyone who will listen to him. He uses grounding when he feels like using and has developed ways to reduce his access to substances. He has been able to maintain his recovery from substances. While going through the topic *Setting Boundaries in*

Relationships he role-played asking his niece to move out as her presence was putting him at risk of losing his housing. While learning *Asking for Help* he made a phone call to his case manager to assist him with his niece, but eventually was successful at overcoming his difficulty by directly setting limits with her until she moved out. He has been learning about *Healthy Relationships* and made the decision to set boundaries with an ex-boyfriend who again "showed up at his doorstep". He is starting to use *Compassion* when he blames himself for the above situations, (which trigger his wanting to use substances) and understands that he learned at an early age that he couldn't say "no", but now recognizes that he can learn to protect himself more. He is working to increase contact with supportive people in his life, especially while learning *Getting Others to Support Your Recovery*; he has also identified a group which he would like to attend to meet more people and receive support. D recently ended treatment. In reflecting on his treatment experience he says, "I never made the connection between the abuse I experienced and using substances. I didn't realize that I could stand up for myself and have better relationships. I didn't realize that I can ask for help and find ways to calm myself down without using substances. Thank you so much for this help."

FUTURE WORK

This chapter highlights clinical and research experiences on the use of Seeking Safety with men. However, much more remains to be done. We have shared our impressions and suggestions, but are aware that all of us have "taken" to the Seeking Safety model. Learning from clinicians and clients who do not like it or who decide not to adopt it would also be important. The research studies thus far provide consistent positive support on use of the model with men; however, they represent an early stage of scientific work. Further Seeking Safety studies with more rigorous designs are needed (randomized controlled trials and multisite trials); such studies have been conducted with women but not as yet on men. Finally, it is essential to remember that gender is one of many influences on clients; others include trauma and substance abuse type; clinician and setting; minority and cultural issues; and subpopulations such as veterans, homeless, criminal justice clients, adolescents; and other factors. Although we have tried to record our observations on men, we recognize that other influences may play an equal or more important role at times than gender. Greater understanding of the interplay between gender and these other factors is also needed in future work.

CONCLUSION

Several general conclusions can be highlighted.
Based on clinical and research experience thus far:

- Both trauma and substance abuse violate the traditional male role of being strong and in control. Men may have to fight these images to accept where they are and to be able to work on achieving genuine strength and control.

- It can be helpful to obtain books or other resources on the psychology of men, especially in relation to trauma and substance abuse.
- Seeking Safety was designed for both men and women, and works well with both genders.
- Seeking Safety has been successfully implemented with diverse men including veterans, men in the criminal justice system, men with histories of childhood abuse, men of various ethnic and racial categories, men of different ages including adolescence, different substance and trauma types, and different settings.
- Four formal research studies have evaluated Seeking Safety with men. All have found the materials highly acceptable as is, and in the three studies that obtained quantitative data, all evidenced significant pre- to post-treatment improvements on various outcomes.
- Early concerns that the material is too feminine have not been supported by either clinical experience or research.
- The overall response to Seeking Safety by men and their clinicians has been highly positive. Both the format and content are perceived as relevant. There are no particular topics or aspects that have thus far been found less useful with men than with women.
- Several typically male themes have been identified. Although these can occur in both genders, we have found them especially prominent with men. Awareness of these can guide implementation of Seeking Safety: (a) bonding in male ways (like warriors, teams); (b) difficulty with feelings; (c) anger; (d) perpetration; (e) sexuality issues; (f) hard to engage in treatment / hard to end treatment; (g) isolation; (h) caretaking problems; (i) issues with authority and control; (j) identity ("Who are you?"); (k) self-hatred (feeling "like a monster"); (l) intimacy; (m) multiple problem areas.
- Seeking Safety emphasizes flexibility, and thus can be adapted as needed (using examples relevant for client subgroups; changing the pacing or length of the treatment; adding in additional materials).
- Suggestions for using Seeking Safety with men include: (a) use language and examples relevant to men; (b) know that men like the treatment format; (c) gently encourage homework ("commitments"); (d) consider mixed-gender groups (e) address men's issues as part of supervision (e) learn from the clients; (f) strive to respond to men's different needs; (g) adapt Seeking Safety to your setting; (h) rehearse the skills; (i) if needed, shorten the check-in.
- Many important aspects of the work transcend gender-- for example, developing a recovery identity, reducing symptoms of trauma and substance abuse, and attaining safety.

Future Work

- Further research is needed, especially randomized controlled trials and multisite trials.
- Further clinical experience will also be helpful. Learning from clinicians and clients who do not like the model or decide not to adopt the model would also be useful.

- It will be important to explore what facets actually relate to gender versus other factors (e.g., trauma and substance abuse type; clinician and setting; minority and cultural issues; and subpopulation).
- More on men, trauma, and addiction is needed, aside from any particular focus on Seeking Safety.

AUTHOR NOTE

Special thanks go to Mark Vargo, PhD and Tommi Leveille, BA at Operation PAR, who were involved with the evaluation and data gathering on their SAMHSA project on Seeking Safety with young African-American men. Roger D. Weiss, MD of McLean Hospital / Harvard Medical School; Joseph Ruzek, PhD of the Palo Alto VA (California); and Joan Cook, PhD formerly of the Philadelphia VA are thanked for their early support and work on Seeking Safety with men clients. Jodie Trafton, PhD, Rachel Kimerling, PhD, and Christopher Weaver, PhD are thanked for their current research on Seeking Safety with men veterans at the Palo Alto VA.

Participation in this paper was as follows: conceptualization and writing of the chapter (LN); clinical notes (LN, MS, KJ, CS, TN, RW); case examples (MS, KJ); provision of research study results (LN, MS, NH); and discussion on a conference call (LN, KR, CS, TN, SN, KW). All of the quotes in this paper are from the co-authors (not LN). All of the co-authors are thanked for their exceptional work and insights on Seeking Safety with men.

REFERENCES

Cook, J. M., Walser, R. D., Kane, V., Ruzek, J. I., and Woody, G. (2006). Dissemination and feasibility of a cognitive-behavioral treatment for substance use disorders and posttraumatic stress disorder in the veterans administration. *Journal of Psychoactive Drugs, 38*, 89-92.

Hamilton, N. (2006). African-American Center for Excellence (AACE) Program; SAMHSA grant number TI14126; final report. Unpublished report, Operation PAR (Largo, Florida).

Lew, Mike (1988). Victims No Longer: Men Recovering From Incest And Other Sexual Child Abuse. New York: Harper and Row.

Najavits, L. M. (2002). *Seeking Safety: A treatment manual for PTSD and substance abuse.* New York, NY: Guilford.

Najavits, L. M. (2004). Treatment for posttraumtic stress disorder and substance abuse: Clinical guidelines for implementing the *Seeking Safety* therapy. *Alcoholism Treatment Quarterly, 22*, 43-62.

Najavits, L. M. (2007). Seeking Safety: An evidence-based model for substance abuse and trauma/ptsd. In K. A. Witkiewitz and G. A. Marlatt (Eds.), *Therapist's guide to evidence based relapse prevention: Practical resources for the mental health professional.* San Diego: Elsevier Press.

Najavits, L. M., Schmitz, M., Gotthardt, S., and Weiss, R. D. (2005). Seeking Safety plus exposure therapy: An outcome study on dual diagnosis men. *Journal of Psychoactive Drugs, 37*, 425-435.

Najavits, L. M., Weiss, R. D., and Liese, B. S. (1996). Group cognitive-behavioral therapy for women with PTSD and substance use disorder. *Journal of Substance Abuse Treatment, 13*, 13-22.

Sonkin, D. J. (1998). Wounded Boys Heroic Men: A Man's Guide to Recovering from Child Abuse Cincinatti: Adams Media.

Shay, J. (1994). *Achilles in Vietnam: Combat trauma and the undoing of character*. New York: Simon and Schuster.

Weaver C.M., Trafton J.A., Walser R.D., Kimerling R.E. (2007). Pilot test of Seeking Safety with male veterans. *Psychiatric Services, 58*, 1012

Peer Review was by Mark Vargo, PhD; Operation PAR (Key Largo, Florida).

ISBN 978-1-60692-098-5

Chapter 3

RELATIONSHIP BETWEEN PERSONALITY SCALES OF IMPULSIVENESS AND DISCOUNTING OF MONETARY GAINS AND LOSSES IN SMOKERS AND NEVER SMOKERS

Taiki Takahashi[1]*, Hidemi Oono[2], Yu Ohmura[3],
Nozomi Kitamura[1] and Mark Radford[4]

1. Department of Behavioral Science, Hokkaido University,Sapporo, Japan
2. Department of Biological Psychiatry, Graduate School of Medicine,
Tohoku University, Sendai, Japan
3. Department of Neuropharmacology, Hokkaido University Graduate School
of Medicine, N15 W7 Kita-ku, Sapporo, 060-8638 Japan
4. Symbiosis Group Limited, P.O. Box 1192, Milton, 4064 Australia

ABSTRACT

Personality scales of impulsiveness have been associated with discounting behavior. It has also been shown that nicotine has an effect on the performance of various tasks measuring impulsivity. This study has two main objectives: (1) to determine the relationship between the impulsive personality and the degrees to which delayed and uncertain monetary gains and losses are discounted, and (2) to examine whether the relationship between the impulsive personality and the four types of discounting differ between smokers and never smokers. 31 current smokers and 32 never smokers participated in this experiment. They were required to choose between immediate and delayed monetary gains (and losses), or between guaranteed and probabilistic rewards (or losses). Following completion of this task, they completed two personality questionnaires – Barratte's Impulsiveness Scale (BIS) and the Sensation Seeking Scale (SSS). Several BIS and SSS subscales were positively correlated with the degrees of discounting for delayed monetary gains and losses, but negatively correlated with uncertain monetary

---

* Corresponding author: Taiki Takahashi: Telephone number: +81-11-706-3057, Fax number: +81-11-706-3066, E-mail: taikitakahashi@gmail.com. Institute for Department of Behavioral Science, Hokkaido University, Sapporo, Japan.

gains. Moreover, when dividing participants by smoking status, we found differences between smokers and never smokers in the correlation pattern between impulsive personality and the four types of discounting. Neuro-psychological bases of impulsive behavior, such as discounting behavior, may differ between smokers and never smokers.

INTRODUCTION

Impulsivity is a core issue in neuropsychiatric illness such as drug-dependence, and many researchers have had an attention to impulsivity mainly in terms of treatment for drug-dependence (e.g. Moeller et al., 2001). Recently, one concept – "delay discounting" – has been proposed as a form of impulsivity. The term "delay discounting" means to choose a smaller reward that may be obtained immediately over a larger reward that may be obtained after a delay (e.g. Rachlin and Green, 1972). People tend to discount the value of delayed outcomes, and often tend to choose immediate small pleasures at the expense of future success (delay discounting of gain), and also tend to put off demanding tasks at hand, despite the fact that by doing so things may become worse in the future (delay discounting of loss). Much previous research has shown that a greater tendency to discount delayed gains is frequently observed in drug dependent subjects (e.g., Kirby and Petry, 2004; Kirby et al., 1999; Bickel et al., 1999; Petry, 2001; Odum et al., 2002; Baker et al., 2003).

People also tend to discount the value of uncertain outcomes; this tendency is called "probability discounting". We often tend to choose certain and safe but small rewards rather than risky but larger rewards (probability discounting of gains), and are more likely to choose large but unlikely damage rather than small but likely damage (probability discounting of loss). Although few studies have focused on the relationship between probability discounting and drug dependence, at least one study has shown that nicotine-dependent individuals discount monetary gains more dramatically than non-drug dependent controls (Reynolds, 2004).

Some studies have shown that personality scales of impulsiveness, such as Barratt's Impulsiveness Scale (BIS) and the Sensation Seeking Scale (SSS) are positively associated with delay and probability discounting of gains (Richards et al., 1999; Reynolds et al., 2004). However, Ostaszewski (1997) showed that these relationships were weak. Moreover, Reynolds and colleagues (2006) found that self-reported scales including BIS-11 were not correlated with delay discounting of gain. These inconsistent results about the relationship between self-reported impulsiveness and delay discounting behavior may partly due to disregarding the effect of smoking behavior. If the effect of smoking behavior is considered, the relationship between self-reported impulsivity and discounting behavior would become clearer.

Moreover, little is known about the relationship between delay and probability discounting of losses and personality scales of impulsiveness despite decision making regarding loss is also closely related to daily decision making. Psychological processes underlying discounting of loss may be different from that underlying discounting of gain.

The first purpose of the present study is to examine the relationship between discounting behavior and scales of impulsiveness. By examining this relationship, we can find which scales or subscales predict discounting behavior and therefore help identify the psychological processes that underlie such behavior.

Table 1. Mean and standard deviations for demographic variables, smoking behavior, and AUCs for current and never smokers

	Current smokers		Never smokers	
	Mean	SD	Mean	SD
Sex (% men)	77.42		69.70	
Age (years)	24.16	3.48	23.82	5.53
Education (% graduate)	65.5		63.6	
Cigarette number (per day)	14.05	6.63		
Smoking history (months)	49.23	50.87		
DD of gain	0.55	0.27	0.61	0.33
PD of gain	0.24	0.14	0.18	0.09
DD of loss	0.70	0.25	0.76	0.29
PD of loss	0.35	0.16	0.39	0.20

In calculating the AUC, the horizontal axis is delay (in delay discounting) or odds-against (=1/probability – 1, in probability discounting), and the vertical axis is the indifference point. Note that smaller AUC values correspond to greater discounting.

Regarding education and cigarette number, two data points are missing due to the participants' omission in answering these questions.

DD Delay discounting, *PD* probability discounting.

A second related purpose is to see whether previous results regarding discounting of gains can be extended to discounting of losses. Considering that several studies have shown that distinct brain regions are activated in response to monetary gains and losses (Knutson et al., 2000; Knutson et al., 2003; Breiter et al., 2001) and that there is a gain-loss asymmetry in decision-making (Tversky and Kahneman, 1981; Thaler, 1981; Baker et al., 2003), it is important to examine whether previous results regarding discounting of gains can be extended to discounting of losses.

A third purpose of this study is to examine whether the relationship between personality and discounting differs between smokers and never smokers. Many studies have demonstrated that nicotine has an effect on several types of behavior and cognitive functioning (e.g., Popke et al., 2000; Ueno et al., 2002; Hahn et al., 2002; Potter and Newhouse, 2004). Further, discounting behavior has been associated with smoking behavior (e.g., Bickel et al., 1999; Mitchell, 1999; Reynolds, 2004; Ohmura et al., 2005). In particular, with respect to delay discounting of gains, it has been shown that nicotine dosage increases the degree of delay discounting of gains in rats (Dallery and Locey, 2005). The results of this study may give us the explanation about the inconsistency of previous findings regarding the relationship between personality and discounting behavior (Osraszewski, 1997; Richards et al., 1999; Reynolds et al., 2004; Reynolds et al., 2006).

METHODS

Participants

Participants were 63 university students, including 31 young-adult current smokers (77.4 % male and 61.3 % graduate) who smoke cigarettes regularly of the past year between 21 and

33 years of age and 32 never smokers (71.9 % male and 65.6 % graduate) between 21 and 28 years of age. They were recruited through advertisements posted on bulletin boards at Hokkaido University in Sapporo, Japan. The characteristics of these subjects are described in more detail in Table 1. Smokers and never smokers in this study did not differ significantly in age, sex, or level of education (graduate-undergraduate). They signed an informed consent form before participating, and received 1000 yen (about US $10) following completion of the experiment.

Materials and Procedure

Participants completed a computerized behavioral choice task followed by two pencil-and-paper personality questionnaires linked to impulsivity.

Behavioral Choice Task

This computerized task consisted of four different types of discounting (i.e., delay of gain, delay of loss, uncertain gain, and uncertain loss). Details of this procedure are described in more detail in our previous study (see Ohmura et al., 2005).

Because Johnson and Bickel (2002) showed a strong correlation (0.80-range) between discounting rates for hypothetical and real monetary gains, and previous studies (Baker et al., 2003; Madden et al., 2004) have demonstrated that discounting rate for hypothetical and real money are not significant different, a computerized procedure consisting of hypothetical monetary outcomes was used to assess discounting in the present study.

Participants were asked to select one of two cards repeatedly displayed on their computer monitor. The left card indicated the sum of money that could be received (or lost) immediately (or certainly, in the probability-discounting tasks), whereas the right card always indicated 100,000 yen (about US $1,000) that could be received (or lost) after a certain delay (or with a certain probability). The sum of money indicated on the left card ranged from 100,000 to 5,000 yen (or from-100,000 to -5,000 yen, in loss-frame tasks) in 5,000 yen increments. In the delay discounting task, the delay indicated on the right card changed between five time frames (1 week, 1 month, 6 months, 1 year, and 5 years). For the probability-discounting task, the right card indicated one of five probability values (90%, 70%, 50%, 30%, and 10%). These changes were computerized according to the algorithm used by Richards et al. (1999). This algorithm is designed to determine the point at which the participant switches his or her preference from the left card (right card) to the right card (left card) by changing the type of task and the sum of money in accordance with previous decisions (for more details, see Richards et al., 1999; Ohmura et al., 2005). The switching point is regarded as the indifference point and was used to calculate the value of the discounting measures.

Personality Questionnaires

Barratt's Impulsiveness Scale, version 11 (BIS-11: Patton et al., 1995)

The BIS-11 Japanese version (Someya et al., 2001) contains a total of 30 items and requires respondents to answer how frequently (rarely/never, occasionally, often, almost always/always) each statement applies to themselves. Because it has been shown that there are three factors (Patton et al., 1995), we analyzed the data using each factor, as well as the total score. Three factors are as follows: *Attentional Impulsiveness*, *Motor Impulsiveness* and *Nonplanning Impulsiveness* (Patton et al., 1995).

Sensation Seeking Scale (SSS, Form IV: Zuckerman et al., 1971)

The SSS (Form IV) Japanese version (Terasaki et al., 1987) contains a total of 38 items, although the original SSS contains 72 items. It should be noted that this revision by Terasaki et al. (1987) is based on the results of a factor analysis with a large sample size (N=889), with the validity of Japanese version being confirmed in a second study (Terasaki et al., 1988). This questionnaire requires respondents to choose one of two statements that best applies to themselves. There are four dimensions: *Thrill and Adventure Seeking*, "a desire to engage in sports or activities involving speed or danger"; *Experience Seeking*, "the seeking of experience through the mind and senses, travel and a nonconforming life style"; *Disinhibition*, "the desire for social and sexual disinhibition"; and *Boredom Susceptibility*, "an aversion to repetition, routine, and dull people, and restlessness when things are unchanging" (Zuckerman, 1971; Zuckerman et al., 1978). We analyzed the data using each factor, as well as the total score.

Data Analysis

In order to determine the degree to which each subjects discounted delayed and uncertain monetary gains and losses, we adopted the Area Under the Curve (AUC; Myerson et al., 2001) for each of the four discounting tasks. The value of AUC is the area under a line graph made by plotting indifference points when normalizing the horizontal axis (delay or odds-against=1/probability-1) and the vertical axis (subjective value) (for the detail of calculation procedure, see Myerson et al., 2001; Ohmura et al., 2005). It should be noted that smaller AUC values indicate more dramatic discounting. The rational for employing AUCs is as follows: (1) previous studies (Lane et al., 2003; Ohmura et al., 2006) have shown that the skewness of the distribution of AUCs is relatively small, in comparison to other discounting parameters calculated by fitting results to specific functions (e.g., hyperbolic k), and (2) because AUCs do not depend on a fitting function, there are no data loss and equation type-dependent systematic errors. Given that the purpose of the present-study was to investigate the relationship between discounting behavior and personality questionnaires rather than to determine the best discounting function to fit the data, AUCs appear to be an appropriate measure.

To test statistical significance of correlations and mean differences, Pearson's product-moment correlation coefficients and independent sample t tests were conducted respectively. Significant level was set at 5% throughout.

Table 2. Pearson product-moment correlation coefficients between the personality questionnaire scales and AUCs

	DDG	DDL	PDG	PDL
BIS (total score)	-0.26*	-0.32*	0.32*	-0.20
Attentional Impulsiveness	-0.05	-0.08	0.30*	-0.20
Motor Impulsiveness	-0.27*	-0.39**	0.21	-0.12
Nonplanning Impulsiveness	-0.29*	-0.30*	0.29*	-0.19
SSS (total score)	-0.09	-0.11	0.37**	-0.16
Thrill and Adventure Seeking	0.02	0.00	0.30*	-0.12
Experience Seeking	-0.13	-0.17	0.16	0.02
Disinhibition	-0.16	-0.10	0.30*	-0.15
Boredom Susceptibility	-0.08	-0.06	0.32*	-0.19

* $p<0.05$, ** $p<0.01$.

Note that a smaller AUC indicates a higher degree of discounting (i.e., negative correlation in this table indicates positive correlation between personality scales and the degree of discounting).

DDG Delay Discounting of Gain, *DDL* Delay Discounting of Loss.

PDG Probability Discounting of Gain, *PDL* Probability Discounting of Loss.

Table 3. Pearson product-moment correlation coefficients between the personality questionnaire scales and AUCs in never smokers and smokers

	never smokers				smokers			
	DDG	DDL	PDG	PDL	DDG	DDL	PDG	PDL
BIS (total score)	-0.32	-0.38*	0.19	-0.12	-0.17	-0.23	0.37*	-0.27
Attentional Impulsivfeness	-0.16	-0.16	0.27	-0.02	0.06	-0.03	0.39*	-0.47**
Motor Impulsiveness	-0.24	-0.31	0.09	-0.14	-0.29	-0.44*	0.17	-0.01
Nonplanning Impulsiveness	-0.38*	-0.45*	0.13	-0.12	-0.17	-0.10	0.38*	-0.25
SSS (total score)	-0.09	-0.08	0.32	-0.22	-0.03	-0.14	0.33	-0.01
Thrill and Adventure Seeking	0.01	-0.01	0.20	-0.15	0.12	0.06	0.29	-0.04
Experience Seeking	-0.12	-0.11	0.16	-0.03	-0.13	-0.16	0.09	0.19
Disinhibition	-0.11	0.00	0.34	-0.26	-0.16	-0.32	0.21	-0.05
Boredom Susceptibility	-0.05	-0.11	0.40*	-0.28	-0.07	0.05	0.20	-0.04

*$p<0.05$, **$p<.01$.

Note that a smaller AUC indicates a higher degree of discounting (i.e., negative correlation in this table indicates positive correlation between personality scales and the degree of discounting).

DDG Delay Discounting of Gain, *DDL* Delay Discounting of Loss,

PDG Probability Discounting of Gain, *PDL* Probability Discounting of Loss.

RESULTS

Demographic Effects on Personality and Discounting Behavior

Participants' age did not correlate with any of the total or subscales' scores for each of the personality scales. There were significant gender differences for total scores of SSS (t(59)=2.20, p<0.05), Thrill and Adventure Seeking (t(60)=2.40, p<0.05) and Disinhibition (t(60)=1.27, p<0.05), which were higher in men. Note that one participant's data had a missing value, so we omitted the data for calculating total scores of SSS.

There were no significant differences for each scale between graduate and undergraduate students. In terms of the relationship between demographics and discounting behavior, no significant correlations or differences were observed.

Relationship between Impulsive Personality and Discounting Behavior

To examine the relationship between personality scales of impulsiveness and discounting behavior, we analyzed the correlations between AUCs and total scores of SSS and BIS-11, and scores of their respective subscales. As shown in Table 2, there were several moderate correlations between AUCs and the different personality scales. The AUCs for delay discounting of gain and loss were significantly negatively correlated with the total BIS-11 score (gain: r(63)=-0.26, p<0.05; loss: r(63)=-0.32, p<0.05), and with it's subscales, Motor Impulsiveness (gain: r(63)=-0.27, p<0,05; loss: r(63)=-0.39, p<0.01) and Nonplanning Impulsiveness (gain: r(63)=-0.29, p<0.05; loss: r(63)=-0.30, p<0.05). The AUC for probability discounting of gain were significantly positively correlated with the total BIS-11 score (r(63)=0.32, p<0.05), and with it's subscales, Attentional Impulsiveness (r(63)=0.30, p<0.05) and Nonplanning Impulsiveness (r(63)=0.29, p<0.05). Moreover, the AUC for probability discounting of gain was significantly positively correlated with the total SSS score (r(62)=0.37, p<0.01), and with it's subscales, Thrill and Adventure Seeking (r(63)=0.30, p<0.05), Disinhibition (r(62)=0.30, p<0.05), and Boredom Susceptibility (r(63)=0.32, p<0.05). The AUC for probability discounting of loss was not significantly correlated with any personality scales and its' subscales. In sum, the person who exhibited high impulsiveness on there personality scales (BIS-11 and SSS) tended to strongly discount future gains and losses, but tended to be less likely to discount uncertain gains.

Differences in the Relationships between Impulsive Personality and Discounting Behavior between Smokers and Never Smokers

To examine whether there are any difference in the correlation pattern between smokers and never smokers, we divided subjects into smokers and never smokers and repeated the correlational analysis. As shown in Table 3, we found a difference in the correlation pattern, and in turn a clearer picture of the correlational relationships between personality scales and discounting behavior. Whereas the AUCs for delay discounting of loss was significantly correlated with the total score of BIS-11 (r(32)=-0.38, p<0.05), and with it's subscale

Nonplanning Impulsivenes (r(32)=-0.45, p<0.05) in never smokers, such correlations were not observed in smokers, and the AUC for delay discounting of loss was significantly correlated with the BIS' subscale Motor Impulsiveness (r(31)=-0.44, p<0.05) in smokers. Furthermore, the AUC for probability discounting of gain was significantly positively correlated with the total score of BIS-11 (r(31)=0.37, p<0.05), and with it's subscales, Attentional Impulsiveness (r(31)=0.39, p<0.39) and Nonplanning Impulsivenes (r(31)=0.38, p<0.05) in smokers. Moreover, the AUC for probability discounting of loss was significantly negatively correlated with BIS-11's subscale Attentional Impulsiveness (r(31)=-0.47, p<0.01) in smokers. However, such correlation patterns were not shown in never smokers. It seems that the difference in the relationship between impulsive personality and discounting behavior between smokers and never smokers was particularly marked at the relationships between BIS and probability discounting behaviors of gain and loss. These findings indicate that there are specific, but different relationships between types of impulsive personality and discounting behavior in smokers and never smokers.

Differences in Impulsive Personality between Smokers and never Smokers

To examine whether a previously reported group difference in impulsive personality between never smokers and smokers was replicated in the present study, we compared personality scale scores between the two groups (Table 4). We observed that impulsivity was significantly higher in smokers, compared to never smokers on several scales, namely, Motor Impulsiveness (t(61)=2.63, p<0.05), total SSS score (t(59)=2.76, p<0.01), Thrill and Adventure Seeking (t(60)=2.65, p<0.05), and Disinhibition (t(59)=2.51, p<0.05). Although, not statistically significant, scores on the other scales for smokers were generally higher than those for never smokers, which is consistent with previous findings (Carton et al., 1994; Mitchell, 1999; Skinner et al., 2004).

Table 4. Mean (and SD) and *t* tests: Comparison of the personality questionnaire scales between smokers and never smokers

	Smokers		Never smokers	t-value
BIS (total score)	70.06 (11.66)		66.59 (10.79)	1.22
Attentional Impulsiveness	17.52 (3.86)		18.25 (3.59)	0.78
Motor Impulsiveness	25.48 (4.90)	>	22.59 (3.78)	2.63*
Nonplanning Impulsiveness	27.06 (5.16)		25.75 (5.31)	1.00
SSS (total score)	23.2 (5.95)	>	18.52 (7.22)	2.76**
Thrill and Adventure Seeking	6.61 (2.59)	>	4.71 (3.05)	2.65*
Experience Seeking	6.06 (1.91)		5.31 (2.25)	1.43
Disinhibition	7.27 (1.86)	>	5.97 (2.17)	2.51*
Boredom Susceptibility	3.40 (1.85)		2.59 (1.64)	1.82

* p<0.50, ** p<0.01

DISCUSSION

Relationship between Impulsive Personality and Discounting of Loss

Our results indicate that the relationship between personality scales of impulsiveness and delay discounting of loss is similar to the relationship between personality scales of impulsiveness and delay discounting of gain overall. This in turn suggests that measures of impulsiveness can be used to predict both delay discounting behavior of loss, as well as discounting behavior of gain. It is possible that the neuro-psychological components involved in impulsive personality may underlie both delay discounting of gain and loss. In contrast, it was not the way in terms of probability discounting of loss. In the future study, researchers need to clarify the psychological process underlying probability discounting of loss by using other personality scales.

Differences on Correlational Patterns with Personality Scales between Delay Discounting and Probability Discounting

The present study showed positive correlations between personality impulsivity and delay discounting of gains and losses, whereas there were negative correlations between personality impulsivity and probability discounting of gains and positive correlation between personality impulsivity and probability discounting of losses. When we analyzed dividing subjects into smokers and never smokers, this asymmetry existed.

Several research evidenced the higher people discount in delay discounting, the less they discount in probability discounting (e.g, Ostaszewski et al., 1998). This reverse discounting behavior is marked particularly in the people who have impulsive traits or anti-social character. They often show gambling habit and they feel subjective large value for large outcomes although involving large uncertainty. Our results that asymmetric correlational pattern with personal impulsivity between delay discounting of gains and probability discounting of gains was consistent with the findings of the people who have impulsive traits or anti-social character.

Differences between Smokers and Never Smokers

We found marked differences between smokers and never smokers in the correlation pattern between the impulsive personality and four type of discounting, particularly it was marked at the relationship between BIS-11 and probability discounting. Specifically, significant correlations between BIS-11 and probability discounting were observed in smokers. This result indicates that we should divide subjects into smokers and never smokers when predicting discounting behavior using these personality scales.

There are at least three possible interpretations for the observed difference in the correlation pattern between smokers and never smokers. First, chronic exposure to nicotine causes significant changes in the central nervous system, as shown in previous studies (e.g., Salokangas et al., 2000; Dagher et al., 2001; Brody et al., 2004; Rahman et al., 2004; Liu and

Jin, 2004), and therefore psychological processes underlying discounting behavior in smokers may be different from those in never smokers. If this is the case, the neuro-psychological effect of chronic smoking may be strong enough to have a significant impact on personality. Second, the personality of smokers may be different from that of never smokers, even before the onset of habitual smoking. In fact, Lipkus et al. (1994) showed that scores on personality scales measured in advance predicted smoking initiation. However, our present results suggest a qualitative, rather than quantitative difference between smokers and never smokers. If the personality of smokers is so different from that of never smokers, it is intriguing to speculate about the factors that may affect character-building.

Relationship of the Present Findings to Previous Studies

When analyzing the merged total sample (consisting of both smokers and never smokers), we observed several correlations between personality scales of impulsiveness and discounting behavior. This correlation pattern in the present study is consistent with the result of Reynolds and collegues' (2004) study showing the correlation between cognitive complexity, one of the BIS-11 subscales, and delay discounting of gain, but it is not consistent with the results of Mitchell's (1999) study. This inconsistency may be partly due to the difference in sampling. Reynolds et al. (2004) employed non smokers or mild smokers, who smoked less than five cigarettes per day, whereas Mitchell (1999) employed never smokers and heavy smokers who smoked 15 cigarettes or more per day. Thus, future research may need to analyze data by dividing the subjects into smokers (heavy and mild smokers as well) and non/never smokers.

Furthermore, we observed that those who exhibited high impulsiveness on these personality scales tended to strongly discount future gains and losses, but were less likely to discount uncertain gains. These results are consistent with the definition of impulsivity broadly accepted by psychiatrists, namely "actions that are poorly conceived, prematurely expressed, unduly risky, or inappropriate to the situation and that often result in undesirable outcomes" (Daruna and Barnes, 1993).

Our results also replicated the difference in impulsive personality between smokers and never smokers. As shown in previous studies (e.g., Carton et al., 1994; Mitchell, 1999; Skinner et al., 2004), smokers were more impulsive than never smokers. This finding seems to be robust regardless of the difference in subjects' characteristics (e.g., nationality and the severity of drug-dependence).

Limitations and Future Directions

Although the results of this study showed some interesting findings, there are at least two limitations. First, because of time constraints, we asked subjects to complete only two personality questionnaire scales and four types of discounting task. In future studies, it would be important to examine whether the difference in correlation patterns between smokers and never smokers extends to other personality scales and behavioral tasks.

Second, this study does not provide an explanation on the observed distinction between smokers and never smokers, in the relationship between impulsive personality and discounting behavior. In future studies, this point needs future analysis. At the moment, we have indicated two possibilities for interpreting the current results – chronic effect of nicotine and initial differences of personality between smokers and never smokers. Researchers should address the two points, because differences between smokers and never smokers may have important implications for clinical treatment for drug abusers. More specifically, if there are really strong distinctions between drug addicts and healthy subjects, clinicians must choose the nature and degree of treatment based on the severity of dependence (e.g., smoking status).

ACKNOWLEDGEMENTS

The research reported in this paper was supported by grants from the Grant-in-Aid for Scientific Research ("21st century center of excellence" grant and grant #17650074) from the Ministry of Education, Culture, Sports, Science and Technology of Japan, and the Yamaguchi endocrinological disorder grant. We are grateful to Dr. Someya for giving us the Japanese version of BIS-11.

REFERENCES

Baker, F., Johnson, M. W., and Bickel, W. K. (2003). Delay discounting in current and never-before cigarette smokers: Similarities and differences across commodity sign and magnitude. *Journal of Abnormal Psychology, 112*, 382-392.

Bickel, W. K., Odum, A. L., and Madden, G. J. (1999). Impulsivity and cigarette smoking: delay discounting in current never and ex-smokers. *Psychopharmacology, 146*, 447-454.

Breiter, H. C., Aharon, I., Kahneman, D., Dale, A., and Shizgal, P. (2001). Functional imaging of neural responses to expectancy and experience of monetary gains and losses. *Neuron, 30*, 619-639.

Brody, A. L., Olmstead, R. E., London, E. D., Farahi, J., Meyer, J. H., Grossman, P., Lee, G. S., Huang, J., Hahn, E. L., and Mandelkern, M. A. (2004). Smoking-induced ventral striatum dopamine release. *American Journal of Psychiatry, 161*, 1211-1218.

Carton, S., Jouvent, R., and Widlocher, D. (1994). Sensation seeling, nicotine dependence, and smoking motivation in female and male smokers. *Addictive Behaviors, 19*, 219-227.

Dagher, A., Bleicher, C., Aston, J. A., Gunn, R. N., Clarke, P. B., and Cumming, P. (2001). Reduced dopamine D1 receptor binding in the ventral striatum of cigarette smokers. *Synapse, 42*, 48-53.

Dallery, J and Locey, M. L. (2005). Effects of acute and chronic nicotine on impulsive choice in rats. *Behavioral Pharmacology, 16*, 15-23.

Daruna, J. H and Barnes, P. A. (1993). A neurodevelopmental view of impulsivity. In: McCown, W. G., Johnson, J. L., and Shure, M. B. (eds) *The impulsive client: theory research and treatment*. American Psychological Association, Washington, D. C., 23-37.

Hahn, B., Shoaib, M., and Stolerman, I. P. (2002). Nicotine-induced enhancement of attention in the five-choice serial reaction time task: the influence of task demands. *Psychopharmacology, 162*, 129-137.

Johnson, M. W and Bickel, W. K. (2002). Within-subject comparison of real and hypothetical money rewards in delay discounting. *Journal of the Experimental Analysis of Behavior*, *77*, 129-146.

Kirby, K. N., Petry, N. M., and Bickel, W. K. (1999). Heroin addicts have higher discount rates for delayed rewards then non-drug-using controls. *Journal of Experimental Psychology; General*, *128*, 78-87.

Kirby, K. N and Petry, N. M. (2004). Heroin and cocaine abusers have higher discount rates for delayed rewards than alcoholics or non-drug-using controls. *Addiction*, *99*, 461-471.

Knutson, B., Westdorp, A., Kaiser, E., and Hommer, D. (2000). FMRI visualization of brain activity during a monetary incentive delay tasl. *Neuroimage*, *12*, 20-27.

Knutson, B., Fong, G. W., Bennett, S. M., Adams, C. M., and Hommer, D. (2003). A region of mesial prefrontal cortex tracks monetarily rewarding outcomes: characterization with rapid event-related fMRI. *Neuroimage*, *18*, 263-272.

Lane, S. D., Cherek, D. R., Pietras, C. J., and Tcheremissine, O. V. (2003). Measurement of delay discounting using trial-by-trial consequences. *Behavioural Processes*, *64*, 287-303.

Lipkus, I. M., Barefoot, J. C., Williams, R. B., and Siegler, I. C. (1994). Personality measures as predictors of smoking initiation and cessation in the UNC Alumni Heart Study. *Health Psychology*, *13*, 149-155.

Liu, Z. H and Jin, W. Q. (2004). Decrease of ventral tegmental area dopamine neuronal activity in nicotine withdrawal rats. *Neuroreport*, *15*, 1479-1481.

Madden, G. J., Raiff, B. R., Lagorio, C. H., Begotka, A. M., Mueller, A. M., Hehli, D. J. and Wegener, A. A. (2004). Delay discounting of potentially real and hypothetical rewards: II. Between- and within-subject comparisons. *Experimental and Clinical Psychopharmacology*, *12*, 251-261.

Mitchell, S. H. (1999). Measures of impulsivity in cigarette smokers and non-smokers. *Psychopharmacology*, *146*, 455-464.

Moeller, F. G., Dougherty, D. M., Barrattt, E. S., Schmitz, J. M., Swann, A. C., and Grabowski, J. (2001). The impact of impulsivity on cocaine use and retention in treatment. *Journal of Substance Abuse Treatment*, *21*, 193-198.

Myerson, J., Green, L., and Warusawitharana, M. (2001). Area under the curve as a measure of discounting. *Journal of the Experimental Analysis of Behavior*, *76*, 2235-243.

Odum, A. L., Madden, G. J., and Bickel, W. K. (2002). Discounting of delayed health gains and losses by current never- and ex-smokers of cigarettes. Nicotine and Tobacco Research, *4*, 195-303.

Ohmura, Y., Takahashi, T., and Kitamura, N. (2005). Discounting delayed and probabilistic monetary gains and losses by smokers of cigarettes. Psychopharmacology Sep 16: online published.

Ohmura, Y., Takahashi, T., Kitamura, N., and Wehr, P. (2006). Three-month stability of delay and probability discounting measures. *Experimental and Clinical Psychopharmacology*, *14*, 318-328.

Ostaszewski, P. (1997). Temperament and the discounting of delayed and probabilistic rewards: Conjoining European and American psychological traditions. *European Psychologist*, *2*, 35-43.

Ostaszewski, P., Green, L., and Myerson, J. (1998). Effects of inflation on the subjective value of delayed and probabilistic rewards. *Psychonomic Bulletin and Review*, *5*, 324-333.

Patton, J. H., Stanford, M. S., and Barratt, E. S. (1995). Factor structure of the Barratt impulsiveness scale. *Journal of Clinical Psychology, 51*, 768-774.

Petry, N. M. (2001). Delay discounting of money and alcohol in actively using alcoholics currently abstinent alcoholics and controls. *Psychopharmacology, 154*, 243-250.

Popke, E. J., Mayorga, A. J., Fogle, C. M., and Paule, M. G. (2000). Effects ofacute nicotine on several operant behaviors in rats. *Pharmacology Biochemistry and Behavior, 65*, 247-254.

Potter, A. S and Newhouse, P. A. (2004). Effects of acute nicotine administration on behavioral inhibition in adolescents with attention-deficit/hyperactivity disorder. *Psychopharmacology, 176*, 182-194.

Rachlin, H and Green, L. (1972). Commitment, choice, and self-control. *Journal of the Experimental Analysis of Behavior, 17*, 15-22.

Rahman, S., Zhang, J., Engleman, E. A., and Corrigall, W. A. (2004). Neuroadaptive changes in the mesoaccumbens dopamine system after chronic self-administration: a microdialysis study. *Neuroscience, 129*, 415-424.

Reynolds, B. (2004). Do high rates of cigarette consumption increase delay discounting? A cross-sectional comparison of adolescent smokers and young-adult smokers and nonsmokers. *Behavioural Processes, 67*, 545-549.

Reynolds, B., Richards, J. B., Dassinger, M., de Wit, H. (2004). Therapeutic doses of diazepam do not alter impulsive behavior in human. *Pharmacology Biochemistry and Behavior, 79*, 17-24.

Reynolds, B., Ortengren, A., Richards, J. B., and Wit, H. (2006). Dimensions of impulsive behavior: personality and behavioral measures. *Personality and Individual Differences, 40*, 305-315.

Richards, J. B., Zhang, L., Mitchell, S. H., and de Wit, H. (1999). Delay or probability discounting in a model of impulsive behavior: effect of alcohol. *Journal of the Experimental Analysis of Behavior, 71*, 121-143.

Salokangas, R. K., Vilkman, H., Ilonen, T., Taiminen, T., Bergman, J., Haaparanta, M., Solin, O., Alanen, A., Syvalahti, E., and Hietala, J. (2000). High levels of dopamine activity in the basal ganglia of cigarette smokers. American Journal of Psychiatry, *157*, 632-634.

Skinner, M. D., Aubin, H. J., and Berlin, I. (2004). Impulsivity in smoking, nonsmoking, and ex-smoking alcoholics. *Addictive Behaviors, 29*, 973-978.

Someya, T., Sakado, K., Seki, T., Kojima, M., Reist, C., Tang, S. W., and Takahashi, S. (2001). The Japanese version of the Barratt Impulsiveness Scale, 11th version (BIS-11): its reliability and validity. *Psychiatry and Clinical Neurosciences, 55*, 111-114.

Terasaki, M and Imada, S. (1988). Sensation seeking and food preferences. *Personality and Individual Differences, 9*, 87-93.

Terasaki, M., Shiomi, K., Kishimoto, Y. and Hiraoka, K. (1987). Nihongoban Sesation-Seeking Scale no sakusei. [A Japanese version of the Sensation-Seeking Scale.] *Shinrigaku Kenkyu [Japanese Journal of Psychology], 58*, 42-48.

Thaler, R. (1981). Some empirical evidence on dynamic inconsistency. Economics Letters, *8*, 201-207.

Tversky, A and Kahneman, D. (1981). The framing of decisions and the psychology of choice. *Science, 211*, 453-458.

Ueno, K., Togashi, J., Matsumoto, M., Ohashi, S., Saito, H., and Yoshioka, M. (2002). Alpha4beta2 nicotinic acetylcholine receptor activation ameliorated impairment of spontaneous alternation behavior in stroke-prone spontaneously hypertensive rats, and animal model of attention deficit hyperactivity disorder. *The Journal of Pharmacology and Experimental Therapeutics, 302,* 95-100.

Zuckerman, M. (1971). Dimensions of sensation seeking. *Journal of Consulting and Clinical Psychology, 36,* 45-52.

Zuckerman, M., Eysenck, S., and Eysenck, H. J. (1978). Sensation seeking in England and America: cross-cultural age, and sex comparisons. *Journal of Consulting and Clinical Psychology, 46,* 139-149.

In: Men and Addictions: New Research
Author: Lyman J. Katlin

ISBN 978-1-60692-098-5
© 2009 Nova Science Publishers, Inc.

Chapter 4

SEXUAL ABUSE IN MEN WITH SUBSTANCE USE PROBLEMS: ASSESSMENT AND TREATMENT ISSUES

Christine M. Courbasson

Head, Eating Disorders and Addiction Clinic
Acting Director of Training, Psychology Practicum Training Program
Centre for Addiction and Mental Health
Assistant Professor, Department of Psychiatry
University of Toronto, Canada

Jim Cullen

Clinic Head/Manager Rainbow Services
Centre for Addiction and Mental Health
Assistant Professor, Factor-Inwentash Faculty of Social Work
University of Toronto, Canada

Karolina Konieczna

Douglas Institute, Montreal, Canada

ABSTRACT

Research suggests that a high prevalence of men with substance use problems have experienced sexual abuse at one point in their life. Men who have been sexually victimized frequently use substances to cope with unpleasant feelings resulting from the abuse, they experience many psychosocial problems and they tend to report sexual abuse much less than women. They also experience more extreme substance use than women with a history of sexual abuse. The present chapter reviews the prevalence and the significance of this problem, outlines significant gaps in the clinical and research literature, discusses the need for gender sensitive assessment approaches, and relevant treatment strategies specific to men that can enhance both substance use treatment and general functioning of these clients.

INTRODUCTION

Over the last few decades, researchers have identified a broad range of negative outcomes associated with childhood sexual abuse (CSA). Undesirable after-effects span the areas of physical, behavioral, and psychological health (Koss et al., 2003; Trickett and McBride-Chang, 1995). One frequently observed outcome is adolescent or adult substance use. For example, in a study using a household probability sample of adolescents, Kilpatrick and colleagues (2000) found that young people who reported sexual assault in the year prior to the study were 2.4 times more likely to report alcohol abuse, 1.6 times more likely to report marijuana use, and 2.6 times more likely to report hard drug use than other youth after controlling for age, sex, ethnicity, familial drug and alcohol problems, and physical assault. In addition, other researches show that the relationship between sexual abuse and substance use persists even after controlling for demographic variables (Kilpatrick et al., 2000), psychopathology (Spak et al., 1998), physical child abuse, parental absence, and family involvement in crime (Dembo et al., 1992).

The prevalence of sexual abuse in men with substance use problems (SUP) range from 6.5% to almost 70% (Ross, 1995). This variation across studies is due to differences in data gathering methods and methodological rigueur. Various studies use different definitions of sexual abuse and thus certain experience may be classified as sexual abuse by some researchers but not by the others. Additionally, respondents may provide different answers depending on the way that a question is worded as well as its open- or closed-ended format. Another important factor is the level of anonymity. Studies, which used telephone interviews, may report different numbers than those with face-to-face interviews. Therefore, the information presented in this chapter needs to be interpreted taking into account these limitations.

The available studies on concomitant SUP and sexual abuse have many limitations. Most studies have documented the prevalence of sexual abuse histories among substance users and non-substance users. There are fewer studies that have measured the reverse, namely, the prevalence of substance use among those who have been sexually abused compared to those who have not. The majority of these studies depended on retrospective ascertainment of childhood sexual abuse, which led to difficulties such as forgotten or non-disclosed abuse and inconsistencies in the reconstruction of abusive experiences to make sense of current distress. Furthermore, most studies focused exclusively on female subjects, with those to have examined males producing inconsistent findings (Spataro et al., 2004).

SEXUAL ABUSE

The Prevalence of Sexual Abuse in the General Population and in Substance Users

The prevalence of childhood sexual abuse (CSA) in the general population is difficult to estimate accurately. Common beliefs about CSA prevalence, which are also shared by researchers, have changed significantly over the last 50 years. A few decades ago CSA was thought to be very rare and was not commonly discussed (Putnam, 2003). Later, sexual abuse was assumed to only affect girls; consequently, male research participants, if they were recruited at all, were reluctant to reveal their CSA histories. Today, researchers face other problems. One of them is inconsistency in definitions of CSA which makes results difficult to compare. Moreover, the methodology of studies varies; researchers use either community or clinical samples and measure CSA using a range of methods (Putnam, 2003). It should not come as a surprise that a literature review from 1992 found that estimates of childhood sexual abuse prevalence vary between 2 and 62 percent (Bolen and Scannapieco, 1992). A community-based study which included nearly 5,000 male residents of Ontario revealed that 4.3% of them had a history of sexual abuse (MacMillan et al., 1997). Dilorio et al. (2002) analyzed data from 2676 men at high risk of contracting HIV and found that 25.2% of them had experienced unwanted sexual activity before the age of 13. A review, which adjusted for some of the measurement biases, calculated that 16.8% of women and 7.9% of men reported having histories of CSA (Gorey and Leslie, 1997). Filkelhor et al. (1990) reported that 27% of women have CSA histories. They used a broader definition of CSA which included touching, kissing, rubbing, having nude pictures taken, etc. In their literature review Simpson and Miller (2002) showed that 15%-32% of women had been exposed to childhood sexual abuse. These numbers are consistent with other findings which showed that women experience more sexual victimization and more dual (both physical and sexual) abuse than men (Ouimette et al., 2000).

Comparison of CSA prevalence among men with substance use problems and men in the general population (Filkelhor et al., 1990) did not reveal significant differences between these two groups. In both cases approximately 16% of men reported having been sexually abused as children. Brems et al. (2004) examined a sample of 274 women and 556 men in detoxification services and found that 6.5% of men with SUP had experienced CSA. Most research, however, suggest higher prevalence rates. Since definitions of sexual abuse vary across studies, the reported numbers are difficult to compare.

In their longitudinal research on people in outpatient drug treatment, Gil-Rivas et al. (1997) found that 13% of men in the sample had been sexually abused. It is of note that studies investigating sexual abuse in individuals with substance use problems have been based on clinical samples and did not include men with substance use problems who were not in treatment for substance use. As a result, the prevalence of sexual abuse based on the above findings have limited applications for the general population of men with SUP as the samples did not include men who were not involved in substance abuse treatment. Simpson and Miller (2002) reviewed 20 studies, selected based on a set of methodological criteria, which examined the presence of histories of childhood sexual abuse among men in substance abuse treatment. The average percentage of CSA in this population was found to be 16.3%.

Similarly as in the general population of women, females with SUP report more sexual abuse histories than men. Gil-Rivas et al. (1997) found that 61% of women in outpatient drug treatment had been sexually abused. A review by Simpson and Miller (2002) showed that women in substance use treatment were approximately 80% more likely to have experienced sexual abuse as children.

Consequences of Sexual Abuse History

Many studies have found that prior physical or sexual abuse is associated with more severe medical, family/social, legal and employment problems (Ouimette et al., 2000) as well as psychiatric issues such as depression, anxiety, phobias, and interpersonal difficulties (Clark et al., 2001; Ellason et al., 1996; Gil-Rivas et al., 1996; Greenfield et al., 2002; Harvey et al., 1994; Ouimette et al., 2000; Rice et al., 2001; Windle et al., 1995). Among a college student sample of approximately 600 participants, those with a history of CSA reported greater psychological distress and posttraumatic stress symptoms compared to participants with a trauma history other than CSA and participants with no trauma history (Marx and Sloan, 2003). Experience of sexual violence is strongly associated with high-risk sex and other harmful behaviours. Other coping mechanisms for survivors of sexual trauma include self-mutilation, avoidance of relationships, and eating disorders, especially bulimia (Briere and Elliott, 1994). Individuals use these coping strategies to empower themselves as well as to regain control over how they feel and experience the world. Unfortunately, substance abuse and high-risk behaviours provide only temporary feelings of control, and ultimately put individuals at risk for re-victimization.

SUBSTANCE USE

The Prevalence of Substance Use Problems in the General Population and in Individuals with Histories of Sexual Abuse

According to the National Household Survey, 9.2% of the US population age 12 and older reports substance dependence or abuse. The prevalence rates are 12.3% among men and 6.3% among women (U.S. Department of Health and Human Services, 2006). Some authors suggest that the actual numbers are likely higher (Simpson and Miller, 2002).

A population-based study on residents of Ontario found that 33.2% of men with childhood sexual abuse CSA histories reported alcohol abuse and dependence (MacMillan et.al., 2001). In another study, Dimock (1988) found that men who had experienced CSA were involved in compulsive behaviours, including substance misuse (60%). Case studies of eight men who had been sexually abused by their mothers found that 63% of them suffered from SUP (Krug, 1989). Similar numbers were reported by findings across studies. A review by Simpson and Miller (2002) revealed that the average prevalence of SUP among male CSA survivors who sought substance abuse treatment is 65%. These prevalence rates are much higher than the ones reported for the general populations and point at a significant role of sexual abuse in SUP.

Molnar et al. (2001) compared the prevalence of drug and alcohol dependence and drug-related problems among men with and without a reported history of CSA. Their analysis of data collected in a national survey revealed that men who had experienced CSA were more often dependent on alcohol (38.7% versus 19.2%) and other drugs (41.4% versus 17.9%). They also reported more drug-related problems (41.4% versus 17.9%). MacMillan et al. (2001) found similar results, with 33.2% of men with CSA histories also experiencing abuse or dependence on alcohol, compared with 18.9% of men in the general population. A study of gay and bisexual men revealed that in this population CSA history is related to an increased likelihood of ever having used tobacco, cocaine, crack, stimulants, hallucinogens, and opiates. This relationship was not found for alcohol, marijuana or nitrites (Bartholow et al., 1994).

Data is also available on the prevalence of SUP in women. A national survey in the United States which compared substance use among women with and without CSA histories (Wilsnack, Vogeltanz, Klassen, and Harris, 1997) showed that women who had been sexually abused in childhood more frequently reported recent use of alcohol (43.6% versus 27.4%), intoxication (30.4% versus 15.9%), drinking-related negative consequences (23.1% versus 8.3%), alcohol dependence syndrome (18.8% versus 5.8%), as well as lifetime use of prescribed psychoactive (63.4% versus 52.9%) and illicit drugs (34.9% versus 13.5%). Generally, approximately 40.5% of women with CSA histories report some substance use problems (SUP) (Simpson and Miller, 2002). Consequently, these prevalence rates for women are not drastically different than of men.

THE RELATIONSHIP BETWEEN SEXUAL ABUSE AND SUBSTANCE USE

A popular perception of the relationship between sexual violence and substance abuse is that being drunk or high makes one more susceptible to sexual abuse or assault. Although this may occur in some situations, the literature suggests that the first incidence of sexual abuse or assault usually precedes first alcohol or drug use. Misuse of psychoactive substances is a common consequence of sexual trauma. Many studies show that those who were abused as children are more likely to drink heavily than those who were not abused (Corbin et al., 2001). Brems et al. (2004) showed that among men who sought detoxification services, those with CSA histories reported an earlier age of alcohol drinking onset. Compared to the general population, men who have experienced sexual abuse have been found to use psychoactive substances more often (Molnar et al., 2001; MacMillan et al., 2001; Dilorio et al., 2002; Bartholow et al., 1994), to have begun using them at younger age (Brems et al., 2004; Bartholow et al., 1994) and to experience more negative consequences with regard to substance use (Liebschutz et al., 2002).

Some studies showed that substance dependence is significantly higher for those with histories of CSA (Kendler et al., 2000; Molnar, Buka, and Kessler, 2001). This effect persisted even after controlling for moderating variables such as familial factors, parental psychopathology (Kendler et al., 2000), and 19 other childhood adversities (Molnar et al., 2001). In Greenfield et al.'s (2002) study of 100 patients hospitalized for alcohol dependence, survival analysis showed that sexual abuse history was associated with shorter times to first drink and to first relapse. Harrison, Fulkerson, and Beebe (1997) also identified the earlier initiation of substance use among victims who were sexually abused as children and adolescents. Mamun and colleagues (2007) found that young adults who had experienced any types of sexual abuse, including non-penetrative, penetrative and self-reported rape before the age of 16 years, had significantly higher rates of nicotine disorder than young adults who had not experienced CSA. Alcohol and drugs may be used by victims in an attempt to cope with the trauma of violence, alleviating the symptoms and anxiety associated with victimization, thereby increasing feelings of mastery and control (Banaji and Steele, 1989; Flannery et al.,

1998; Runtz and Schallow, 1997). This suggests that victims may use alcohol and other drugs as a form of self-medication (Jasinski et al., 2000; Spatz et al., 1995).

A very recent study by Schneider et al. (2008) revealed that men with histories of sexual or physical abuse report more severe SUP at the beginning of treatment than their non-abused counterparts. However, many earlier studies failed to find such a relationship; they reported that men with histories of sexual abuse had more severe psychiatric, but not substance use problems than other groups when entering addiction treatment (Gil-Rivas et al., 1996; Greenfield et al., 2002; Pirard et al., 2005; Windle et al., 1995; Marx and Sloan, 2003; Spataro et al., 2004). It has been suggested that the lack of differences in alcohol and drug-related problems among those with and without histories of childhood sexual abuse (CSA) may be due to the methodology adopted. For example, Spataro et al. (2004) implemented a diagnostic hierarchy in which substance use problems accompanied by other psychiatric disorders were counted as comorbid conditions not as substance use problems. It is important to know that comorbidity between substance use disorders and other psychiatric disorders is consistently reported (e.g. Kessler et al., 1997). Thus, it is suggested that what these studies do not demonstrate is in fact an association between child sexual abuse and more pure forms of substance use disorders (Langeland and van den Brink, 2004).

CONSEQUENCES OF COMORBID SUBSTANCE USE AND SEXUAL ABUSE HISTORIES

There are relatively few studies on the impact of sexual abuse on the psychosocial and medical problems in men and even fewer that have investigated this impact in men who have SUP. The few existing studies focus mainly on the psychosocial functioning of survivors of sexual abuse with SUP. Some potential reasons for this lack of information are the reluctance of men to disclose these concomitant issues and the fact that more recent studies use prison populations as subjects. As Banyard, Williams, and Siegel (2004) revealed, some victims of childhood sexual abuse did not recall or did not wish to report their CSA experiences. In addition, most available studies and measurements have a retrospective character and fail to capture some problems related to coexisting sexual abuse and SUP.

Research suggests that men with SUP and sexual trauma histories report more severe psychiatric problems and distress than men with SUP who have no histories of sexual abuse (Medrano, 2002; Pirard et al., 2005; Rosen et al., 2002; Schneider, 2008). They also are more likely to think about or have attempted suicide (Schneider, 2008). A case study of eight men who had experienced childhood sexual abuse (CSA) revealed that concomitant histories of CSA and SUP might be associated with depression and difficulties in maintaining relationships (Krug, 1989). However, Krug's findings cannot be generalized to the whole population of men with CSA and SUP histories without further exploration of these relationships in larger samples. A study of gay and bisexual men suggested that, in this population, histories of sexual abuse, but not substance use, are associated with greater prevalence of subclinical bulimia and other subclinical or full-syndrome eating disorders (Feldman and Meyer, 2007). Other studies found that in patients with alcohol disorders, CSA but not child physical abuse (CPA) is associated with antisocial personality disorder, suicide attempts and posttraumatic stress disorder (Langeland, Draijer and van den Brink, 2004;

Windle et al., 1995). In fact, 48% of CSA survivors meet the DSM-IV criteria for a diagnosis of Post-Traumatic Stress Disorder (PTSD), and their symptoms are often more intense and severe than non-sexual abuse victims with PTSD (Briere and Elliott, 1994; Corbin, et al., 2001). Also, sexual abuse survivors are 4 times more likely to be diagnosed with major depression, and 5 times more likely to be diagnosed with an anxiety disorder. One out of six survivors of sexual violence reports at least one suicide attempt (Briere and Elliott, 1994).

Beyond these findings, some of the psychosocial and medical problems of sexually abused men with SUP may only be deduced from studies on either men with sexual trauma or substance use problems. However, the lack of data on the psychosocial and medical problems of men with both SUP and sexual abuse histories specifically, make the significance of these problems very difficult to assess. Further research is necessary to understand the nature and significance of problems faced by men with both SUP and CSA histories in order to effectively assess and plan for treatment.

GENDER-SENSITIVE ASSESSMENT APPROACHES

The available literature on validated gender-sensitive assessment approaches as applied to men with both substance use problems and a history of sexual abuse/trauma points to a significant scarcity of information on this important issue. This should not be surprising as there are many complicating factors, including the tendency of male survivors to either delay disclosure of sexual abuse/trauma or not report its occurrence at all in fear of being seen as a victim or homosexual (Allagia, 2005). Another issue which complicates identification and treatment of concomitant sexual abuse and SUP is that various screeners were developed and are being used routinely in separate settings but little effort has been made to consolidate the findings to refine the instruments and identify men who need a more specialized treatment (Sacks et al, 2007).

There is also a scarcity of assessment instruments that address both sexual abuse and substance use problems. An example of such an instrument is the revised Substance Abuse and Incest Survey (SAIS-R, Janikowski et al., 1997). Most studies that explored the relationships between sexual abuse and SUP used separate measurements for these two variables. Some of the measurements used were the Computer Assisted Maltreatment Inventory (CAMI), the revised Childhood Trauma Questionnaire (CTQ, DiLillo et al., 2006), the Sexual and Physical Abuse Questionnaire - SPAQ (Kooiman et al., 2002), the Addiction Severity Index (ASI, Branstetter et al., 2008; Rosen et al, 2002) and the Inventory of Drug Use Consequences (InDUC, Liebschutz et al., 2002). While some of these screening tools can be used in both scientific research and clinical practice, clinical research suggests that interviews are more successful in identifying the presence of sexual and physical abuse histories than questionnaires. Questionnaires should not then be solely relied on (Wyatt and Peters, 1986 as cited in Kooiman et al., 2002). There is a need for research aimed at developing psychometrically sound instruments to assess both the history of sexual abuse and its relationship with substance use.

SEXUAL ABUSE, SUBSTANCE USE AND THEIR TREATMENT

The literature, which explores the effects of, combined SUP and sexual abuse on treatment outcomes is sparse and inconsistent. Some studies found that those with prior sexual abuse may have a higher risk of problematic treatment outcomes. For example, in a study by Rosen and colleagues (2002), male (n = 19,989) and female (n = 622) veterans with substance use disorders were assessed with the Addiction Severity Index (ASI) early in treatment and reassessed an average of 12 months later. Treatment outcomes were compared for patients who did and did not report prior physical or sexual abuse in the initial ASI interview. Results showed that lifetime physical or sexual abuse predicted worse outcomes in six of seven domains of functioning, after controlling for baseline functioning, psychiatric diagnoses and demographic variables. Although women were more likely than men to report being abused, the effect of abuse on treatment outcomes was similar for both genders. The study concluded that individuals with substance use disorders who have a history of physical or sexual abuse may be at higher risk for problematic treatment outcomes as a result of greater psychiatric problems, deficits in social support and possible difficulties in establishing treatment alliance. The authors suggested that clinicians might consider increasing the duration and intensity of treatment to temper the negative effects of abuse on later functioning (Rosen et al. 2002). Other research has shown that alcohol abusers with history of sexual abuse were at greater risk of lapsing and relapsing after inpatient treatment than those without such a history (Greenfield et al., 2002).

Conversely, other studies have failed to show that prior physical or sexual abuse compromised treatment outcomes (Fiorentine et al., 1999; Gil-Rivas et al., 1997). For example, in a study of 330 individuals with substance use disorders who participated in 26 outpatient treatment programs, it was found that sexual abuse had no impact on drug use or treatment participation at short-term follow-up; at a two-year follow-up the impact was minimal (Fiorentine et al., 1999). Charney and colleagues (2007) found similar results. At six-month follow-up, they found no differences between patients with and without sexual abuse histories in their response to treatment, or their utilization of treatment services. These inconsistent results regarding the relationship between abuse experiences and response to treatment may be attributed to the diversity of the samples (e.g. only alcohol abusers or a primarily male veteran sample) and the failure to distinguish between the effects of physical and sexual abuse, among others (Charney et al. 2007). The fact that men tend not to disclose histories of sexual abuse as often as women (Langeland et al., 2001) may have also contributed to these results.

TREATMENT PROGRAM RECOMMENDATIONS

As the literature on the concomitance of substance use and mental health problems has grown, many researchers and institutions, including Health Canada (2007), have recognized the importance of creating treatment programs that address the needs of clients who have concurrent disorders. In its 2007 report on best practices, Health Canada recommended integrating treatments of coexisting substance use and mental health problems. A similar need was expressed by professionals who work with people suffering from both sexual trauma and

SUP. However, no data is yet available to support the effectiveness of modified or intensified treatment approach in addressing specific needs of the sexually abused patients in substance use treatment (Charney et al., 2007).

Studies revealed that men with concomitant sexual abuse histories and SUP report more severe psychiatric, family and substance use problems (Branstetter et al., 2008; Ouimette, Kimerling, Shaw, and Moos, 2000; Schneider, 2008) than their non-abused counterparts. Although the treatment offered to men with SUP and sexual abuse histories helps with substance use problems, the psychiatric distress persists (Pirard et al., 2005; Schneider, 2008). Pirard and colleagues (2005) noticed that, despite similar utilization of alcohol and drug treatment as well as overall improvement in alcohol and drug use, sexually abused substance users reported a significantly higher utilization rate of psychiatric treatments. Since the use of psychoactive substances often serves as a coping mechanism for distress related to sexual trauma, failure to address this trauma in treatment may cause relapse into substance use. It is thus very important to create comprehensive therapy programs for this population that would address a broad range of psychiatric problems and distress experienced by this population. Such programs are likely to improve the efficacy and lower the costs of treatment for this population. This is further supported by results of studies conducted on substance abusers with PTSD, showing that treatments addressing trauma-related symptoms in addition to substance use problems yielded better treatment outcomes (Brady et al., 2001; Hien and Levin, 1994; Najavits et al., 1998; Ouimette et al., 1998; 2000; Sullivan and Evans, 1994; Zweben et al., 1994). Since identifying the history of sexual abuse is one of the important challenges in working with men who suffer from coexisting SUP and sexual abuse, additional research on effective ways to identify such coexisting problems is needed. Rohsenow et al. (1988) pointed to the effectiveness of asking clients direct questions about sexual abuse. Their study revealed that adding a routine question about sexual abuse into substance use treatment increased the rates of CSA disclosed by male patients by 350%.

Although the need for specific treatments for concomitant sexual abuse and SUP has been broadly acknowledged in the literature, very few treatment models have been presented. The few papers that exist focus mainly on the female population. Research by Wadsworth and Spampneto (1995) showed that addressing sexual abuse in gender-sensitive groups is more effective than in mixed groups of both men and women. Hiebert-Murphy and Richert (2000) showed that a solution-based group treatment can be beneficial for women with concurrent substance use and childhood sexual abuse problems. Other authors recommended the Seeking Safety therapeutic model for women with concomitant trauma and substance use. This therapy focuses on teaching coping skills and can be used for both individuals and groups (Gatz et al., 2007; Schaefer and Najavits, 2007). Although most of these findings can be applied to male clients, further empirical investigation is required to assess their effectiveness in this population.

CONCLUSION AND FUTURE DIRECTIONS

There exists a paucity of literature to address a significant problem that men who struggle with sexual abuse and substance abuse face. Furthermore the lack of clinical studies that provide solid evidence or promising practices is a barrier for these men to improve their lives.

We know that gender specific programs that concurrently examine and intervene in both areas of substance abuse and trauma have had success with women but appear to have had limited application with men.

The treatment community must focus on prevention strategies, early identification and concurrent programs that meet the needs of men with these difficult histories. As research has indicated the prevalence rates are significant, and given an underreporting analysis, it is even more urgent that gender specific concurrent treatments be created to meet this need. While studies are limited there may exist promising practices that could contribute to the overall knowledge base and well being of these individuals. More dialogue needs to exist within treatment communities to share these programs, interventions and strategies, that may might meet the criteria as evidence based, but show promise in assisting people who are in need.

REFERENCES

Al Mamun, A., Alati, R., O'Callaghan, M., Hayatbakhsh, M.R., O'Callaghan, F.V., and Najman et al. (2007). Does childhood sexual abuse have an effect on young adults' nicotine disorder (dependence or withdrawal)? Evidence from a birth cohort study. *Addiction, 102*(4), 647-654.

Allagia, R. (2005). Disclosing the trauma of sexual abuse: A gender analysis. *Journal of Loss and Trauma*, 10, 453-470.

Bailey, J.A., and McCloskey, L.A. (2005). Pathways to adolescent substance use among sexually abused girls. *Journal of Abnormal Child Psychology, 33*(1), 39–53.

Banaji, M., and Steele, C. (1989). Alcohol and self-evaluation: Is a social cognition approach beneficial? *Social Cognition, 7*(2), 137-151.

Banyard, V.L., Williams, L.M., and Siegel, J.A. (2004). Childhood sexual abuse: A gender perspective on context and consequences. *Child Maltreatment, 9*(3), 223-238.

Barthorolow, B.N., Doll, L.S., Joy, D., Douglas, J.M., Jr., Bolan, G., Harrison, J.S et al. (1994). Emotional, behavioral, and hiv risks associated with sexual abuse among adult homosexual and bisexual men. *Child Abuse and Neglect, 18*(9), 747-761.

Bell, C.C. and Jenkins, E.J. (1991).Traumatic stress and children. *Journal of Health Care for the Poor and Underserved*, 2(1), 175-185.

Bolen, R.M., and Scannapieco, M. (1999). Prevalence of child sexual abuse: A corrective metanalysis. *The Social Service Review, 73*(3), 281-309.

Brady, K.T., Dansky, B.S., Back, S.E., Foa, E.B., and Carroll, K.M. (2001). Exposure therapy in the treatment of PTSD among cocaine-dependent individuals: preliminary findings. *Journal of Substance Abuse Treatment, 21,* 47–54.

Branstetter, S.A., Bower, E.H., Kamien, J., and Amass, L. (2008). A history of sexual, emotional, or physical abuse predicts adjustment during opioid maintenance treatment. *Journal of Substance Abuse Treatment, 34,* 208-214.

Brems, Ch., Johnson, M.E., Neal, D., and Freemon, M. (2004). Childhood abuse history and substance use among men and women receiving detoxification services. *The American Journal of Drug and Alcohol Abuse, 30*(4), 799-821.

Briere, J.N., and Elliott, D.M. (1994). Immediate and long-term impacts of child sexual abuse. *Sexual Abuse of Children, 4,* 54-69.

Charney, D.A., Palacios-Boix, J., and Gill, K.J. (2007). Sexual abuse and the outcome of addiction treatment. *The American Journal on Addictions, 16,* 93-100.

Clark, H.W., Masson, C.L., Delucchi, K.L., Hall, S.M., Sees, K.L., (2001). Violent traumatic events and drug abuse severity. *Journal of Substance Abuse Treatment, 20,* 121–127.

Corbin, W.R., Bernat, J.A., Calhoun, K.S., McNair, L.D., and Seals, K.L. (2001). The role of alcohol expectancies and alcohol consumption among sexually victimized and nonvictimized college women. *Journal of Interpersonal Violence, 16,* 297-311.

Dembo, R., Williams, L., Wothke, W., Schmeidler, J., and Brown, C. H. (1992). The role of family factors, physical abuse, and sexual victimization experiences in hi-risk youths' alcohol and other drug use and delinquency: A longitudinal model. *Violence and Victims, 7,* 245–266.

DiLillo, D., Fortier, M.A., Hayes, S.A., Trask, E., Perry, A.R., Messman-Moore, T. et al. (2006). Retrospective assessment of childhood sexual and physical abuse. *Assessment, 13*(3), 297-312.

Dilorio, C., Hartwell, T., and Hansen, N. (2002). Childhood sexual abuse and risk behaviors among men at high risk for HIV infection. *American Journal of Public Health, 92,* 214-219.

Dimock, P.T. (1988). Adult males sexually abused as children: Characteristics and implications for treatment. *Journal of Interpersonal Violence, 3,* 203-221.

Dunn, G.E., Ryan, J.J., and Dunn, C.E., (1994). Trauma symptoms in substance abusers with and without histories of childhood abuse. *Journal of Psychoactive Drugs, 26,* 357–360.

Ellason, J.W., Ross, C.A., Sainton, K., and Mayran, L.W., (1996). Axis I and II comorbidity and childhood trauma history in chemical dependency. *Bulletin of the Menninger Clinic, 60,* 39–51.

Feldman, M.B., and Meyer, I.L. (2007). Childhood abuse and eating disorders in gay and bisexual men. *International Journal of Eating Disorders, 40*(5), 418-423.

Finkelhor, D., Hotaling, G., Lewis, I.A., and Smith, Ch. (1990). Sexual abuse in a national survey of adult men and women: Prevalence, characteristics, and risk factors. *Child Abuse and Neglect, 14,* 19-28.

Fiorentine, R., Pilati, M.L., and Hillhouse, M.P., 1999. Drug treatment outcomes: investigating the long-term effects of sexual and physical abuse histories. *Journal of Psychoactive Drugs, 31,* 363–372.

Flannery, D., Singer, M., Williams, L., and Castro, P. (1998). Adolescent violence exposure and victimization at home: Coping and psychological trauma symptoms. *International Review of Victimology, 6*(1), 29-48.

Gatz, M., Brown, V., Hennigan, K., Rechberger, E., O'Keefe, M., Rose, T. et al. (2007). Effectiveness of an integrated, trauma-informed approach to treating women with co-occurring disorders and histories of trauma: the Los Angeles site experience. *Journal of Community Psychology, 35*(7), 863–878.

Gil-Rivas, V., Fiorentine, R., Anglin, M.D., (1996). Sexual abuse, physical abuse, and posttraumatic stress disorder among women participating in outpatient drug abuse treatment. *Journal of Psychoactive Drugs, 28,* 95–102.

Gil-Rivas, V., Fiorentine, R., Anglin, M.D., and Taylor, E. (1997). Sexual and physical abuse: Do they compromise drug treatment outcomes? *Journal of substance abuse treatment, 14*(4), 351-358.

Gorey K., and Leslie, D. (1997), The prevalence of child sexual abuse: integrative review adjustment for potential response and measurement bias. *Child Abuse and Neglect, 21,* 391–398.

Greenfield, S.F., Kolodziej, M.E., Sugarman, D.E., Muenz, L.R., Vagge, L.M., He, D.Y., Weiss, R.D., (2002). History of abuse and drinking outcomes following inpatient alcohol treatment: a prospective study. *Drug and Alcohol Dependence, 67,* 227–234.

Harrison, P. A., Fulkerson, J. A., and Beebe, T. J. (1997). Multiple substance use among adolescent physical and sexual abuse victims. *Child Abuse and Neglect, 21*(6), 529-539.

Harvey, E.M., Rawson, R.A., and Obert, J.L., (1994). History of sexual assault and the treatment of substance abuse disorders. *Journal of Psychoactive Drugs, 26,* 361–367.

Health Canada (2007). *Best practices - concurrent mental health and substance use disorders.* Retrieved March 17, 2008 from http://www.hc-sc.gc.ca/hl-vs/pubs/adp-apd/bp_disorder-mp_concomitants/intro_e.html

Hiebert-Murphy, D., and Richert, M. (2000). A parenting group for women dealing with childhood sexual abuse and substance abuse. *International Journal of Group Psychotherapy, 50*(3), 397-405.

Hien, D.A., and Levin, F.R., (1994). Trauma and trauma-related disorders for women on methadone: prevalence and treatment considerations. *Journal of Psychoactive Drugs, 26,* 421–429.

Janikowski, T.P., Bordieri, J.E., and Glover, N.M. (1997). Client perception of incest and substance abuse. *Addictive Behaviors, 22*(4), 447-459.

Jasinski, J. L.,Williams, L.,and Siegel, J. (2000). Childhood physical and sexual abuse as risk factors for heavy drinking among African-American women: A prospective study. *Child Abuse and Neglect, 24*(8): 1061-1071.

Kaukinen, C., and DeMaris, A. (2005). Age at first sexual assault and current substance use and depression. *Journal of Interpersonal Violence, 20*(10): 1244-1270.

Kendler, K. S., Bulik, C. M., Silberg, J.,Hettema, J.M.,Myers, J., and Prescott, C. A. (2000). Childhood sexual abuse and adult psychiatric and substance use disorders in women. An epidemiological and co-twin control analysis. *Archives of General Psychiatry, 57,* 953–959.

Kessler, R. C., Crum, R. M., Warner, L. A., Nelson, C.B., Schulenberg, J. and Anthony, J.C. (1997). Lifetime co-occurrence of DSM - III - R alcohol abuse and dependence with other psychiatric disorders in the national comorbidity survey. *Archives of General Psychiatry, 54,* 313 -321.

Kilpatrick, D. G., Acierno, R., Saunders, B. E., Resnick, H. S., Best, C. L., and Schnurr, P. P. (2000). Risk factors for adolescent substance abuse and dependence: Data from a national sample. *Journal of Consulting and Clinical Psychology, 68,* 19–30.

Kooiman, C.G., Ouwehand, A.W., and ter Kuile, M.M. (2002). The sexual and physical abuse questionnaire (SPAQ) a screening instrument for adults to assess past and current experiences of abuse. *Child abuse and neglect, 26*(9) 939-953.

Koss, M. P., Bailey, J. A., Yuan, N. P., Herrera, V. M., and Lichter, E. L. (2003). Depression, PTSD, and health problems in survivors of male violence: Research and training initiatives to facilitate recovery. *Psychology of Women Quarterly, 27,* 130–142.

Krug, R.S. (1989). Adult male report of childhood sexual abuse by mothers: case descriptions, motivations and long-term consequences. *Child abuse and neglect, 13,* 111-119.

Ladwig, G.B., and Andersen, M.D., (1989). Substance abuse in women: relationship between chemical dependency of women and past reports of physical and/or sexual abuse. *Int. J. Addict.* 24: 739–754.

Langeland, W., Draijer, N., and van den Brink,W. (2004). Psychiatric comorbidity in treatment-seeking alcoholics: The role of childhood trauma and perceived parental dysfunction. *Alcoholism: Clinical and Experimental Research, 28,* 441–447.

Langeland, W., and van den Brink, W. (2004). Child sexual abuse and substance use disorders: role of psychiatric comorbidity. *The British Journal of Psychiatry, 185,* 353.

Langeland, W., van den Brink, W., Draijer, N., and Hartgers, C. (2001). Sensitivity of the addiction severity index physical and sexual assault items: preliminary findings on gender differences. *European Addiction Research, 7*(4), 193-197.

Liebschutz, J., Savetsky, J.B., Saitz, R., Horton, N.J., Lloyd-Travaglini, Ch., and Samet, J.H. (2002). The relationship between sexual and physical abuse and substance abuse consequences. *Journal of Substance Abuse Treatment, 22,* 121-128.

MacMillan, H.L., Fleming, J.E., Streiner, D.L., Lin, E., Boyle, M.H., Jamieson, E., et al. (2001). Childhood abuse and lifetime psychopathology in a community sample. *The American Journal of Psychiatry, 158*(11), 1878-1883.

MacMillan, H.L., Fleming, J.E., Trocme, N., Boyle, M., Wong, M., Racine, Y.A., et al. (1997). Prevalence of child physical and sexual abuse in the community: results from the Ontario Health Supplement. *The Journal of American Medical Association, 278*(2), 131-135.

Marx, B.P., and Sloan, D.M. (2003). The effects of trauma history, gender, and race on alcohol use and posttraumatic stress symptoms in a college student sample. *Addictive Behaviors, 28,* 1631–1647.

Medrano, M.A., Hatch, J.P., Zule, W.A., and Desmond, D.P. (2002). Psychological distress in childhood trauma survivors who abuse drugs. *American Journal of Drug and Alcohol abuse, 28*(1), 1-13.

Miller, B.A., Downs, W.R., and Testa, M., 1993. Interrelationships between victimization experiences and women's alcohol use. *Journal of Studies on Alcohol (suppl. 11),* 109–117.

Molnar, B.E., Buka, S.L., and Kessler, R.C. (2001). Child sexual abuse and subsequent psychopathology: results from the National Comorbidity Survey. *American Journal of Public Health, 91*(5), 753-760.

Moncrieff, J., Drummond, D.C., Candy, B., Checinski, K., and Farmer, R.(1996). Sexual abuse in people with alcohol problems. A study of the prevalence of sexual abuse and its relationship to drinking behavior. *British Journal of Psychiatry, 169,* 355–360.

Najavits, L.M., Gastfriend, D.R., Barber, J.P., Reif, S., Muenz, L.R., Blaine, J. et al. (1998). Cocaine Dependence with and without PTSD in the NIDA Cocaine Collaborative Study. *American Journal of Psychiatry, 155,* 214–219.

Ouimette, P.C., Brown, P.J., and Najavits, L.M., (1998). Course and treatment of patients with both substance use and posttraumatic stress disorders. *Addictive Behavior, 23,* 785–795.

Ouimette, P.C., Kimerling, R., Shaw, J., and Moos, R.H. (2000). Physical and sexual abuse among women and men with substance use disorders. *Alcoholism Treatment Quarterly, 18*(3), 7-17.

Pirard, S., Sharon, E., Kang, S. K., Angarita, G. A., and Gastfriend, D. R. (2005). Prevalence of physical and sexual abuse among substance abuse patients and impact on treatment outcomes. *Drug and Alcohol Dependence, 78,* 57-64.

Putnam, F.W. (2003). Ten-year research update review: child sexual abuse. *Journal of the American Academy of Child and Adolescent Psychiatry, 42*(3), 269-278

Rohsenow, D.J., Corbett, R., and Devine, D. (1988). Molested as children: a hidden contribution to substance abuse? *Journal of Substance Abuse Treatment, 5,* 13-18.

Rosen, C. S., Ouimette, P. C., Sheikh, J. I., Gregg, J. A., and Moos, R. H. (2002). Physical and sexual abuse history and addiction treatment outcomes. *Journal of Studies on Alcohol, 63,* 683-687.

Runtz, M., and Schallow, J. (1997). Social support and coping strategies as mediators of adult adjustment following childhood maltreatment. *Child Abuse and Neglect, 21*(2), 211-226.

Sacks, J.Y., McKendrick, K., and Kressel, D. (2007). Measuring offender progress in treatment using the Client Assessment Inventory. *Criminal Justice and Behavior, 34*(9), 1131-1142.

Sanders-Philips, K., Moisan, P. A.,Wadlinton, S., Morgan, S., and English, K. (1995). Ethnic differences in psychological functioning among Black and Latino sexually abused girls. *Child Abuse and Neglect, 19*(6), 691-706.

Schaefer, I., and Najavits, L.M. (2007). Clinical challenges in the treatment of patients with posttraumatic stress disorder and substance abuse. *Current Opinion in Psychiatry, 20,* 614-618.

Schneider, R., Cronkite, R., and Timko, C. (2008). Lifetime physical and sexual abuse and substance use treatment outcomes in men. *Journal of Substance Abuse Treatment.* 35(4):353-61.

Simpson, T.L., and Miller, W.R. (2002). Concomitance between childhood sexual and physical abuse and substance use problems. A review. *Clinical Psychology Review, 22,* 27-77.

Spak, L., Spak, F., and Allebeck, P. (1998). Sexual abuse and alcoholism in a female population. *Addiction, 93,* 1365–1373.

Spataro, J., Mullen, P. E., Burgess, P. M., Wells, D., and Moss, S. (2004). Impact of child sexual abuse on mental health. Prospective study in males and females. *British Journal of Psychiatry, 184,* 416 -421.

Spatz, Widom, C., Ireland, T., and Glynn, P. J. (1995). Alcohol abuse in abused and neglected children followed up: Are they at increased risk? *Journal of Studies on Alcohol, 56,* 207-217.

Trickett, P. K., and McBride-Chang, C. (1995). The developmental impact of different forms of child abuse and neglect. *Developmental Review, 15*(3), 311–337.

U.S. Department of Health and Human Services (2006). 2006 National Survey on Drug Use and Health: detailed tables. Retrieved March 10, 2008, from http://www.oas.samhsa.gov/NSDUH/2k6NSDUH/tabs/Sect5peTabs1to56.htm

Wadsworth, R., and Spampneto, A. (1995). The role of sexual trauma in the treatment of chemically dependent women. *Journal of Counseling and Development, 73*(4), 401-407.

Wilsnack, S.C., Vogeltanz, N.D., Klassen, A.D., and Harris, T.R. (1997). Childhood sexual abuse and women's substance abuse: national survey findings. *Journal of Studies on Alcohol, 58,* 264-271.

Windle M, Windle RC, Scheidt DM, Miller GB. (1995). Physical and sexual abuse and associated mental disorders among alcoholic inpatients. *American Journal of Psychiatry, 152,* 1322–1328.

Wyatt, G.E., and Peters, S.D. (1986). Methodological considerations in research on the prevalence of child sexual abuse. *Child Abuse and Neglect, 10,* 241–251.

Zlotnick, C., Johnson, D.M., Stout, R.L., Zywiak, W.H., Johnson, J.E., and Schneider, R.J. (2006). Childhood abuse and intake severity in alcohol disorder patients. *Journal of Traumatic Stress, 19*(6), 949-959.

Zweben, J.E., Clark, H.W., and Smith, D.E., (1994). Traumatic experiences and substance abuse: mapping the territory. *Journal of Psychoactive Drugs, 26,* 327–344.

In: Men and Addictions: New Research
Author: Lyman J. Katlin

ISBN 978-1-60692-098-5

Chapter 5

EXPLAINING TYPE 2 DIABETES: COMPARING PATIENTS' AND PHYSICIANS' MODELS IN MEXICO

Raminta Daniulaityte[1], Javier E. García de Alba García[2] and Ana L. Salcedo Rocha[2]

[1] Center for Interventions, Treatment and Addictions Research,
Wright State Univ., School of Medicine, Dayton, OH, USA
[2] Social Epidemiological and Health Services Research Unit (UISESS),
Guadalajara, Mexico

ABSTRACT

Conducted in Guadalajara, Mexico, the study focuses on patients' and physicians' beliefs about diabetes causality. The study was conducted in two stages and used cultural consensus model. First, qualitative interviews were conducted with a convenience sample of 28 Type 2 diabetes patients. On the basis of the elicited themes, 21 scenarios on diabetes causes were developed. In the second stage, a convenience sample of 46 Type 2 diabetes patients and 25 physicians working at the primary care level was recruited. Participants were asked to rate each scenario on a three-point scale. Scenario-type interviews were consensus analyzed using ANTHROPAC. Patients and physicians shared very different cultural models of diabetes causality. The patient model included emotional, environmental, some behavioral, and hereditary causes of diabetes. The physician model emphasized heredity as a single most important cause of diabetes. Differences between patient and physician views of diabetes causality may contribute to mistrust and miscommunication in medical interactions. There is a need for clinical practice that would include psychosocial stress and environmental factors in diabetes prevention and care.

Keywords: Type 2 diabetes, Mexico, cultural consensus model, health care providers, patients.

INTRODUCTION

Type 2 diabetes presents a very challenging and growing problem in Mexico and many countries around the world. According to the World Health Organization estimates, the total number of people with diabetes worldwide is projected to rise from 177 million in 2000 to 366 million in 2030 (Wild et al. 2004). In Mexico, prevalence rates of Type 2 diabetes among adults have increased from 8.8% in 1993 to 11.4% in 1999 (Jimenez-Cruz and Bacardi-Gascon 2004). Since 2000, diabetes has become the principle cause of death among women and the second among men in Mexico (Rull et al. 2005). Research shows that only about 15% of treated patients in Mexico are able to control Type 2 diabetes at favorable levels (García de Alba García et al. 2005).

The successful management of diabetes involves significant life-style changes. One's daily life routines have to be modified to incorporate dietary and physical activity regiments, stress management, medication, and blood glucose monitoring. It has been recognized that differences between patient and provider conceptions of the disease may be a serious barrier to effective communication and favorable treatment outcomes in diabetes and other health conditions (Clark and Hampson 2003; Freeman and Loewe 2000; Garcia de Alba-Garcia et al. 2002; Helman 1985; Kleinman 1980; Lipton et al. 1998).

Studies of diabetes-related knowledge have most commonly used standardized instruments to assess individual knowledge in terms of the "correct" biomedical model of the disease (Bautista-Martinez et al. 1999; Clark and Hampson 2003; Valadez-Figueroa, Aldrete-Rodriguez, and Alfaro-Alfaro 1993). However, integration of qualitative or ethnographic methodologies has been recognized as a valuable tool in eliciting insider attitudes, knowledge, and beliefs about diabetes. Such insider-focused approaches may provide a better insight into personal meanings of diabetes, one of the key areas for diabetes education interventions (Anderson 1986).

Most qualitatively oriented research on diabetes-related knowledge has focused on patient perceptions in various ethnic groups. Research conducted in various Mexican and Mexican American communities found varying degrees of congruence between lay and scientific models of diabetes, but generally identified an emphasis on social and emotional factors in lay explanations of diabetes (Arganis-Juarez 1998; Daniulaityte 2004; Hunt, Valenzuela, and Pugh 1998; Jezewski and Poss 2002; Mercado-Martinez and Ramos-Herrera 2002; Poss and Jezewski 2002; Torres-Lopez, Sandoval-Diaz, and Pando-Moreno 2005; Weller et al. 1999).

Despite research showing that biomedicine may adapt the values of a larger culture in which it is embedded (Baer et al. 2004; Finkler 1991), biomedical knowledge is typically viewed as an objective, "value-free" enterprise. As a result, besides a few notable exceptions, researchers have paid less attention to the study of health care provider knowledge and attitudes about diabetes (Larme and Pugh 1998; Loewe et al. 1998). Similarly, there are relatively few studies that aimed to systematically examine differences in diabetes-related knowledge between patients and health care providers. A few existing studies that used qualitative approach described substantial differences between patient and practitioner conceptions of diabetes. Medical professionals focused on biochemical, physiological and "numerical" aspects of the disease, while the patients emphasized social and psychological domains (Cohen et al. 1994; Freeman and Loewe 2000; Loewe and Freeman 2000).

Furthermore, a study conducted by Cohen and colleagues found that patients with normal glycosylated hemoglobin levels tended to have explanatory models that were more congruent with the physician model (Cohen et al. 1994).

A paper by Hunt and colleagues (Hunt, Arar, and Larme 1998) is among the very few published studies on variation in patient and practitioner perspectives on diabetes among people of Mexican origin. The study, conducted in South Texas, identified substantial differences between patient and health care provider attitudes. Practitioners assumed that high blood sugar meant uncooperativeness on the part of the patients. In contrast, the patients were committed to the control of their illness, but they lacked access to behavioral options due to their poverty and lack of social resources (Hunt, Arar, and Larme 1998). Another study, conducted in Nuevo Leon, Mexico, used a standardized instrument (The Diabetes Attitude Scale) to assess differences in attitudes between diabetic patients and health care providers in all three health care sectors—private, social security and welfare. The study found that diabetic patient and health care provider attitudes differed in most domains, including the severity of the disease, value of tight control of glucose levels and patient autonomy (Salinas-Martinez et al. 2004).

In this article, we report on a study conducted in Guadalajara, Mexico in the clinics managed by the Social Security Administration that provides health care benefits to working people throughout the country. The aim of this paper is to explore variation in causal explanations of diabetes between Type 2 diabetes patients and physicians, practicing at the primary care level. It has been suggested that causal explanations comprise a domain of medical knowledge that is powerfully affected by cultural categories (Chrisman and Kleinman 1983). Previous research has shown that causal beliefs often form a core of medical knowledge and have an important role in shaping illness behavior (Finkler 1991; McMullin et al. 2005; Weller et al. 1999)

This study uses cultural consensus model (Romney, Weller, and Batchelder 1986) and scenario-type interviews (Caulkins et al. 2000) which integrate qualitative and quantitative perspectives. The cultural consensus model builds on the definition of culture as shared information and knowledge, and is able to perform three tasks. First, it determines the degree to which a group of study participants share knowledge of some cultural domain. If knowledge is shared, it is reasonable to infer that they are all drawing on a single cultural model of that domain. Second, it provides a "culturally best" estimate of the correct answer to each question asked of the informants. Third, cultural consensus analysis estimates how much each individual's responses correspond to the group shared responses (the level of cultural knowledge). Different from the standardized instruments that tend to impose researcher categories, or the methodological difficulties of qualitative studies to address intra-cultural variation (Carey 1993), the cultural consensus model is able to both elicit insider perspectives and provide for systematic comparisons across different social groups.

RESEARCH SETTING

Guadalajara, a capital of the state of Jalisco, is the second largest city in Mexico, and currently has a population of more than four million people. It is located in the western part of the country, which is considered one of the most prosperous regions. Guadalajara started growing rapidly after World War II, and has become an important industrial center (Gobierno del Estado de Jalisco, 2006).

The Social Security system in Mexico covers disability and old age insurance, and provides medical benefits for the economically active population working in the formal private sector. It is managed by the government-run Mexican Institute of Social Security (*Instituto Mexicano del Seguro Social*, IMSS) and covers more than 35 million people. IMSS is the major public and health agency in Mexico, supplying primary, secondary and tertiary health care to working people throughout the country. In the state of Jalisco, about 53% of the population is covered by the social security system (Gobierno del Estado de Jalisco, 2006; Guttierrez Trujillo et al. 2006). However, some research conducted in Mexico suggested that many patients with chronic illness, including diabetes, report negative experience with primary care services at the Social Security clinics (Meracado Martinez, Herrera, Valadez Curiel, 2000).

The study participants were recruited at the Social Security clinics that mostly serve population residing in the *Sector Libertad*, which is the largest and most densely populated neighborhood in the city. Much of the migrant population that contributed to the rapid growth of Guadalajara in the 40s to 60s settled in this part of the city (Padilla-Dieste and Niembro-Díaz, 1990). *Sector Libertad* is considered a working class neighborhood, although socio-economic diversity of its population has been increasing.

METHODS

In the first stage, qualitative interviews were conducted with 28 individuals in various community and hospital settings to obtain a broad understanding of the meanings and experiences of diabetes among Type 2 diabetes patients (Daniulaityte 2004). Participant recruitment was facilitated by the Social, Epidemiological and Health Services Research Unit (UISESS), located in the Western Medical Center in Guadalajara (Garcia de Alba et al. 2005). On the basis of the elicited themes, a series of scenarios about diabetes causation were constructed that were used for systematic interviewing in the second stage of the study. A scenario is defined as a brief one or two-sentence description that illustrates identified themes related to diabetes causation (Caulkins et al. 2000). To make sure that scenarios conveyed the intended meaning, they were pre-tested with a small group of diabetes patents. The final list included 21 scenarios on diabetes causation (table 1).

Table 1. A list of scenarios and their ratings (range from 3 = strongly agree to 1 = disagree) according to cultural models based on patient and physician responses

No.	Scenario	Patients	Physic.
1	Señor Toño used to drink a lot and most likely this was the cause of his diabetes.	2.06	1.62
2	Señor Jose thinks that his diabetes is caused by what he used to eat. He was used to eating a lot. And most likely this was one of the causes.	2.23	1.92
3	Señora Ceci thinks that she developed diabetes because she used to eat lots of sweets, lots of chocolate, and things like that.	2.36	1.83
4	Señora Elena says that her diabetes is hereditary, because her father was diabetic, and he died from that.	2.51	2.76

Table 1. (Continued)

No.	Scenario	Patients	Physic.
5	Señor Alvarez has doubts that his diabetes is hereditary, because his parents developed diabetes when they were old. Because of that he thinks that his diabetes does not come from his parents.	2.11	1.60
6	There are different types of diabetes, some hereditary, others from angry spells, and others from frights or other things.	2.65	1.17
7	Señor Tacho became diabetic because of one very strong medicine that he had taken for another illness.	1.66	1.25
8	Señora Elena is diabetic, and she is a very fat lady. Most likely her diabetes comes from fatness.	2.61	2.15
9	Don José became diabetic because of a fright that he experienced when somebody tried to rob their house. He got very frightened, and because of that he got diabetes.	2.93	1.46
10	Señora Veronica became diabetic when her daughter passed away, and from the grief she got diabetes.	2.77	1.33
11	Señora Elena became diabetic because she had so many angry spells in her life. Her husband used to upset her a lot. She suffered so much with him that she became diabetic.	2.88	1.21
12	These days there are many people with diabetes. People in the olden days did not have so much diabetes.	2.69	1.55
13	There are so many people with diabetes these days because they consume lots of fat, lots of pork.	2.68	1.89
14	Now there are so many people with diabetes because we live in a large city with lots of pressures, lots of hurry; before there were not so many people, or so much traffic, and life was more peaceful.	2.73	2.05
15	There are many pressures in our times. Due to monetary problems, and lack of jobs, people get anxious and worried, and because of that there are more people with diabetes.	2.69	1.74
16	Nowadays there are many people with diabetes because of the pollution and smog in large cities.	1.90	1.19
17	Before there was not as much diabetes because food was more healthy. And now everything is contaminated, processed, with preservatives.	2.79	1.78
18	(18) Señor Javier developed diabetes 2 years ago, and his wife has had diabetes for 10 years now. None of his parents was diabetic, and so he thinks that he most likely got his diabetes from his wife.	1.17	1.05
19	Señora Juana became diabetic because she used to eat a lot of vegetables and fruit.	1.07	1.05
20	Señor José became diabetic because he had a very peaceful life, without any worries, without anything.	1.07	1.02
21	Before there were not that many people with diabetes because people used to walk more. Now many jobs are sedentary, and people exercise less.	2.50	2.22

In the second stage, consensus-type interviews were conducted with Type 2 diabetes patients and physicians working at the primary care level in the Social Security clinics. Social workers and other medical staff assisted in identifying adult individuals diagnosed with Type 2 diabetes who then were invited to participate in the study (see Daniulaityte 2004). Physicians were recruited and interviewed by the UISESS staff. All interviews were conducted in Spanish.

According to the estimates by Romney and colleagues (1986), cultural consensus analysis can generate stable results with a fairly small group of informants. Assuming that participants would have 0.5 level of cultural knowledge, a sample size of 17 participants would be sufficient to achieve a 95% confidence level and 95% validity (Romney, Weller, and Batchelder 1986). The sample included 46 Type 2 diabetes patients and 25 physicians, and was sufficient to conduct cultural consensus analysis separately for the data generated by the two groups.

On average, each interview lasted about 30 minutes. The interview protocol included scenario-type questions, and a number of questions on demographic and clinical information. To avoid introducing order bias, scenarios were read to each participant in a random order. The participants had to rate each of the scenarios on a 3-point scale. A situation described in the scenario that was considered very true and common was rated "3," somewhat true, or possibly true, was "2," and, not true at all/not common, was "1." Participants were instructed that scenarios are not questions about their personal experiences, and that when evaluating each scenario they should think in general terms about situations that they have seen or heard in their social environment.

Consensus analysis was performed separately for the two groups using ANTHROPAC (Borgatti 1996). Other statistical analysis was performed using SPSS. The cultural consensus routine in ANTHROPAC conducts factor analysis and extracts three un-rotated factors. If the ratio between the first and second eigenvalues is greater than 3:1, there is a single-factor solution, or a "cultural" level of agreement. The higher the ratio, the more cultural sharing there is. To make a decision about the cultural sharing, it is important to take into account average level of cultural knowledge, standard deviation and the percentage of the variance explained by the first factor.

RESULTS

Participant Characteristics

In the first stage, 28 participants were interviewed; 14 of them were women. The age ranged from 39 to 87 years, with a mean about 64 years. The sample included individuals whose education varied from no school to a university degree. The mean duration of diabetes was around 12 years. Data obtained from 28 individual qualitative interviews were used to construct the scenarios and describe a cultural model of diabetes causation.

In the second stage, women comprised 52% of all patient respondents and 48% of all physicians interviewed. Patients were older than physicians (58.8, std. dev. 11.3, vs. 45.2, std. dev. 9.0), and had much lower educational levels than the medical professionals. About 22% of patients had no formal education, about 37% reported incomplete primary education, and 24% complete primary education. Only about 9% of patients had a university diploma. Among patients, the mean duration of diabetes was around 12 years.

Cultural Sharing among Patients and Physicians

Cultural consensus analysis revealed that when patient and physician responses were analyzed together, the ratio between the first and second eigenvalues was 2.9, the average level of cultural knowledge was 0.54, st. dev. 0.23., and 63.4% of the variance was explained by the first factor. The level of sharing did not reach an acceptable "cut off" point indicating a single cultural model of diabetes causes. Mean level of cultural knowledge (or agreement) among physicians was 0.38, and among patients 0.62. In other words, on average, physicians "knew" or matched correctly about 38% of the items that described culturally shared model of diabetes causes. In contrast, patients matched correctly about 62% of all items. Visual representation of the differences in cultural knowledge scores is presented in figure 1 which shows little overlap between the two groups. Two-way analysis of variance confirmed significant differences in cultural knowledge scores between patients and physicians, and gender-related interaction effects (table 2).

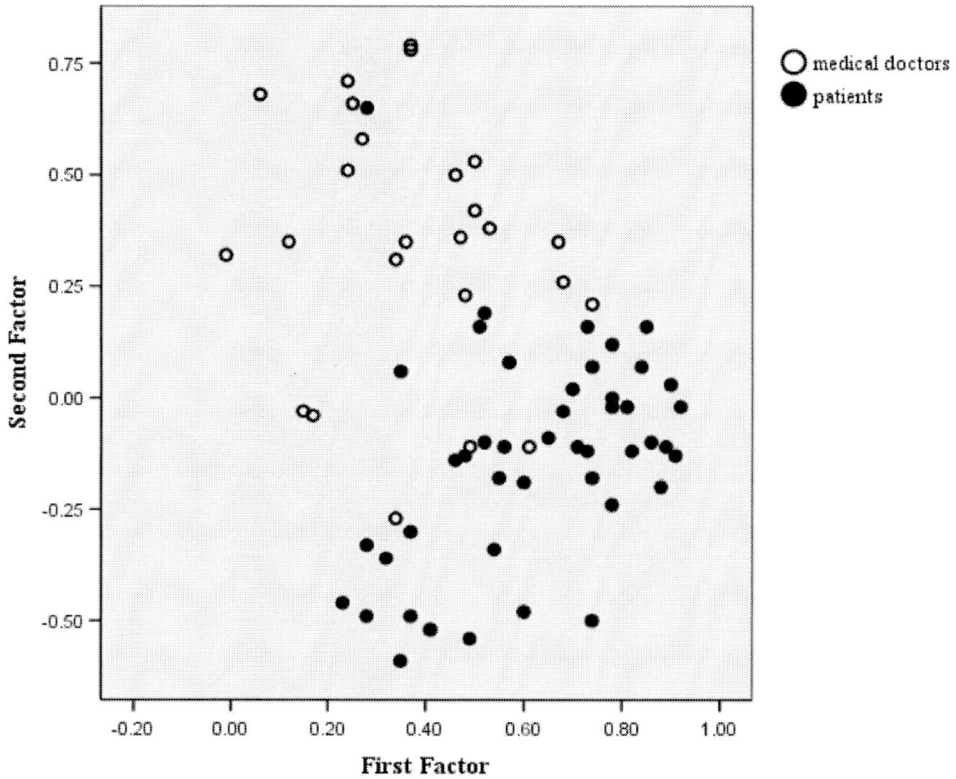

[1]

Figure 1. Visual representation of participant agreement about diabetes causal explanations (knowledge scores on first and second factors).

Table 2. Analysis of variance of cultural knowledge scores on diabetes causes

Source	df	Sum of Squares	Mean Square	F	p value
Participant type	1	0.96	.96	26.48	<0.001
Gender	1	0.12	.12	3.34	0.07
Interaction	1	0.16	.16	4.02	0.05
Error	67	2.43	.04		
Total	70	3.80			

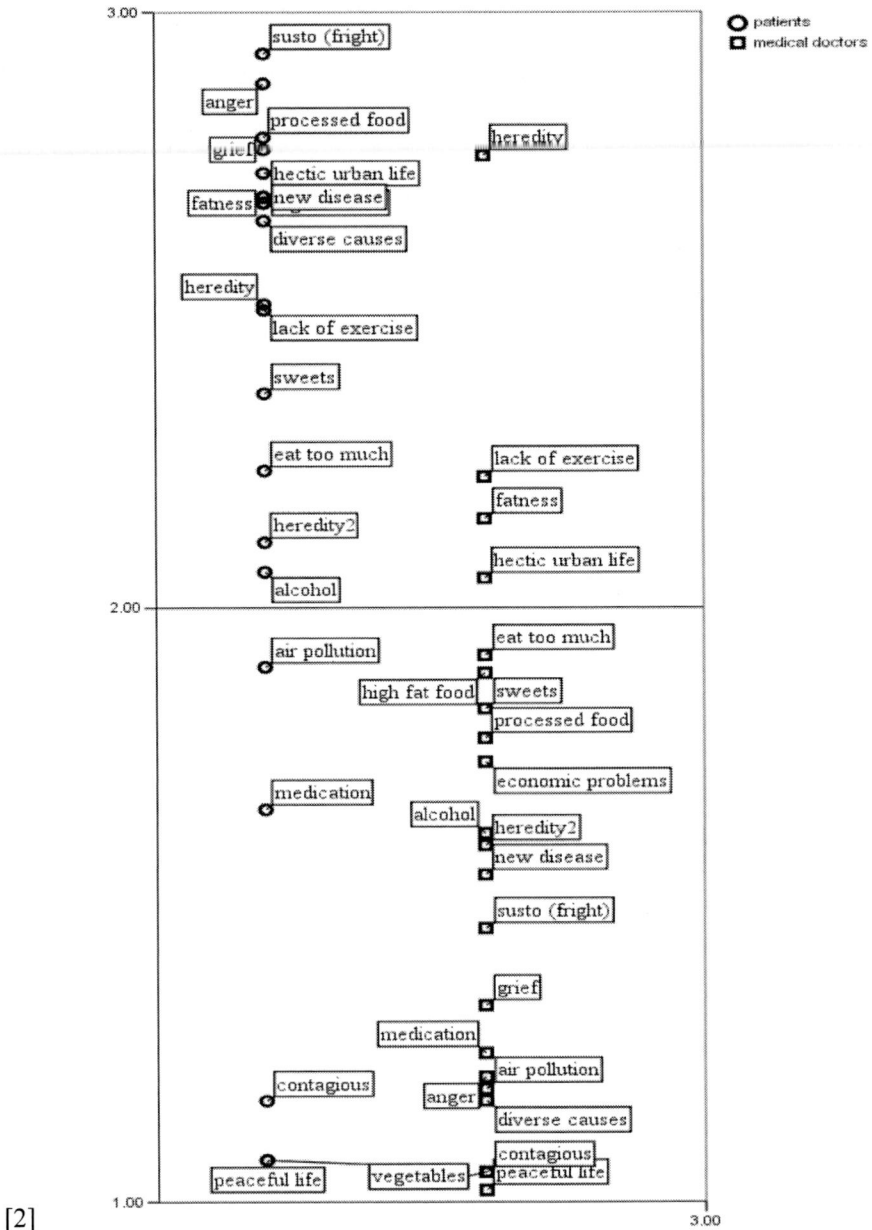

[2]

Figure 2. Ranking of 21 scenarios on diabetes causes according to patients and physicians.

When patients were analyzed as a separate group, the ratio between the first and second eigenvalues was 4.3. The level of variance explained by the first factor was 74.3%, and the average level of knowledge was 0.64 (std. dev. 0.19). These results suggest a fairly high level of agreement among respondents and an existence of a single cultural model of diabetes causality. In terms of gender differences, female patients had a higher level of knowledge than male patients (0.72, std. dev. 0.17 vs. 0.55, std. dev. 0.18). This difference was found to be statistically significant (t = 3.27, df = 44, p<0.01) (more on gender differences among patients see Daniulaityte 2004).

When physician responses were analyzed as a separate group, the ratio between the first and second eigenvalues barely reached a formal "cut off" point of 3. The level of variance explained by the first factor was 64%, and the average level of cultural knowledge was 0.53 (std. dev. 0.24). There was no statistically significant difference between the average level of knowledge shared by male and female physicians. Although consensus analysis revealed that physicians, similar to patients, did share a single model of diabetes causality, the level of sharing among physicians was lower than among patients. In other words, there was greater variability among physicians than among patients.

Patients and Physicians Models of Diabetes Causes

Besides the level of cultural sharing, cultural consensus analysis revealed that patients and physicians shared very different models of diabetes causality, as seen from the table 1 and figure 2. Patient model depicted diabetes as a multi-causal disease, and emphasized psychosocial stress, environmental changes, heredity, and some behavioral factors. For example, some of these themes are illustrated in the following interviews conducted with Type 2 diabetes patients in the first stage of the study:

> I think that disorderly nutrition [contributes to diabetes]. Another factor is sedentary life style, lack of exercise. Today most jobs are office-based. Stress related to the modern way of life is also a factor. I also think that our foods may contribute [to diabetes]. Most foods today are with additives; many foods are "synthetic"... Also, the economic factor, unemployment, high rates of unemployment, and this popular trend now to go to the United States.... People get stress out—every day there are more tensions and worries.... (60-year-old man)

> I became diabetic after the death of my daughter, the oldest one. She was in the hospital, because she had problems with her pregnancy, and so we took her to this hospital over there. And so she was there. And I went to visit her, and she was very sick, very sick. I went to see her on Friday. On Saturday they call me from the hospital and tell me that she had a cardiac arrest and is dead.... Oh my God!... I felt such a terrible pain... I felt like I was dying... And this all affected me so much, that it made me diabetic. It made me diabetic. (69-year-old woman)

In the physician model, the major emphasis was placed on hereditary causation of diabetes. Lack of exercise and fatness were also rated fairly high by physicians, although these issues were rated as more significant causes in the patient model. Other behavioral factors such as "eating too much" and "high fat foods" were also rated as more significant causes by patients than by medical doctors. Causes related to emotional distress and some environmental changes were rated as untrue in the physician model, while in the patient model, these items received a very high rating. Patient and physician models were similar in that both excluded such factors as contagiousness of diabetes, peaceful life leading to diabetes, and eating fruit and vegetables.

These differences between patients and provider views regarding diabetes causation were discussed by some of the participants in the first stage qualitative interviews. For example, a 68-year-old man indicated, "In our Mexican culture, those who do not have medical knowledge [training], we all relate diabetes causes to frights, strong positive emotions, sadness, depression….” Similarly, another participant, a 70-year-old woman, discussed her views about diabetes causes, and pointed out that her physician had a different opinion:

> Who knows, I say I became diabetic because I used to fight a lot with my mother-in-law, she used to make me mad a lot. I think because of that…. We lived on the other side [of the house], but we had a small window that was left uncovered. And she used to shout at me, tell me so many things… Sometimes she used to tell me such things… that I would get really angry. And I think that all these angers and frustrations contributed to diabetes. I told to one doctor that my diabetes was caused by the angers. And he said no, that angers could not cause diabetes. But I say, “What else?” Neither my mother nor my father were diabetics. I did not have diabetics in the family… .

DISCUSSION

Our findings demonstrate substantial differences between physician and patient attitudes about diabetes causality which may hinder effective communication and contribute to a lack of trust in medical advice on the part of the patient (Helman 1985). Interestingly, consensus analysis results suggested greater variability among physicians than among the group of Type 2 diabetes patients regarding their views about diabetes causality. These findings contrast with research conducted in the USA that show higher coherence in health-related views among medical professionals than lay individuals (Chavez et al. 1995). Conversely, our findings are consistent with other research conducted in Mexico showing that professional education among psychology students increased diversity in health-related views (García de Alba García et al. 1999).

Contrary to previous research showing cultural influences on a number of domains in Mexican biomedicine (Finkler 1991), our findings indicate that the physicians’ model excluded most of the lay views about diabetes causation. The issue of emotional distress represents a key discrepancy between patient and physician models of diabetes causality and may be an important contributor to mistrust and miscommunication in medical interactions. Low rating of emotional distress in the physicians’ model presents a contradiction to the current state of knowledge about psychosocial stress and its role in the processes of chronic health conditions. Previous research conducted among various ethnic groups demonstrated that psychosocial stress related to major stressful life events, acculturation and socio-economic inequalities in modern societies is linked to the increased risk for developing Type 2 diabetes (Dressler, Bindon, and Gilliland 1996; Helz and Templeton 1990; Mooy et al. 2000; Scheder 1988; Surwit and Schneider 1993; Szathmary and Ferrel 1990). Our findings suggest that clinical medicine in Mexico, similar to the clinical medicine in other countries, tends to minimize psychosocial factors, including emotional distress, in the medical teachings and management of diabetes (Helz and Templeton 1990; Loewe and Freeman 2000).

The lay model depicted diabetes as a multi-causal disease, while the physician model focused on heredity as a single most important cause of diabetes. Such emphasis on heredity, although accepted as a plausible cause of diabetes in the patient model, may seem irrelevant to some of the patients who did not have family history of diabetes, or who were the first generation of diagnosed diabetics in the family. This focus on a single-factor explanation among physicians may reflect a background in medical education molded according to the acute or infectious disease model that is inadequate in explaining or managing chronic health conditions such as diabetes, a problem faced by physicians practicing in other socio-cultural settings (Larme and Pugh 1998)

The physician model also excluded most of the environmental explanations of diabetes which were rated fairly high in the patient model. This orientation is consistent with clinical practice that focuses primarily on individual sickness and pays little attention to public health knowledge and concerns about environmental processes in diabetes etiology and care.

Consensus analysis shows that patients rated fairly high most of the behavioral factors related to the increased risk of developing Type 2 diabetes, but excluded alcohol consumption as a plausible cause of diabetes. Similarly, alcohol abuse was rated fairly low in the physician model (table 1, figure 2), although it has been recognized as one of the important risk factors for developing diabetes in men (Monterrosa et al. 1995).

Our findings are limited to patients and physicians recruited at the Social Security clinics in a large urban center. Physician knowledge was assessed using themes elicited in patient interviews. Although additional qualitative interviews with health care practitioners might have given a better insight into the physician model of diabetes, many of the causes elicited from patient interviews include factors of biomedical relevance.

The study suggests that besides transfer of new medical information, continuing medical education programs should focus on addressing and changing some of the health care provider beliefs and attitudes about diabetes (Weinberger, Cohen, and Mazzuca 1984). There is a need for clinical practice that would include psychosocial stress as an important domain in diabetes education and management, and would integrate public health knowledge about environmental influences in diabetes etiology and care. A practitioner who is aware of and integrates the above subjects into diabetes care should be able to establish a better understanding of the patients' view of illness, which eventually would contribute to better communication and trust in medical interactions.

REFERENCES

Anderson, R. M. 1986 The personal meaning of having diabetes: Implications for patient behaviour and education or kicking the bucket theory. *Diabetic Medicine.* 3: 85-89.

Arganis-Juarez, E. N. 1998 Ideas populares acerca de diabetes y su tratamiento. *Revista De Medicina De IMSS.* 36: 383-387.

Baer, R. D., S. C. Weller, J. García de Alba García, J., and A. L. Salcedo Rocha. 2004 A comparison of community and physician explanatory models of AIDS in Mexico and the United states. *Medical Anthropology Quarterly.* 18: 3-22.

Bautista-Martinez, S., C. A. Aguilar-Salinas, I. Lerman, M. L. Velasco, R. Castellanos, E. Zenteno, and L. E. Guillen, et al. 1999 Diabetes knowledge and its determinants in a Mexican population. *The Diabetes Educator.* 25: 374-381.

Borgatti, S. P. 1996 *Anthropac* 4 [software]. Analytic Technologies: Natick, MA.Carey, J. W. 1993 Linking qualitative and quantitative methods: Integrating cultural factors into public health. *Qualitative Health Research.* 3: 298-318.

Caulkins, D. D., C. Trosset, A. Painter, and M. Good. 2000 Using scenarios to construct models of identity in multiethnic setting. *Field Methods.* 12: 267-281.

Chavez, L. R., F. A. Hubbell, J. M. McMullin, R. G. Martinez, and S. I. Mishra.1995 Structure and meaning in models of breast and cervical cancer risk factors: A comparison of perceptions among Latinas, Anglo women, and physicians. *Medical Anthropology Quarterly.* 9: 40-74.

Chrisman, N. J., and A. Kleinman 1983 Popular health care, social networks, and cultural meanings: The orientation of medical anthropology. In *Handbook of health, health care, and the health professions*, ed. D. Mechanic, 569-590. New York: The Free Press.

Clark, M., and S. E. Hampson Comparison of patients' and healthcare professionals' beliefs about and attitudes towards Type 2 diabetes. *Diabetic Medicine.* 20: 152-154.

Gobierno del Estado de Jalisco 2006 Monografía. Guadalajara, México.

Cohen, M. Z., T. Tripp-Reimer, C. Smith, B. Sorofman, and S. Lively. Explanatory models of diabetes: Patient practitioner variation. *Social Science and Medicine.* 38: 59-66.

Daniulaityte, R. Making sense of diabetes: Cultural models, gender and individual adjustment to Type 2 diabetes in a Mexican community. *Social Science and Medicine.*59:1899-1912.

Dressler, W. W., J. R. Bindon, and M. J. Gilliland 1996 Sociocultural and behavioral influences on health status among the Mississippi Choctaw. *Medical Anthropology.*17: 165-180.

Finkler, K. 1991 Physicians at work, patients in pain: Biomedical practice and patient responses in Mexico. Boulder, CO: Westview.

Freeman, J., and R. Loewe Briers to communication about diabetes mellitus: Patients' and physicians' different view of the disease. *The Journal of Family Practice.*49: 507-512.

García de Alba, J.E., A.L. Salcedo Rocha, C. Colunga Rodriguez, J.A. Gonzalez Barrera, E. Herrera Solis, and M.E. Milke Najar 2005 UISESS scale for staging and classifying clinical-epidemiological risk in Type 2 diabetes mellitus and for establishing multidisciplinary preventive actions. *Preventive Medicine.*41:211-218, 2005

García de Alba García, J. E., A. L. Salcedo Rocha, A. R. Plascencia Campos, and H. A. Gomez Rodriguez 1999 Algunas consideraciones sobre el dominio cultural de las complicaciones de la diabetes mellitus en dos grupos de estudiantes de psicología. *Salud Mental.*22: 27-33.

García de Alba García, J. E., A. J. Rubel, C. C. Moore, M. Marquez-Amezcua, S. Casasola, and C. Von Glascoe 2005 Various anthropologic features of the physician-patient encounter with pulmonary tuberculosis in western Mexico. *Gaceta Medica De México.*138: 211-216.

Guttierrez Trujillo, G. et al. 2006 Estrategia de prestación y evaluación de servicios preventivos. *Revista Medica del Instituto Mexicano del Seguro Social,* 44 (Supl1): S3-S21.

Helman, C. G. 1985 Communication in primary care: The role of patient and practitioner explanatory models. *Social Science and Medicine.*20: 923-931.

Helz, J. W., and B. Templeton 1990 Evidence of the role of psychosocial factors in diabetes mellitus: A review. *The American Journal of Psychiatry.*147: 1275-1282.

Hunt, L. M., N. H. Arar, and A. C. Larme 1998 Contrasting patient and practitioner perspectives in Type 2 diabetes management. *Western Journal of Nursing Research.*20: 656-76.

Hunt, L. M., M. A. Valenzuela, and J. A. Pugh 1998 Porqué me tocó a mi? Mexican American diabetes patients' causal stories and their relationship to treatment behaviors. *Social Science and Medicine.*46: 959-969.

Jezewski, M. A., and J. Poss 2002 Mexican Americans' explanatory model of Type 2 diabetes. *Western Journal of Nursing Research.* 24: 840-58.

Jimenez-Cruz, A., and M. Bacardi-Gascon 2004 The fattening burden of Type 2 diabetes on Mexicans: Projections from early growth to adulthood. *Diabetes Care.* 27: 1213-1215.

Kleinman, A. 1980 *Patients and healers in the context of culture.* Berkeley: University of California Press.

Larme, A. C., and J. A. Pugh 1998 Attitudes of primary care providers toward diabetes: Barriers to guideline implementation. *Diabetes Care.* 21: 1391-1396.

Lipton, R. B., L. M. Losey, A. Giachello, J. Mendez, and M. H. Girotti 1998 Attitudes and issues in treating Latino patients with Type 2 diabetes: Views of healthcare providers. *The Diabetes Educator.* 24: 67-71.

Loewe, R., and J. Freeman 2000 Interpreting diabetes mellitus: Differences between patient and provider models of disease and their implications for clinical practice. *Culture, Medicine and Psychiatry.* 24: 379-401.

Loewe, R., J. Schwartzman, J. Freeman, L. Quinn, and S. Zuckerman 1998 Doctor talk and diabetes: Towards an analysis of the clinical construction of chronic illness. *Social Science and Medicine.* 47: 1267-1276.

McMullin, J. M., I. De Alba, L. R. Chavez, and F. A. Hubbell 2005 Influence of beliefs about cervical cancer etiology on Pap smear use among Latina immigrants. *Ethnicity and Health.* 10: 3-18.

Mercado-Martinez, F. J., and I. M. Ramos-Herrera 2002 Diabetes: The layperson's theories of causality. *Qualitative Health Research.* 12: 792-806.

Monterrosa, A. E., S. M. Haffner, M. P. Stern, and H. P. Hazuda 1995 Sex difference in lifestyle factors predictive of diabetes in Mexican-Americans. *Diabetes Care.* 18: 448-456.

Mooy, J. M., H. de Vries, P. A. Grootenhuis, L. M. Bouter, and R. J. Heine 2000 Major stressful life events in relation to prevalence of undetected Type 2 diabetes: The Hoorn study. *Diabetes Care.* 23: 197-201.

Poss, J., and M. A. Jezewski, 2002 The role and meaning of susto in Mexican Americans' explanatory model of Type 2 diabetes. *Medical Anthropology Quarterly.* 16: 360-377.

Romney, A. K., C. S. Weller, and H. W. Batchelder, 1986 Culture as consensus: A theory of culture and informant accuracy. *American Anthropologist.* 88: 313-338.

Rull, J. A., C. A. Aguilar-Salinas, R. Rojas, J. M. Rios-Torres, F. J. Gomez-Perez, and G. Olaiz, 2005 Epidemiology of Type 2 diabetes in Mexico. *Archives of Medical Research.* 36: 188-196.

Scheder, J. C. 1988 A sickly sweet harvest: Farmworker diabetes and social equality. *Medical Anthropology Quarterly.* 2: 251-277.

Surwit, R. S., and M. S. Schneider, 1993 Role of stress in the etiology and treatment of diabetes mellitus. *Psychosomatic Medicine.* 55: 380-393.

Szathmary, E. J. E., and R. E. Ferrel, 1990 Glucose level, acculturation, and glycosylated hemoglobin: An example of biocultural interaction. *Medical Anthropology Quarterly.* 4: 315-341.

Torres-Lopez, T. M., M. Sandoval-Diaz, and M. Pando-Moreno, 2005 "Blood and sugar": Social representations of diabetes mellitus by chronic patients in Guadalajara, Mexico. *Cadernos De Saude Publica.* 21: 101-110.

Valadez-Figueroa, I. A., M. G. Aldrete-Rodriguez, and N. Alfaro-Alfaro 1993 Family influence in the metabolic control of the Type 2 diabetic. *Salud Publica De México.* 35: 464-470.

Weinberger, M., S. J. Cohen, and S. A. Mazzuca, 1984 The role of physicians' knowledge and attitudes in effective diabetes management. *Social Science and Medicine.* 19: 965-969.

Weller, S. C., R. D. Baer, L. M. Pachter, R. T. Trotter, M. Glazer, J. E. García de Alba García, and R. E. Klein, 1999 Latino beliefs about diabetes. *Diabetes Care.* 22: 722-728.

In: Men and Addictions: New Research   ISBN 978-1-60692-098-5
Author: Lyman J. Katlin   © 2009 Nova Science Publishers, Inc.

Chapter 6

COGNITIVE DYSFUNCTION IN COCAINE ABUSE: EVIDENCE FOR IMPAIRMENTS IN IMPULSE CONTROL AND DECISION-MAKING

Laurie M. Rilling[1]† and Bryon Adinoff †,‡
†University of Texas Southwestern Medical Center, Dallas, TX, USA
‡VA North Texas Health Care System, Dallas, TX, USA

ABSTRACT

Cocaine is one of the most widely abused psychoactive substances in the United States, with an estimated 1.3 million Americans using the drug on a regular (at least monthly) basis. Even occasional cocaine use can result in serious medical complications, such as cardiac damage, vascular ischemia, respiratory failure, and persistent alterations in neural function. In this chapter, we will examine the most recent research on impulsivity and decision-making in cocaine use. First, we will present a brief overview of the cognitive processes affected by cocaine use. Next, we will review the relevant literature detailing the status of inhibitory control and decision-making in cocaine users, as well as their proposed neuroanatomical correlates. Finally, we will attempt to integrate these findings with the current view of cocaine addiction and relapse, with an emphasis on the role of impulsivity and decision-making in continued cocaine use despite the elevated risk of negative consequences.

Cocaine is one of the most widely abused psychoactive substances in the United States, with an estimated 1.3 million Americans using the drug on a regular (at least monthly) basis (Department of Health and Human Services, 1994). Even occasional cocaine use can result in serious medical complications, such as cardiac damage, vascular ischemia, respiratory failure, and persistent alterations in neural function (Bartzokis et al, 1999; Bolouri and Small, 2004; Frishman et al, 2003; Neiman, Haapaniemi, and Hillbom, 2000; Qureshi et al, 2001; Su et al., 2003; Vallee et al., 2003; Velasquez, et al., 2004; Wilson and Saukkonen, 2004). The

---

[1] Correspondence: Laurie M. Rilling, Ph.D., UT Southwestern Medical Center, 5323 Harry Hines Blvd., Dallas Texas 75390-8846; Telephone: (214) 648-4646; E-mail: laurie.rilling@utsouthwestern.edu

neurologic sequelae associated with these serious medical complications can include seizures, hypertensive encephalopathy, cerebral vasculitis, ischemic stroke and cerebral hemorrhage, and may result in severe and permanent cognitive disability in those who survive the acute phase of these potentially fatal conditions (Bolouri and Small, 2004; Keller and Chappell, 1997; Konzen et al., 1995; Nolte et al., 1996; Reeves, McWilliams, Fitz-Gerald, 1995; Strickland, Miller, Kowell, and Stein, 1998; Tolat, O'Dell, Golamco-Estrella, and Avella, 2000, Valee et al, 2003).

In addition to an acute medical event, alterations in neural structure, receptor action and cerebral blood flow occur with repeated exposure (Franklin et al, 2002; Matochik et al, 2003), leading to the persistent cognitive and functional declines that accompany the state of addiction (Ardila et al., 1991; Bolla, Cadet, and London, 1998; Franken, 2003; Di Sclafani et al., 2002; Strickland and Stein, 1995; see also Neiman, Haapaniemi, and Hillborn, 2000). Together, these neurophysiological and neurocognitive changes likely account for the reduced impulse control and poor decision-making that perpetuates the abuse and undermines attempts at prolonged abstinence.

In this chapter, we will examine the most recent research on impulsivity and decision-making in cocaine use. First, we will present a brief overview of the cognitive processes affected by cocaine use. Next, we will review the relevant literature detailing the status of inhibitory control and decision-making in cocaine users, as well as their proposed neuroanatomical correlates. Finally, we will attempt to integrate these findings with the current view of cocaine addiction and relapse, with an emphasis on the role of impulsivity and decision-making in continued cocaine use despite the elevated risk of negative consequences.

COCAINE USE AND COGNITIVE IMPAIRMENT

There is a growing body of evidence to support the relationship between chronic cocaine use and impaired neurocognitive functioning. Varying degrees of impairment have been reported in specific cognitive domains, including memory, verbal fluency, spatial relations, psychomotor speed, and grip strength (Hoff et al., 1996; Manschreck et al., 1990; O'Malley et al., 1990; Roberts and Bauer, 1993; Strickland and Stein, 1995). In contrast, several investigators have found that cocaine users demonstrate enhanced performance on select cognitive measures (Bauer, 1993; O'Malley et al., 1990, 1992; Sevy et al., 1990; Manschreck et al., 1990), but this likely reflects methodological differences among studies, such as sample characteristics, patterns of cocaine use, or the specific task employed. Despite these conflicting findings, two areas of cognition that appear to be consistently impaired are select aspects of attention and executive functioning, namely inhibitory control and decision-making.

COMPONENTS OF ATTENTION AND EXECUTIVE FUNCTIONS

The concept of attention is complex and engenders much debate among cognitive scientists. Several investigators have developed theoretical models of attention in which various cognitive mechanisms are identified as being responsible for the component processes of attentional function. For example, Shallice (1982) has proposed that two adaptive mechanisms underlie the process of attention: contention scheduling and supervisory attentional control. The first mechanism, *contention scheduling*, can be thought of as an automatic selection process which is elicited through external stimuli and involves little or no conscious awareness (e.g., bottom-up processing). It is ideal for handling routine behaviors which occur under well-known circumstances. In contrast, the second mechanism, *supervisory attentional control*, serves as a top-down process by which attention is modulated via inhibitory control over externally activated schemas held in working or short-term memory (see van Zomeren and Brouwer, 1994). This mechanism is similar to the *central executive* in the model of working memory proposed by Baddeley (1986). In the Baddeley model, the central executive modulates attention by exerting inhibitory control over a number of subsidiary *slave* systems (see van Zomeren and Brouwer, 1994 for a comprehensive review of attentional theories).

Although the supervisory attentional system (SAS) and central executive were conceptualized within the framework of attentional models, these complex attentional mechanisms are commonly associated with the cognitive construct of *executive functions.* This term refers set of higher-order cognitive processes involved in the monitoring and modulation of behavior. These include such functions as planning, organization, problem-solving and decision-making through the generation and implementation of strategies, the evaluation of behavioral outcomes, integration of feedback, and the consideration of response alternatives (Brandt and Blysma, 1993; Huber and Shuttlewoth, 1990). Both complex attentional mechanisms and executive functions have been neuroanatomically associated with distinct regions of the frontal cortex, as well as frontal-subcortical circuits (Salmon, Heindel, and Hamilton, 2001; Baddeley and Della Sala, 1998). This growing body of literature will be reviewed in greater detail in subsequent sections.

INHIBITORY CONTROL AND IMPULSIVITY IN COCAINE USE

The process of addiction is a complex phenomenon that involves reciprocal alterations in neurochemical and behavioral responses. Historically, the mesolimbic dopamine system and motivational processes have played a dominant role in the study of drug abuse and addiction (Taylor, 1985; Salamone et al., 1997; Adinoff et al., 2004). Increasingly, however, researchers interested in the effects of chronic drug abuse are turning their attention toward regions of the frontal cortex involved in inhibitory control (Ardila et al., 1991, Biggins et al. 1997; Fillmore, Rush, and Hays, 2002; Fuchs et al., 2004; Goldstein et al., 2001; Horner et al., 1996; Moeller et al., 2004; Volkow et al., 1996).

Evidence derived from the study of rodents and primates suggests that dysfunction of the frontostriatal system may be particularly important in the compulsive reward-seeking behavior observed in chronic drug abuse (Baylis and Gaffin, 1991; Butter, 1968; Dias et al., 1996a, 1996b; Rosenkilde, 1979). Based upon these and other supporting studies (e.g., Weissenborn et al., 1997), Jentsch and Taylor (1999) have proposed a theoretical model which predicts that chronic drug use results in the disruption of normal frontostriatal function (specifically corticostriatal projections from the medial prefrontal cortex to the caudate nucleus and nucleus accumbens) which controls inhibitory modulation. Further, they propose that compulsive drug-seeking behaviors are perpetuated by the "functional synergism between impairments in inhibitory control and augmentations in conditioned reward (which) manifest as an overwhelming control of behavior by drugs and conditioned reinforcers," (p. 384). This model provides an excellent framework within which the emerging human data can be considered.

Inhibitory control serves as a top-down regulatory process through which a prepotent response can be suppressed or terminated. This control mechanism can be applied to both internal cognitive processes and overt behavioral actions. For example, in chronic cocaine use, the individual may be unable to suppress the recurrent thoughts of using cocaine, as well as the behavioral response triggered by cocaine-associated stimuli. Given the inherent difficulty in measuring internal thought processes, much of the research to date has focused on chronic cocaine use and its effect on impulsivity and behavioral inhibition.

Evidence from both animal and human research has consistently supported an association between long-term cocaine use and reduced behavioral inhibition (Ardila et al, 1991; Biggins et al, 1997; Butros et al., 1994, 1997; Fillmore, Rush, and Hays, 2002; Fuchs et al, 2994; Hester and Garavan, 2004; Horner et al, 1996; Volkow et al, 1996). Studies examining inhibitory function in humans have employed a variety of neuropsychological and cognitive paradigms, including traditional and computerized versions of the Stroop task (Stroop, 1935), continuous performance tasks, go/no-go tasks, and the stop-signal task. These tasks are commonly used to demonstrate impaired behavioral inhibition in non-substance abusing populations with impulse control disorders, such as Attention-Deficit-Hyperactivity Disorder (ADHD) and Oppositional/Defiant Disorder (e.g., Nigg, 1999; Oosterlaan and Sergeant, 1996; Schachar et al, 1995), as well as traumatic brain injury (Levin et al., 2004; O'Keeffe, et al., 2004; Whyte et al., 1998) and stroke (Reding et al., 1993).

Due to their excellent sensitivity, substance abuse investigators are increasingly utilizing these cognitive tasks to examine the role of behavioral inhibition in chronic drug abuse and addiction. In the stop-signal paradigm, response inhibition and execution are examined using a computerized choice reaction time (RT) task that requires the participant to respond or inhibit responding to a "go-signal" or a "stop-signal," respectively. Signals are presented at different ratios and the inter-stimulus-interval (ISI) may vary from 50 to 350 ms, with the probability of inhibiting decreasing in a linear fashion as the ISI increases (Fillmore et al, 2001, Fillmore and Vogel-Sprott, 1999, 2000). Response inhibition is measured by examining the number of successfully inhibited responses relative to the total number of stop-signals presented (i.e., probability of inhibition) and the estimated mean latency to inhibit a response (e.g., stop-signal RT; see Logan, 1994 for calculation details). Fillmore and colleagues (2002a, 2002b) employed the stop-signal task in a series of studies examining inhibitory control in adults with a history of chronic cocaine use. Results from these studies indicated that inhibitory control was reduced relative to non-cocaine using controls, both in terms of their ability to inhibit a response and the amount of time required to do so. Furthermore, inhibitory deficits were similar for chronic cocaine users who had used cocaine within one week of testing (Fillmore et al, 2002a) and those who received oral cocaine immediately prior to testing as part of a placebo-controlled inpatient design (Fillmore, Rush, and Hays, 2002b), independent of the inhibitory response latencies. Speed and accuracy performance to go-signals, as opposed to stop-signals, was unaffected in both cocaine groups. Taken together, these findings suggest that while cocaine has a negative effect on inhibitory control, it is not necessarily due to slowed inhibitory function but rather a disruption of the inhibitory process itself.

Similar to the stop-signal task, the go/no-go task requires the individual to inhibit a prepotent motor response to environmentally triggered stimuli (see Rubia et al, 2003 for a review of how these two tasks differ). Using a standard go/no-go paradigm, Kaufman and colleagues (2003) examined inhibitory control in sample of 13 active cocaine users with an average of 11 years of use. Compared to age-matched healthy controls, the cocaine users demonstrated significantly worse inhibitory control as measured by the number of commission errors (i.e., failure to inhibit a response to a non-target). . When this task was employed in conjunction with event-related functional magnetic imaging (fMRI), a neuroimaging technique used to assess brain function, cocaine users showed reduced activation following both successful STOPS and ERRORS in frontal and midline areas, including the anterior cingulate cortex (ACC) or Brodmann areas (BAs) 6 and 32. These areas are believed to be involved in error-detection and have been implicated in inhibitory dysfunction in other populations, such as schizophrenia (Carter et al, 2001) and obsessive-compulsive disorder (Ursu et al, 2001). Using a somewhat modified version of the go/no-go task, Hester and Garavan (2004) found that, relative to healthy controls, the magnitude of the cocaine users' inhibitory impairment tended to increase proportionally with the demand on executive (or inhibitory) control. Under even-related fMRI conditions, the inhibitory control deficit in cocaine users was associated with reduced activation in the ACC (BAs 32/34), pre-supplementary motor cortex (BA 6), and right superior frontal gyrus (BAs 10/9), relative to controls. Furthermore, unlike the controls, the cocaine users did not demonstrate any increased ACC activation in response to the increased executive demand; rather they exhibited an unexpected hyperactivation of the left cerebellum. This latter finding highlights the disruption of not only frontal cortical regions in chronic cocaine users, but perhaps the entire network of frontal-subcortical-cerebellar connections. Other brain regions that have been implicated in cocaine-related reductions in inhibitory control include the orbitofrontal cortex (Goldstein et al, 2001; Fuchs et al, 2004) and the anterior corpus callosum (Moeller et al, 2005).

In summary, the evidence supporting an association between chronic cocaine use and impaired inhibitory control is quite compelling, though admittedly still preliminary in nature. Replication of these results would provide additional support for this important link between impulsivity and the difficulties such individuals encounter when faced with the environmental triggers that entice them to use again. Moreover, although there is some evidence that ACC dysfunction may serve as the neural substrate for this impairment, the extent to which habitual cocaine use may disrupt other frontal, subcortical, and even cerebellar regions is yet to be determined. Clearly, this is an area of research that deserves continued attention from the scientific community.

COCAINE USE AND DECISION MAKING

One of the most difficult challenges substance abusers face when attempting to remain abstinent is resisting the urge to use when they encounter drug-related cues in the environment (Luborsky et al., 1995). In this situation, the individual is presented with the choice of whether they will resume their drug use or maintain their abstinence. This decision will undoubtedly be associated with positive and negative consequences, some of which will be short-lived and others which will be long-lasting. For those who have not developed a chemical addiction (or dependency), the decision to abstain from drug use in order to avoid potentially adverse consequences may seem relatively logical and straightforward. However, one of the hallmarks of addiction is the persistent use of chemical substances despite the likelihood of seriously negative long-term effects (Grant et al, 2000; WHO, 1992).

Individuals who engage in drug use are often described as "risk-takers" or "sensation seekers," both of which highlight the some of the variables involved in this decision-making process. For those who are able to postpone their response long enough to engage in the decision-making process (i.e., those with relatively preserved impulse control), they are compelled to engage in a spontaneous cost/benefit analysis. In other words, they must ask themselves, "What are the costs and benefits of returning to drug use versus maintaining abstinence?" This decision is highly influenced by multiple factors, including prior experiences, the expected rewards, and possible punishments. In the case of drug use, the reward typically involves a rapid transition from an unpleasant to a pleasant physiological (and perhaps psychological) state. Thus, the temptation of the immediate reward must be weighed against the reality of the delayed cost. There is a substantial scientific literature devoted to the study of decision-making in healthy individuals (see Tversky and Kahneman, 1981). The relationship between impaired decision-making and chronic cocaine use, however, is still somewhat preliminary and continues to be an area of intense study.

One of the most common paradigms used to examine human risk-taking and decision-making is the gambling task (GT). This measure was developed to assess behavioral patterns in the context of a reward-punishment situation and has proven to be quite sensitive to decision-making deficits in patients with ventromedial prefrontal cortex lesions (Bechara et al., 1994, 1999, 2000) as well as individuals with a history of chronic substance abuse (Grant et al., 2000; Petry et al., 1998; Mazas et al., 2000). In the computerized version of this task, subjects are required to choose between two options; one with the possibility of large immediate rewards and a risk of large punishments and a second with the possibility of small rewards and a risk of small punishments. Reward-punishment ratios are fixed so that the first option will result in a net loss and the second option will result in a net gain upon completion of the task. Optimal performance on this measure requires the subject to make conservative choices (e.g., smaller rewards) and delay the gratification achieved by receiving a larger payout until the end of the task.

There is a strong tendency, however, for humans (and animals) to "discount" delayed outcomes (Monterosso et al., 2001). As such, those who seek immediate gratification will more often choose a larger immediate reward despite the greater risk of long-term negative consequences. Indeed, findings from studies of drug-abusing individuals suggest that those who more steeply discount the future suffer from a kind of "temporal myopia," in which the overwhelming desire for immediate gratification interferes with their ability to contemplate future consequences (Bickle, Odum, & Madden, 1999; Kirby et al., 1999; Madden, Bickle, & Jacobs, 1999; Mitchell, 1999; Vuchinch & Simpson, 1998). This myopic perspective may predispose these individuals to problematic drug use even before they are exposed to their drug of choice (Bechara et l., 1994; Bickel & Marsch, 2001; Herrnstein & Prelec, 1992; Monterosso et al., 2001; Vuchinch & Tucker, 1988). It has also been suggested that chronic under-arousal in a subset of drug abusing individuals may serve to increase their tendency toward "risk-seeking" behavior. This phenomenon, combined with a myopic outlook, may elevate the risk of recurrent relapse following chemical dependency treatment (Bartzokis et al., 2000; Quay, 1965; Zuckerman, 1979, 1994). The interaction between perception of risk (e.g., risk-discounting) and the preference for risk (e.g., sensation-seeking) in the perpetuation of drug abuse has not been well studied however, and warrants further systematic examination.

Despite the controversies surrounding the role of risk-taking versus sensation-seeking, there is growing support in the scientific literature for an association between impaired decision-making and chronic drug abuse. Numerous studies have reported that drug-dependent individuals are impaired on the GT relative to matched controls (Bartzokis et al., 2000; Bechara et l., 2001; Ernst et al., 2003; Fishbein, 2000; Grant, Contoreggi & London, 2000; Mazas, Finn, & Steinmetz, 2000; Rotheram-Fuller, et al., 2004). For example, Grant and colleagues (2000) utilized the GT in conjunction with the Wisconsin Card Sorting Test (WCST) to examine decision-making in a group of active polysubstance abusers and drug-naïve controls. The majority of substance abusers acknowledged using cocaine (28/30 subjects) and over half endorsed using heroin (19/30 subjects). Most substance-abusing subjects also endorsed using marijuana, alcohol, and nicotine, while the only substance a majority of controls endorsed using was alcohol (16/24 subjects). After controlling for IQ differences, results indicated that drug abusers performed significantly worse than controls in terms of their net score on the GT, with almost 50% of the drug abusing subjects yielding net scores in the negative range as compared to only 8% of the controls. In a subsequent study, Ernst and colleagues (2003) examined GT performance over five blocks of 20-card choices and found that a similar sample of active substance abusers performed significantly worse than controls during the third block. The authors interpreted this finding as reflecting a critical "hunch" time-period when respondents should begin to internalize the reward/penalty differences between decks. Similar decision-making deficits have also been reported using a somewhat different version of the gambling task paradigm (Heyman & Dunn, 2002).

In contrast, several recent studies that examined cocaine-dependent individuals reported no differences in GT performance between these individuals and control subjects (Adinoff et al, 2003; Bolla et al., 2003; Tucker et al, 2004). Upon closer inspection, it appears that differences in methodology and sample characteristics may at least partially explain these conflicting findings. For example, subjects in the studies with negative findings consisted of patients who identified cocaine as their drug of choice, as opposed to individuals in the earlier described studies who acknowledged concurrent use of heroin and cocaine. In addition, studies with negative findings limited their sample to subjects who were abstinent for a specified period of time, many of whom were either enrolled in a residential chemical dependency treatment program or had recently completed such a program. This is in contrast to the "active" substance abusers who were included in the studies reporting group differences. Differences in gender distribution among patient and control samples may have also contributed to discrepant findings, as there is some evidence to suggest that males perform slightly better than females on gambling tasks (LeLand et al, 1998; Reavis et al., 1998). Finally, variability in the task parameters, administration procedures, and methods for computing primary outcome variables may also contribute to the inconsistencies among studies employing the GT.

Although the GT performance data reported in the literature thus far is equivocal at best, there is emerging evidence to support an association between cocaine use and alterations in brain function as measured by neuroimaging. Several recent studies have examined resting cerebral blood flow (rCBF) in cocaine-dependent individuals using single-photon emission computed tomography (SPECT) and positron emission tomography (PET), with a focus on frontal cortical regions believed to be involved in decision-making. One area of particular interest has been the orbitofrontal cortex (OFC). This brain region is an important part of the neural networks involved in positive reinforcement in primates (Rolls and Baylis, 1994) and has reciprocal connections with many brain regions that mediate the rewarding effects of cocaine in humans (Rolls, 2000; Volkow and Fowler, 2000). Damage to the OFC may produce changes in personality, social behavior, and judgment characterized by irresponsibility and repetition of inappropriate or self-destructive behaviors.

Studies using PET to examine the role of the OFC in drug addiction have revealed increases in activation in the OFC, anterior cingulate, right insular region, and the amygdala in response to cocaine-related cues (Bonson et al., 2002, Childress et al., 1999; Grant et al., 1996; Wang et al., 1999). Alterations in the striato-thalamo-orbitofrontal network have also been reported in association with cocaine addicted individuals' performance on tasks of impulsivity and conflict monitoring (Goldstein et al., 2001). Using PET to examine the neural activation patterns associated with decision-making, Bolla and colleagues (2003) found that cocaine abusers who were abstinent for an average of 24 days showed increased right OFC activation during the GT as compared to non-drug using controls. Moreover, they reported that the amount of cocaine used (grams/week) prior to their period of abstinence was negatively correlated with activation in the left OFC. Similar increases in rCBF have been found using SPECT in a sample of abstinent cocaine-dependent individuals (Tucker et al., 2004). Others have reported no association between OFC activation and GT performance in this population (Adinoff et al., 2003), but indicate a relative decrease in resting rCBF in cocaine-dependent subjects compared to controls (Adinoff et al., 2001, Volkow et. 1992). Other brain regions associated with GT performance in cocaine users include the ACC and the dorsolateral prefrontal cortex (DLPFC) (Adinoff et al, 2003; Bolla et al., 2003; Tucker et al., 2004). Taken together, these findings suggest that chronic cocaine users show persistent functional abnormalities in prefrontal regions involved in decision-making.

SUMMARY

Based on the currently available data, it is clear that cocaine use is associated with alterations in neural activation. How these changes are manifested in terms of cognitive dysfunction and treatment outcome, however, remains unclear. Historically, models of addiction have emphasized such constructs as incentive motivation and the subjective phenomenon of craving (Bindra, 1992; Cox and Klinger, 1988; Robinson and Berridge, 2000; Toates, 1994), with a focus on mesolimbic-dopamine system. In the field of addictions research, however, there is a growing interest in the role of cognitive factors and how they may influence the addictions process, as well as the likelihood of a successful treatment outcome. Studies thus far have provided preliminary data to support an association between cocaine use and impaired inhibitory control (i.e., impulsivity), with the ACC emerging as the likely neural substrate for the observed cognitive dysfunction. Evidence for a decision-making deficit in cocaine users is equivocal, but alterations in OFC activation, as well as the

ACC and DLPC, suggest a disruption of frontal neural networks even in the absence of any overt performance decrement.

Despite these promising findings, the etiology of impaired "frontal" function and inhibitory control remains poorly delineated. For example, it is not known whether persons who engage in chronic cocaine use suffer from a preexisting neurocognitive impairment that places them at risk for addiction or whether the use of cocaine itself produces alterations in brain structure and function that ultimately result in the addiction despite an individuals' baseline susceptibility for developing such a disorder. It is likely that the truth lies somewhere between these two extremes. In other words, the majority of individuals who struggle with addiction likely carry an elevated premorbid risk due to impaired inhibitory function that is further exacerbated by alterations in neural function secondary to their prolonged use of the drug in question (e.g., cocaine). Beyond the etiology question lies a host of methodological issues that make interpretation of these intriguing findings even more challenging. Future studies would benefit from including greater detail regarding sample characteristics and drug use history (e.g., amount, duration, and method of use), as well as more comprehensive assessment of intellectual, neuropsychological, and psychosocial functioning. Such improvements in data collection and reporting would facilitate comparisons across studies and likely enhance our ability to isolate potentially critical cognitive mechanisms for successful treatment outcome. Given that prevention of relapse is a primary goal of treatment, there is clearly a need to better understand the role of impulsivity and decision-making in chronic drug use in order to tailor interventions to address these important factors.

REFERENCES

Adinoff, B., Devous, M. D., Cooper, D. B., et al. Resting regional cerebral blood flow and gambling task performance in cocaine-dependent subjects and healthy comparison subjects. *American Journal of Psychiatry* (2003) 160(10):1892-1894.

Ardila, A., Rosselli, M., and Strumwasser, S. Neuropsychological Deficits in Chronic Cocaine Abusers. *International Journal of Neuroscience* (1991) 57(1-2):73-79.

Baddeley, A., and Della Sala, S. Working Memory and Executive Control. In A. C. Roberts, T. W. Robbins, and L. Weiskrantz, eds., *The Prefrontal Cortex.* Oxford University Press, 1998.

Baddeley, A. D. *Working Memory.* Oxford University Press, 1986.

Bartzokis, G., Beckson, M., Hance, D. B., et al. Magnetic resonance imaging evidence of "silent" cerebrovascular toxicity in cocaine dependence. *Biological Psychiatry* (1999) 45(9):1203-1211.

Bartzokis, G., Lu, P. H., Beckson, M., et al. Abstinence from cocaine reduces high-risk responses on a gambling task. *Neuropsychopharmacology* (2000) 22(1):102-103.

Bauer, L. O. Eye-Movements in Recovering Substance-Abusers - a Prospective-Study. *Addictive Behaviors* (1993) 18(4):465-472.

Baylis, L. L., and Gaffan, D. Amygdalectomy and Ventromedial Prefrontal Ablation Produce Similar Deficits in Food Choice and in Simple Object Discrimination-Learning for an Unseen Reward. *Experimental Brain Research* (1991) 86(3):617-622.

Bechara, A., Damasio, A. R., Damasio, H., et al. Insensitivity to Future Consequences Following Damage to Human Prefrontal Cortex. *Cognition* (1994) 50(1-3):7-15.

Bechara, A., Damasio, H., and Damasio, A. R. Emotion, decision making and the orbitofrontal cortex. *Cerebral Cortex* (2000) 10(3):295-307.

Bechara, A., Damasio, H., Damasio, A. R., et al. Different contributions of the human amygdala and ventromedial prefrontal cortex to decision-making. *Journal of Neuroscience* (1999) 19(13):5473-5481.

Bechara, A., Dolan, S., Denburg, N., et al. Decision-malting deficits, linked to a dysfunctional ventromedial prefrontal cortex, revealed in alcohol and stimulant abusers. *Neuropsychologia* (2001) 39(4):376-389.

Bickel, W. K., and Marsch, L. A. Toward a behavioral economic understanding of drug dependence: delay discounting processes. *Addiction* (2001) 96(1):73-86.

Bickel, W. K., Odum, A. L., and Madden, G. J. Impulsivity and cigarette smoking: delay discounting in current, never, and ex-smokers. *Psychopharmacology* (1999) 146(4):447-454.

Biggins, C. A., MacKay, S., Clark, W., et al. Event-related potential evidence for frontal cortex effects of chronic cocaine dependence. *Biological Psychiatry* (1997) 42(6):472-485.

Bindra, D. Motivation, the Brain, and Psychological Theory. In S. Koch and D. Leary, eds., *A Century of Psychology as Science.* American Psychological Association, 1992.

Bolla, K. I., Cadet, J. L., and London, E. D. The neuropsychiatry of chronic cocaine abuse. *Journal of Neuropsychiatry & Clinical Neurosciences* (1998) 10(3):280-9.

Bolla, K. I., Eldreth, D. A., London, E. D., et al. Orbitofrontal cortex dysfunction in abstinent cocaine abusers performing a decision-making task. *Neuroimage* (2003) 19(3):1085-94.

Bolouri, M., and Small, G. Neuroimaging of hypoxia and cocaine-induced hippocampal stroke. *J Neuroimaging* (2004) 14(3):290-1.

Bonson, K., Grant, S., Contoreggi, C., et al. Neural systems and cue-induced cocaine craving. *Neuropsychopharmacology* (2002) 26:376-386.

Brandt, J., and Blysma, F. The neuropsychology of Huntington's disease. *Trends in Neurosciences* (1993) 9:118-120.

Butros, N., Uretsky, N., Bernston, G., et al. Effects of cocaine on sensory inhibition in rats: preliminary data. *Soc Biol Psychit* (1994) 36:242-248.

Butter, C. Perseveration in extinction and in discrimination reversal following selective frontal ablations in *Macaca mulatta. Psychiol Behav* (1968) 4:163-171.

Carter, C. S., MacDonald, A. W., Ross, L. L., et al. Anterior cingulate cortex activity and impaired self-monitoring of performance in patients with schizophrenia: An event-related fMRI study. *American Journal of Psychiatry* (2001) 158(9):1423-1428.

Childress, A. R., Mozley, P. D., McElgin, W., et al. Limbic activation during cue-induced cocaine craving. *American Journal of Psychiatry* (1999) 156(1):11-18.

Cox, W. M., and Klinger, E. A Motivational Model of Alcohol-Use. *Journal of Abnormal Psychology* (1988) 97(2):168-180.

Department of Health and Human Services. HHS releases 1993 household drug survery., *HHS News,* 1994.

Di Scalfani, V., Tolou-Shams, M., Price, L., et al. Neuropsychological performance of individuals dependent on crack-cocaine or crack-cocaine and alcohol, at 6 weeks and 6 months of abstinence. *Drug and Alcohol Dependence* (2002) 66:161-171.

Dias, R., Robbins, T. W., and Roberts, A. C. Dissociation in prefrontal cortex of affective and attentional shifts. *Nature* (1996a) 380(6569):69-72.

Dias, R., Robbins, T. W., and Roberts, A. C. Primate analogue of the Wisconsin Card Sorting Test: Effects of excitotoxic lesions of the prefrontal cortex in the marmoset. *Behavioral Neuroscience* (1996b) 110(5):872-886.

Ernst, M., Grant, S. J., London, E. D., et al. Decision making in adolescents with behavior disorders and adults with substance abuse. *American Journal of Psychiatry* (2003) 160(1):33-40.

Fillmore, M. T., and Rush, C. R. Alcohol effects on inhibitory and activational response strategies in the acquisition of alcohol and other reinforcers: Priming the motivation to drink. *Journal of Studies on Alcohol* (2001) 62(5):646-656.

Fillmore, M. T., and Rush, C. R. Impaired inhibitory control of behavior in chronic cocaine users. *Drug and Alcohol Dependence* (2002) 66(3):265-273.

Fillmore, M. T., Rush, C. R., and Hays, L. Acute effects of oral cocaine on inhibitory control of behavior in humans. *Drug and Alcohol Dependence* (2002) 67(2):157-167.

Fillmore, M. T., and Vogel-Sprott, M. An alcohol model of impaired inhibitory control and its treatment in humans. *Experimental and Clinical Psychopharmacology* (1999) 7(1):49-55.

Fillmore, M. T., and Vogel-Sprott, M. Response inhibition under alcohol: Effects of cognitive and motivational conflict. *Journal of Studies on Alcohol* (2000) 61(2):239-246.

Fishbein, D. Neuropsychological function, drug abuse, and violence - A conceptual framework. *Criminal Justice and Behavior* (2000) 27(2):139-159.

Franklin, T. R., Acton, P. D., Maldjian, J. A., et al. Decreased gray matter concentration in the insular, orbitofrontal, cingulate, and temporal cortices of cocaine patients. *Biological Psychiatry* (2002) 51(2):134-142.

Frishman, W., DelVecchio, A., Sanal, S., et al. Cardiovascular manifestations of substance abuse: part 2: alcohol, amphetamines, heroin, cannabis, and caffeine. *Heart Dis* (2003) 5(4):253-71.

Fuchs, R. A., Evans, K. A., Parker, M. C., et al. Differential involvement of the core and shell subregions of the nucleus accumbens in conditioned cue-induced reinstatement of cocaine seeking in rats. *Psychopharmacology* (2004) 176(3-4):459-465.

Goldstein, R. Z., Leskovjan, A. C., Hoff, A. L., et al. Severity of neuropsychological impairment in cocaine and alcohol addiction: association with metabolism in the prefrontal cortex. *Neuropsychologia* (2004) 42(11):1447-58.

Goldstein, R. Z., Volkow, N. D., Wang, G. J., et al. Addiction changes orbitofrontal gyrus function: involvement in response inhibition. *Neuroreport* (2001) 12(11):2595-2599.

Grant, S., Contoreggi, C., and London, E. D. Drug abusers show impaired performance in a laboratory test of decision making. *Neuropsychologia* (2000) 38(8):1180-1187.

Grant, S., London, E. D., Newlin, D. B., et al. Activation of memory circuits during cue-elicited cocaine craving. *Proceedings of the National Academy of Sciences of the United States of America* (1996) 93(21):12040-12045.

Herrstein, R., and Prelec, D. A theory of addiction. In G. Lowenstein and J. Elster, eds., *Choice over Time.* Russell Sage Press, 1992.

Hester, R., and Garavan, H. Executive dysfunction in cocaine addiction: Evidence for discordant frontal, cingulate, and cerebellar activity. *The Journal of Neuroscience* (2004) 24(49):11017-11022.

Heyman, G. M., and Dunn, B. Decision biases and persistent illicit drug use: an experimental study of distributed choice and addiction. *Drug and Alcohol Dependence* (2002) 67(2):193-203.

Hoff, A. L., Riordan, H., Morris, L., et al. Effects of crack cocaine on neurocognitive function. *Psychiatry Research* (1996) 60(2-3):167-176.

Horner, B., Scheibe, K., and Stine, S. Cocaine abuse and attention-deficit hyperactivity disorder: Implications of adult symptomatology. *Psychology of Addictive Behaviors* (1996) 10(1):55-60.

Huber, S., and Shuttleworth, E. Huntington's disease. In J. Cummings, ed., *Subcortical Dementia*. Oxford University Press, 1990.

Jentsch, J. D., and Taylor, J. R. Impulsivity resulting from frontostriatal dysfunction in drug abuse: implications for the control of behavior by reward-related stimuli. *Psychopharmacology* (1999) 146(4):373-390.

Kaufman, J. N., Ross, T. J., Stein, E. A., et al. Cingulate hypoactivity in cocaine users during a GO-NOGO task as revealed by event-related functional magnetic resonance imaging. *Journal of Neuroscience* (2003) 23(21):7839-7843.

Keller, T. M., and Chappell, E. T. Spontaneous acute subdural hematoma precipitated by cocaine abuse: Case report. *Surgical Neurology* (1997) 47(1):12-14.

Kirby, K., Petry, N., and Bickel, W. K. Heroin addicts have higher discount rates for delayed rewards than non-drug using controls. *J Exp Psychol* (1999) 128:78-87.

Konzen, J., Levine, S., and Garcia, J. Vasospasm and thrombus formation as possible mechanism of stroke related to alkaloidal cocaine. *Stroke* (1995) 26(6):1114-8.

LeLand, D., Richardson, J., Vankov, A., et al. Decision-making and associated ERPS in low- and high-dependence smokers performing the Iowa gambling task. *Society for Neuroscience Abstracts* (1998) 24:1175.

Levin, H. S., Hanten, G., Zhang, L. F., et al. Selective impairment of inhibition after TBI in children. *Journal of Clinical and Experimental Neuropsychology* (2004) 26(5):589-597.

Logan, G. On the ability to inhibit thought and action: a users' guide to the stop-signal paradigm. In D. Dagenbach and T. Carr, eds., *Inhibitory Processes in Attention, Memory, and Language*. Academic Press, 1994.

Luborsky, L., McKay, J., Mercer, D., et al. To use or refuse cocaine: The deciding factors. *J Substance Abuse* (1995) 7:293-310.

Madden, G. J., Bickel, W. K., and Jacobs, E. A. Discounting of delayed rewards in opioid-dependent outpatients: Exponential or hyperbolic discounting functions? *Experimental and Clinical Psychopharmacology* (1999) 7(3):284-293.

Manschreck, T. C., Schneyer, M. L., Weisstein, C. C., et al. Freebase Cocaine and Memory. *Comprehensive Psychiatry* (1990) 31(4):369-375.

Matochik, J. A., London, E. D., Eldreth, D. A., et al. Frontal cortical tissue composition in abstinent cocaine abusers: a magnetic resonance imaging study. *Neuroimage* (2003) 19(3):1095-1102.

Mazas, C. A., Finn, P. R., and Steinmetz, J. E. Decision-making biases, antisocial personality, and early-onset alcoholism. *Alcoholism-Clinical and Experimental Research* (2000) 24(7):1036-1040.

Mitchell, S. H. Measures of impulsivity in cigarette smokers and non-smokers. *Psychopharmacology* (1999) 146(4):455-464.

Mitchell, S. L., and Lawson, F. M. E. Decision-making for long-term tube-feeding in cognitively impaired elderly people. *Canadian Medical Association Journal* (1999) 160(12):1705-1709.

Moeller, F. G., Barratt, E. S., Fischer, C. J., et al. P300 event-related potential amplitude and impulsivity in cocaine-dependent subjects. *Neuropsychobiology* (2004) 50(2):167-173.

Moeller, F. G., Hasan, K. M., Steinberg, J. L., et al. Reduced anterior corpus callosum white matter integrity is related to increased impulsivity and reduced discriminability in cocaine-dependent subjects: Diffusion tensor imaging. *Neuropsychopharmacology* (2005) 30(3):610-617.

Monterosso, J., Ehrman, R., Napier, K. L., et al. Three decision-making tasks in cocaine-dependent patients: do they measure the same construct? *Addiction* (2001) 96(12):1825-1837.

Neimann, J., Haapanieme, H., and Hillbom, M. Neurological complications of drug abuse: pathophysiological mechanisms. *Eur J Neurol* (2000) 7(6):595-606.

Nigg, J. T. The ADHD response-inhibition deficit as measured by the stop task: Replication with DSM-IV combined type, extension, and qualification. *Journal of Abnormal Child Psychology* (1999) 27(5):393-402.

Nolte, K., Brass, L., and Fletterick, C. Intracranial hemorrhage associated with cocaine abuse: a prospective autopsy study. *Neurology* (1996) 46(5):1291-6.

O'Keeffe, F., Dockree, P., and Robertson, I. Poor insight in traumatic brain injury mediated by impaired error processing? Evidence from electrodermal activity. *Cognitive Brain Research* (2004) 22(1):101-112.

O'Malley, S., Adamse, M., Heaton, R., et al. Neuropsychological impairment in chronic cocaine abusers. *Am J Drug Alcohol Abuse* (1992) 18:131-144.

O'Malley, S., and Gawin, F. Abstinence symptomatology and neuropsychological impairment in chronic cocaine abusers. *NIDA Research Monographs* (1990) 101:179-190.

Oosterlaan, J., and Sergeant, J. A. Inhibition in ADHD, aggressive, and anxious children: A biologically based model of child psychopathology. *Journal of Abnormal Child Psychology* (1996) 24(1):19-36.

Petry, N. Substance abuse, pathological gambling, and impulsiveness. *Drug and Alcohol Dependence* (2001) 63:29-38.

Quay, H. Psychopathic personality as pathological stimulation seeking. *Am J Psychiatry* (1965) 122:180-183.

Qureshi, A. I., Suri, M. F. K., Guterman, L. R., et al. Cocaine use and the likelihood of nonfatal myocardial infarction and stroke - Data from the Third National Health and Nutrition Examination survey. *Circulation* (2001) 103(4):502-506.

Reavis, R., Overman, W., Hendrix, S., et al. Possible double dissociation of function between adult males and females in two brain system. *Society for Neuroscience Abstracts* (1998) 24:1177.

Reding, M., Gardner, C., Hainline, B., et al. Neuropsychiatric problems interfering with inpatient stroke rehabilitation. *J Neurol Rehab* (1993) 7(1):1-7.

Reeves, R. R., Mcwilliams, M. E., and Fitzgerald, M. Cocaine-Induced Ischemic Cerebral Infarction Mistaken for a Psychiatric Syndrome. *Southern Medical Journal* (1995) 88(3):352-354.

Roberts, L. A., and Bauer, L. O. Reaction-Time during Cocaine Versus Alcohol-Withdrawal - Longitudinal Measures of Visual and Auditory Suppression. *Psychiatry Research* (1993) 46(3):229-237.

Robinson, T. E., and Berridge, K. C. The psychology and neurobiology of addiction: an incentive-sensitization view. *Addiction* (2000) 95(8):S91-S117.

Rolls, E. T. The orbitofrontal cortex and reward. *Cerebral Cortex* (2000) 10(3):284-294.

Rolls, E. T., and Baylis, L. L. Gustatory, Olfactory, and Visual Convergence within the Primate Orbitofrontal Cortex. *Journal of Neuroscience* (1994) 14(9):5437-5452.

Rosenkilde, C. E. Functional-Heterogeneity of the Prefrontal Cortex in the Monkey - Review. *Behavioral and Neural Biology* (1979) 25(3):301-345.

Rotheram-Fuller, E., Shoptaw, S., Berman, S., et al. Impaired performance in a test of decision-making by opiate-dependent tobacco smokers. *Drug and Alcohol Dependence* (2004) 73:79-86.

Rubia, K., Smith, A. B., Brammer, M. J., et al. Right inferior prefrontal cortex mediates response inhibition while mesial prefrontal cortex is responsible for error detection. *Neuroimage* (2003) 20(1):351-358.

Salamone, J. D., Cousins, M. S., and Snyder, B. J. Behavioral functions of nucleus accumbens dopamine: Empirical and conceptual problems with the anhedonia hypothesis. *Neuroscience and Biobehavioral Reviews* (1997) 21(3):341-359.

Salmon, D., Heindel, W., and Hamilton, J. Cognitive Abilities Mediated by Frontal-Subcortical Circuits. In D. Lichter and J. Cummings, eds., *Frontal-Subcortical Circuits in Psychiatric and Neurologic Disorders.* The Guilford Press, 2001.

Schachar, R., Tannock, R., and Marriott, M. Deficient inhibitory control in attention deficit hyperactivity disorder. *J Abnorm Child Psychol* (1995) 23:411-437.

Sevy. (1990).

Sevy, S., Kay, S. R., Opler, L. A., et al. Significance of Cocaine History in Schizophrenia. *Journal of Nervous and Mental Disease* (1990) 178(10):642-648.

Shallice, T. Specific Impairments of Planning. *Philosophical Transactions of the Royal Society of London Series B-Biological Sciences* (1982) 298(1089):199-209.

Strickland, T. L., Miller, B. L., Kowell, A., et al. Neurobiology of cocaine-induced organic brain impairment: Contributions from functional neuroimaging. *Neuropsychology Review* (1998) 8(1):1-9.

Strickland, T. L., and Stein, R. Cocaine-Induced Cerebrovascular Impairment - Challenges to Neuropsychological Assessment. *Neuropsychology Review* (1995) 5(1):69-79.

Su, J., Li, J., Li, W., et al. Cocaine induces apoptosis in cerebral vascular muscle cells: potential roles in strokes and brain damage. *Eur J Pharmacol* (2003) 482(1-3):61-6.

Taylor, J. R. Neural mechanisms of the potentiation of conditioned reinforcement by psychomotor stimulant drugs, *Department of Experimental Psychology.* University of Cambridge, 1985.

Toates, F. Comparing Motivational Systems-An Incentive Motivation Perspective. In C. Legg and D. Booth, eds., *Appetite: Neural and Behavioural Bases.* Oxford University Press, 1994.

Tolat, R. D., O'Dell, M. W., Golamco-Estrella, S. P., et al. Cocaine-associated stroke: three cases and rehabilitation considerations. *Brain Injury* (2000) 14(4):383-391.

Tucker, K. A., Potenza, M. N., Beauvais, J. E., et al. Perfusion abnormalities and decision making in cocaine dependence. *Biological Psychiatry* (2004) 56(7):527-530.

Tversky, A., and Kahneman, D. The Framing of Decisions and the Psychology of Choice. *Science* (1981) 211(4481):453-458.

Ursu, S., van Veen, V., Siegle, G., et al. Executive control and self-evaluation in obsessive-compulsive disorder: an event-related fMRI study . Presented at conference, "Cognitive Neuroscience Society Meeting." New York, NY, 2001.

Vallee, J. N., Crozier, S., Guillevin, R., et al. Acute basilar artery occlusion treated by thromboaspiration in a cocaine and ecstasy abuser. *Neurology* (2003) 61(6):839-841.

van Zomeren, A., and Brouwer, W. *Clinical Neuropsychology of Attention.* Oxford University Press, 1994.

Velasquez, E., Anand, R., Newman, W., et al. Cardiovascular complications associated with cocaine use. *J La State Med Soc* (2004) 156(6):302-10.

Volkow, N. D., Ding, Y. S., Fowler, J. S., et al. Cocaine addiction: Hypothesis derived from imaging studies with PET. *Journal of Addictive Diseases* (1996) 15(4):55-71.

Volkow, N. D., Fowler, J. S., and Wang, G. J. Imaging studies on the role of dopamine in cocaine reinforcement and addiction in humans. *Journal of Psychopharmacology* (1999) 13(4):337-345.

Vuchinich, R. E., and Simpson, C. A. Hyperbolic temporal discounting in social drinkers and problem drinkers. *Experimental and Clinical Psychopharmacology* (1998) 6(3):292-305.

Wang, G. J., Volkow, N. D., Fowler, J. S., et al. Regional brain metabolic activation during craving elicited by recall of previous drug experiences. *Life Sciences* (1999) 64(9):775-784.

Weissenborn, R., Robbins, T. W., and Everitt, B. Effects of medial prefrontal or anterior cingulate cortex lesions on responding for cocaine under fixed-ratio and second-order schedules of reinforcement in rats. *Psychopharmacology* (1997) 134:242-257.

Whyte, J., Fleming, M., Polansky, M., et al. The effects of visual distraction following traumatic brain injury. *Journal of the International Neuropsychological Society* (1998) 4(2):127-136.

Wilson, K., and Saukkonen, J. Acute respiratory failure from abused substances. *J Intensive Care Med* (2004) 19(4):183-93.

World Health Organization. International statistical classification of diseases and related health problems (10th revision). 1992.

Zuckerman, M. *Sensation Seeking: Beyond the Optimal Level of Arousal.* Lawrence Erlbaum, 1979.

Zuckerman, M. *Behavioral Expressions and Biosocial Bases of Sensation Seeking.* Cambridge University Press, 1994.

In: Men and Addictions: New Research
Author: Lyman J. Katlin

ISBN 978-1-60692-098-5
© 2009 Nova Science Publishers, Inc.

Chapter 7

CURRENT CONTROVERSIES IN THE ASSESSMENT AND TREATMENT OF HEROIN ADDICTION

Robert J. Craig[2]

Jesse Brown VA Medical Center, Chicago, IL USA

ABSTRACT

This paper addresses controversial topics in the assessment and treatment of heroin addiction. Included in the discussion are issues of dose and outcome, difficulties with toxicology screens, the role of co-occurring Axis I and Axis II disorders, the introduction (and extinction) of newer medications to treat heroin dependence, difficulties of measuring treatment outcome, models of heroin dependence, the role of user personality, and the question of heroin maintenance treatment.

HEROIN DEPENDENCE: DEFINITION AND OVERVIEW OF THE SYNDROME

Heroin is morphine treated with acetic acid, so technically it is diacetylmorphine and considered a semi-synthetic opioid. Historically it was developed to treat morphine dependence and thought not to be addictive. Official diagnostic nomenclature (e.g., DSM-IV) (APA, 1994) says "The essential feature of Substance Dependence is a cluster of cognitive, behavioral, and physiological symptoms…(with) continued use …despite significant substance-related problems" (p176). This use results in tolerance, withdrawal and compulsive drug-taking behavior. By tolerance we mean the need for more of the drug to achieve the intended effect or substantially reduced effects when using the same amount of the drug. Withdrawal is a pattern of stage-specific patterns of signs and symptoms associated with the discontinuance of the drug. Compulsive substance use is manifested by continued use in the presence of adverse consequences, taking more of the drug than originally intended,

---

[2] Address inquiries concerning this paper to rjcraig41@comcast.net

manifestation of a persistent desire to cut down followed by continued use, daily behavior consumed by activities designed to procure the drug, and reduced social, occupational, recreational, and spiritual activities.

While opiates are used medically to treat pain, diarrhea, and cough, heroin has no accepted medical use. Heroin is usually taken intraveneously (IV – "mainlined"), or nasally (.e.g., "snorted" (insufflation). It is also administered by subcutaneous injections – a process known as "skin-popping".

Heroin intoxication is manifested by initial euphoria and impaired judgment followed by pupillary constriction (or pupillary dilation due to anoxia from an overdose), drowsiness ("nodding") (or coma if severe), slurred speech, impairment in memory or attention and motor disturbance. Medically, it causes dry mouth, a slowing of gastrointestinal activity and constipation. Chronic IV use can result in sclerosed veins and puncture marks at the injection sites giving the appearance of "railroad tracks". Abscesses are also possible, as is bacterial endocarditis, Hepatitis, and HIV infections, and positive PPD tests. Erectile dysfunction in males and irregular menses in females may occur, but loss of desire is probably the most common effect of chronic use. In addition to deaths from diseases, heroin addicts also die from overdose, accidents, and murder.

Heroin withdrawal is often stage-sequenced and occurs following cessation of use. Depending on habit strength and amount of the drug taken, this pattern of withdrawal occurs anywhere from hours to three days following the discontinuance of the drug. The individual experiences yawning, muscle aches, lacrimation or rhinorrhea, diaphoresis, fever, insomnia, nausea and vomiting. These symptoms are nearly identical to symptoms associated with influenza.

The most common laboratory test used to detect the presence of heroin is the urine toxicology screen. The acetic acid is metabolized and excreted and the urine tests positive for morphine. Urine samples are likely to test positive for morphine for up to three days following use in heroin-dependent patients. This will depend, however, on many other factors, including the specific procedures use to detect the drug (see section below on urine toxicology screens). Liver enzymes may also be elevated, and many heroin-addicted patients will test positive for Hepatitis C antibody (indicating past infection) or for the hepatitis antigen indicating an active infection.

Prevalence of heroin abuse/addiction will vary according to the population sampled. In the *Monitoring the Future (2004)* – a survey of drug abuse reported by high school teenagers, the prevalence of lifetime use of heroin was generally 1.5% among 8th, 10th, and 12th graders. According to the National Survey on Drug Use and Health (2003), among the general population age 12 and older, 404,000 had used heroin annually. NIDA estimates that there are over 1,000,000 heroin addicts in the U. S.

Pharmacology and Pharmacokinetics

Heroin is transformed into MAM (6-momo-acetylmorphine) by hydrosis and then metabolized into morphine once it reaches the brain. Because of greater lipid (fat) solubility, heroin easily crosses the blood-brain barrier and acts on the same receptors as the natural opioid system (i.e., endorphins). The areas of the brain that are most sensitive to morphine and therefore also most sensitive to heroin are the hypothalamus, thalamus, and the amygdala.

MODELS OF ETIOLOGY

Researchers have invoked biological, psychological, and sociological theories to explain why some people become addicted to opiates while others do not. Biological and pharmacological variables form the necessary but perhaps not the sufficient explanation for addiction.

Biological Theories

Biological explanations for understanding of the central processes associated with addiction, especially tolerance, the addictive euphoria, and withdrawal are well-understood at the physiological level and at the anatomical level. We understand and can explain in microscopic detail what happens in the brain when molecules of heroin enter the brain, act upon the brain, and distributed through the body and finally metabolized and excreted. Where we are deficient is in biological understandings as to why some gravitate and become addicted in the first place. While variables of dose are relevant as a physical explanation, it is also true that most patients do not become addicted when given opiates for medical conditions. It is only a small percentage that develop an addiction.

The heroin "high" occurs when heroin molecules enter the brain and occupy the mu receptors activating the mesolimbic (midbrain) system that signals the ventral tegmental (VTA) area causing the release of dopamine in the nucleus accumbens. This results in feelings of pleasure. Tolerance occurs when the opiate receptors become less responsive to opiate stimulation so that more opiates are required to stimulate the VTA cells to release the same amount of dopamine in the nucleus accumbens.

Intoxication occurs when opiate molecules link to the mu receptors on brain cells in the locus cerulus. This linkage system activates an enzyme that converts adenosine triphosphate (ATP) into cyclic adenosine monophosphate (cAMP), which then triggers the release of noradrenaline. This linkage also results in the inhibition of the enzyme that converts ATP to cAMP, so that less cAMp is produced and hence less noradrenaline is released. This results in the classic symptoms associated with the heroin "rush" –slowed respiration, drowsiness, low blood pressure, and shallow breathing.

When opiates are not present to suppress the locus cerulus' enhanced activity, the neurons produce abnormally high levels of cAMP, leading to an excessive amount of noradrenaline, resulting in anxiety, muscle cramps and diarrhea – the classic opiate withdrawal syndrome. (Other areas of the brain also contribute to these symptoms, including the mesolimbic reward system.)

Classical Conditioning

Classical conditioning involves a process whereby a neutral stimulus, called the unconditioned stimulus, is paired with a stimulus that evokes a response that is either rewarding or punishing. This process usually occurs several times until the neutral stimulus has the power to evoke the response alone. In the classic example, a hungry dog is presented with meat (the unconditioned stimulus) which evokes salivation (the unconditioned response). In the next phase, the presentation of the meat is preceded by a tone – perhaps a bell. After multiple pairing, the presentation of the bell is able to produce the response. The bell is now termed the conditioned stimulus and salivation after the bell is now termed the conditioned response.

Classical conditioning contributes to the perceived effects of heroin and also to withdrawal. Heroin is taken within certain environments and preceded by a series of behaviors (i.e., deciding to get the drug, driving to the spot where drugs are sold, reaching into one's pocket for the money to pay for the drug, giving the money to the dealer, seeing and receiving the bag of heroin, getting out one's "works" (i.e., needle if one is using IV), or preparing the drug to be sniffed, and finally receiving the rush as the drug impacts on the brain). This sequence is referred to as a "behavioral chain" and each behavior in the chain can be classically conditioned to cues in the environment that becomes associated with taking the drug. As one prepares to engage in this behavioral chain, these classically conditioned interoceptive (internal sensory receptors) and exteroceptive (stimuli in the environment) cues emerge. The patient has become conditioned to learn that a certain feeling will be associated with the end result of this chain and begins to feel anticipatory excitement (Wikler, 1973).

Classical conditioning also contributes to withdrawal. As one approaches an environment previously associated with the use of drugs, the presence of these environmental cues is sufficient enough to begin to experience a withdrawal syndrome that is relieved upon use of the drug. This explains why patients, following release from prison, have been known to go into withdrawal when re-entering their previous copping area even though they have not used heroin in several years.

Classical conditioning is more of an explanatory model to relapse than it is for onset of addiction in the first place.

Psychodynamic Theories

Several psychodynamic theories have been proposed to explain why some, growing up in the same environment, and with similar parentage, develop a problem with heroin addiction while others do not (Blatt, McDonald, Sugarman, & Wilber, 1984; Lettieir, Sayers, & Perason, HW, 1980). These theories argue that heroin addiction is (a) related to feelings of childhood emotional deprivation and use heroin to experience a soothing, infantile, symbiotic bond, (b) an attempt to deal with excessively aggressive impulses and thereby preventing their expression, (c) a reaction to guilt, shame, and feelings of worthlessness, or (d) an attempt to self-medicate an underlying psychiatric disorder (Khantzian, 1985).

Family Functioning Theories

It has been recognized for some time that the families of opiate addicts function differently than most other families (Alexander & Dibb, 1975;Harbin & Mazier, 1975). These theories have changed little in the intervening years (Stanton, 1997).This research has concluded that addict families are characterized by poor communication, unsuccessful attempts of parents to control the addict behavior combined with an unsuccessful attempt by the addict to emotionally separate from the nuclear family, a tendency of the father to dominate the mother or to be seen a week and submissive and subordinate to an aggressive wife. The addict's mother is described as enmeshed with the son (the addict) in a dyad that perversely excludes the father, who feels emasculated. From a family systems perspective the addict's behavior within the family is an attempt to maintain overall family homeostasis and related to an intense fear of separation and individuation. The addict's role is to act in ways to bring the familial dysfunction to the attention of mental health specialists through the addictive behavior.

Socioeconomic Theories

Socioeconomic theories emphasize environmental variables that presage the onset of addiction. These include such factors to poverty, lack of economic opportunities, poor role models within the community, embattled and gang-infested neighborhoods, inadequate schools, estrangement from community instructions such as churches, etc.

Summary and Conclusions

Theories of addiction have changed little in the past fifty years. It is also likely that all of these factors – biological, psychological, sociological, and in some cases, familial – play a role in the phases of addiction (onset, continuation, addiction, cessation, relapse, abstinence). Attention has changed from testing these theories to developing more effective treatment interventions for the disorder

THE ASSESSMENT OF OPIATE ADDICTION

Urine Toxicology Screens

Besides clinical examinations and evaluations, the toxicology screen for drugs of abuse is the most common physical test to aid in the diagnosis of heroin abuse (Craig, 2004). After ingestion, the acetic acid is metabolized and the excreted urine results in a positive finding for the presence of morphine in urine. While this is a simple principle, there are several factors to consider when evaluating the toxicology screen results.

1) The urine sample should be taken under direct observation and chain of custody of the sample must also be assured. Drug addicts – especially males – have many ways to falsify a urine sample to avoid detection. For example, they purchase "clean" urine from a non-user and then switch urine prior to returning it to the technician. This is quite easily done if the sample is unobserved. Even when observed, unless the area is free from blind spots, addicts can substitute the urine by placing it in a balloon under the arm with a tube leading to the genital area. While appearing to urinate, they are actually squeezing the bulb thereby allowing the contents (i.e., clean urine) to flow

into the test vial. Sometimes addict work in pairs, distracting the technician while the partner makes the switch on the urine cart. Some may make the switch by accidentally dropping the real sample and then substituting the forged sample.

2) A number of products are available on the internet and are available for purchase (Cleartest.com, 2006). All of these products allege an ability to be able to falsify the urine results. Many of these products have clever and alluring names. For example, "The Urinator" consists of a small electric, self-contained module containing thermostatically controlled water maintained at the correct temperature for up to four hours. The water is mixed with a concentrated clean synthetic urine substitute. The device is small enough to hold in your hand and thereby easy to conceal. "Urine Luck" is a chemical solution which allegedly destroys unwanted substances (i.e., heroin). Similar products, such as "Zip-n-Flip, "Ready Clean", XXtra Clean" purport similar outcomes. "Clear Choice Shampoo" is available if hair testing is done instead of urine testing. It is questionable whether or not any of these devices or products can beat a toxicology screen. They are probably most often used for pre-employment physicals rather than for routine use in drug treatment programs.

3) Addicts try to add water brought from home or drink an excessive amount of water or substitute water scooped from the toilet bowl to try and change the Ph level of urine and thereby diluting the sample. Adding a colorant to the toilet bowl will defeat these attempts. They also have been known to drink vinegar, which theoretically would be effective except that the patient would have to ingest such a large amount that it would become toxic. Addicts also try and add chemicals or bleach, or water-purification tablets to the urine however these products have a recognizable odor.

4) Some addicts make a small pinhole in the collection tube (if plastic). This hole is too small to be detected at the collection site, but during shipping to the lab, the fluid slowly leaks out, resulting in an insufficient volume for testing.

Thus it is imperative that the technician be fully trained on these methods and make a conscientious effort to ensure that the sample analyzed is the actual specimen taken from the patient. The best method to defeat these efforts is a competent and well-trained technician, who directly observes the specimen collected with no distractions. A blue colorant may be added to the toilet bowl, and urine collection bottles are available for purchase which automatically records the temperature of the urine in the bottle, which should be the same as body temperature. Finally, one may test for the specific gravity of the sample, which, if less than 1.010, then the specimen is suspect.

While urine screens are the most common method to detect drugs of abuse, blood, hair, sweat, and saliva can also be used. Blood is more invasive - one needs about 40 strands of hair for each sample, thereby creating patient resistance, and use of sweat and saliva has collection problems. Urine toxicology tests are either screening tests or confirmatory tests. A good lab will employ both types of methods when reporting the results. Screening tests are used to rule out negative results. They are usually quick and cost-effective. When a positive result if found on a screening test, the sample should be tested by a more sensitive method, referred to as a confirmatory test. The likelihood that these two methods will result in a false positive is next to zero. Also, there are different laboratory techniques to assay the sample, each with advantages and disadvantages. These are presented in Tables 1 and 2.

Table 1. Overview of Drug Use Detection Methods

Method	Cost	Detection Period	Detection of Poppy Seed	Cheating Potential	Problems
Urine	About 6$ for each unconfirmed test	1-5 days for most drugs; up to 1 month for marijuana	Will test positive for opiates	Problematic	Testing methods differ in sensitivity and specificity
Hair	About $40/test	Up to 90 days 1 one 1/2" sample	Will not test positive for opiates	Impervious to cheating	Does not detect methadone, alcohol or semi-synthetic opiates*
Sweat	variable	undetermined	Distinguishes between opiates and poppy seed	Impervious to cheating	Does not detect methadone, or semi-synthetic opiates*
Saliva	Similar to costs of urine tox screens	undetermined	Depends on method used	Resistant to Cheating	Less effective in identifying marijuana
Blood	variable	Days	Able to differentiate opiates from poppy seed	Not susceptible to cheating	Invasive

* Labs have screens set up for the five commonly sued drugs required for workplace drug testing, which is a big source of revenue. These methods could detect methadone and other opiates if someone was willing to pay the additional costs. Hospital-based labs could also detect these drugs when so requested.

Most labs use immunoassays because they are reliable, easy-to-use, and have ways to eliminate the vast number of negative tests from the few that will be positive. However, this method cross-reacts with chemically similar drugs in the same class and that can result in false positive findings. Most labs use a combination of gas chromatography (GC) and mass spectrometry as a confirmatory technique.

The sensitivity of a drug is that level of concentration of a drug in urine below which the assay can no longer detect it. The laboratory technician will set the threshold level for a positive finding with different labs possibly setting different threshold levels and thereby reporting different results.

Table 2. Common Methods Used for Urine Toxicology Screens

Method	Use	Turn-Around Time	Sensitivity	Specificity	Benefits	Problem
Chromatography						
Thin-Layer (TLC)	Mass Screening	2 hrs	reasonable	reasonable	Useful for large volume operations	Qualitative results only (pos.neg); results need confirmation; Specificity affected by environmental condition
Gas Liquid (GLC)	Used as a confirming test	2 hrs	Greater than TLC but time-consuming	Utmost specificity	Low incidence of false positives;	Only a single specimen can assay a sample at any one time; ,more costly overall
Spectral Methods						
Spectro-photo-fluometry	Often used to confirm results from immuno-Assays				Can handle high volume output; simple to use	High false positive rates; virtually used for morphine detection only.
immuno-assays (in general)		rapid	Very sensitive	poor	Adaptable to high volume operations; can detect smaller amounts of drug in urine than TLC	Cross-reactive with similar drugs, resulting in false positives
Free Radical Assay	Used for mass screening	5 seconds to 2-3 minutes	High rate of false positives	low	Relatively inexpensive and requires little technical expertise	High equipment costs; results need confirmation by GC/TLC
Enzyme Multipied Immuno-Assay	Allows for high-volume testing	5 seconds to 2-3 minutes	High sensitivity	High specificity	Detects a wide range of substances; results very reliable when confirmed by GC/TLC	High instrument costs; results need confirmation by another method

Table 2. Common Methods Used for Urine Toxicology Screens (Continued)

Method	Use	Turn-Around Time	Sensitivity	Specificity	Benefits	Problem
immuno-assays (in general						
Radio Immuno-Assays	Intended for screening with another method to confirm the results	1-2 hours		Doesn't detect a full range of drugs	More sensitive that FRAT/EMIT; low rate of false positives	Very costly; doesn't detect a wide range of drugs
Hemaglutin-ation	High volume	90 minutes	High	Not able to detect a wide range of drugs	Inexpensive; uses uncomplicated equipment	Limited number of samples assayed each day; high equipment costs.

The results will be reported as either positive or negative. The clinician needs to know what method was used to obtain the results and whether they were confirmed. I am personally aware of one situation where results were coming back which contradicted what the patients were telling their counselors and physicians. In many cases the patient was observed drinking methadone but then the results came back negative for methadone. When this was brought to the attention of responsible officials, we were chastised for not believing the lab results and charged with succumbing to the "charm" and manipulations of our patients. Accordingly, we split the next day's collection and sent them down as separate samples (without telling the lab) and then compared the results. The evidence was clear. The results were generally unreliable. When this evidenced was reported to these same responsible officials, it was then learned that the lab was not confirming the results due to costs and lack of personnel.

This is not necessarily an isolated occurrence. In a study reported in *JAMA*, the performance of 13 laboratories, serving 262 methadone maintenance treatment facilities, was evaluated by submitting pre-tested patient urine samples for blind testing. The false positive and false negative error rates for samples containing (or not containing) morphine, amphetamines, methadone, codeine, and barbiturates, ranged from 0% to 100% depending on the drug tested. These very same labs had detection rates in the 99% percentile for samples submitted to the Center for Disease Control (CDC) as quality checks. The results suggested that greater care was taken for samples to be submitted to CDC than for routine samples, and laboratories were often unable to detect the presence of illicit drugs at levels required of in their contracts. The authors recommended that drug treatment facilities monitor the performance of their laboratories with quality control samples and blind testing (Hansen, Caudill, & Boon, 1985). Subsequently NIDA developed proficiency standards for accrediting laboratories based on this study and others (Davis, Hawks, & Blanke, 1988).

In our own program, periodically we become suspect of urine results. Fortunately we have the cooperation of laboratory personnel to detect the source of the problem. Occasionally it is due to improper cleaning of the equipment between uses resulting in traces of drugs (usually cocaine), remaining in the equipment and thereby pickup up a positive reading for cocaine. At other times the standard is not able to detect the presence of methadone at extremely low doses. The point here is that one needs to have a good working relationship with the lab and the results from the lab require continued scrutiny.

ASI (and its Problems)

The Addiction Severity Index (McLellan et al, 1992) was developed under contract from NIDA as a screening measure to assess the domains known to be effected by alcohol and drug abuse. These domains are medical, employment, family/social, legal, and psychological/psychiatric. The instrument also provides severity levels for both alcohol and drug abuse. It is questionnaire-based and takes about 45-minutes to administer. At the end of each section the patient provides a severity ranking for each domain and a rating of importance for inclusion in treatment. The clinician also provides a severity rating. Where there is agreement, then that would lead to congruent treatment goals, whereas widely discrepant ratings between clinician and counselor suggest probable denial and treatment resistance.

The ASI has consistently demonstrated its concurrent and predictive validity for both alcohol and drug-dependent patients. For example, in a recent study, low ASI severity scores in drug predicted good outcomes for patients on methadone maintenance treatment after one year of treatment; low scores on ASI psychological/psychiatric predicted attendance at counseling sessions, and low scores on ASI employment predicted full time employment. Correspondingly, high scores in those domains predicted continuing drug abuse, unemployment and treatment non-compliance in counseling (Craig & Olson, 2004).

The ASI has become the standard instrument to assess severity levels in addiction, at least in research studies, and the Department of Veterans Affairs require it as a standard measure at treatment intake as well as every six months thereafter, to assess treatment progress. However, its use has not become a mainstream assessment instrument among most treatment programs, despite its demonstrated validity. This is a concern to NIDA, which lists it as one area of technology transfer that remains lacking in treatment programs.

Role of Personality

A datum in medicine is that it is just as important to know the person who has the disease as it is to know what disease the person has. In the case of psychiatric disorders, this datum is ever more true. In the Diagnostic Manual of Mental Disorders, 4 edition (1994) of the American Psychiatric Association, Axis I disorders (i.e., clinical syndromes) put one at risk for developing Axis II disorders (i.e., personality disorders). Similarly, having an Axis II disorder increases the risk of having certain Axis II disorders. This is referred to as comorbidity. For example, having an Axis II antisocial personality disorder increases the likelihood that the person will also develop a substance use disorder, either alcohol or drugs. Having a dependent personality disorder increases the risk of developing a clinical depression or a panic disorder.

Researchers have extensively evaluated the relationship between substance abuse and various Axis II disorders and this research has recently been summarized (Craig, 2003). Whether one uses a structured clinical interview or a self-report questionnaire to make a personality diagnosis, the personality disorder of Antisocial is the most common personality disorder associated with heroin addict, with prevalence rates ranging up to 62%, depending on the setting and the method used to make the diagnosis.

TREATMENT OF HEROIN ADDICTION

Methadone Maintenance Treatment

Methadone is D,1-4, 4-diphenyl-6-dimethyl-amino-3-hepatone, with the L isomer accounting for much of its activity (Weddington, 1995). It is available in tablet/wafer, power and injectable forms but oral use is the most common. It was initially developed as an analgesic but now is more currently used for opiate detoxification and for the treatment of the opiate abstinence syndrome and for maintenance treatment of opiate addiction. Its subjective effects include sedation, analgesia and changes in mood and is not substantially different form those of other opiates except for a longer duration. It depresses the respiratory center, has antitussive actions, inhibits gastrointestinal tone and propulsion, and produces mild hyperglycemia and hypothermia.

Methadone is absorbed quickly and plasma levels can be detected within 30 minutes of oral ingestion. Peak plasma levels are attained in about four hours. In non-tolerant patients, the mean half-life of the drug is about 15 hours, whereas after chronic administration the mean half-life is 22 hours (Weddington, 1995).

In 1964, Vincent Dole MD, an internist at Rockefeller University and Marie Nyswander MD, a New York psychiatrist began treating patients addicted to heroin with methadone hydrochloride. Patient were accepted into the treatment protocol if they were 20 and 40 years of age, had been using heroin for at least four years with repeated relapses, had no psychosis or serious medical illness, and were no coerced into treatment by the courts. They were hospitalized and placed on a gradual stabilizing dose of methadone.

Methadone induction began with low doses of 10 to 20mg/day and gradually increased over a period of from four to six week. This was done to avoid narcotic against effects. After patients had been stabilized on doses from 80 to 120mg/day, they were maintained on a single oral daily dose without further dose increases and, at the end of the six week trial, the patients were discharged to outpatient clinics where they continued to receive daily methadone. Urine toxicology screens were taken as a means to determine treatment effectiveness. These clinician/researchers were quick to add that, while counseling was available, the essential treatment was a medical approach to the heroin addiction.

Of the 1007 applicants interviewed as possible candidates, 60% were accepted.

Their initial report was based on 304 of these patients. The authors found dramatic improvement in patients treated with methadone. A total of 91% remained in treatment, 70% were employed or were in school, while the remaining 30% had discontinued heroin use and antisocial behavior, although they had not yet become socially productive. This favorable response to a medical therapy was not expected in a sample of patients with slum backgrounds, school dropouts, prison records, and minority group status. The authors questioned psychogenic theories of addiction etiology that stressed character defects in these patients as the seminal etiology of the disorder. Instead, they argued that heroin addiction was a metabolic disease caused by repeated exposure to narcotic drugs (Dole, Nyswander, & Kreek, 1966; Dole & Nyswander, 1967).

Over the past 40 years, methadone has become one of the most studied medications. This research has documented its effectiveness as well as the absence of any long-term side effects or complications in over 300 published studies (Hubbard & Marsden, 1986; Sells, Demaree, & Hornick, 1979). While on methadone, consumption of all illicit drugs declines to less than 40% of pre-treatment levels during the first year of treatment and to 15% of pre-treatment levels for patients who remain on methadone for two or more years (Ball & Ross, 1991). Furthermore, crime is substantially reduced. In the most detailed study of treatment outcome, Ball and Ross (1991) found that criminal activity was reduced by more that 70% during the first four months of treatment. Patients on methadone showed reduced rates of HIV infection – an outcome referred to as harm reduction. In one study, 5% of patients on methadone contracted HIV compared to a cohort of patients not on methadone whose rate of HIV infection was 26% (Metzger, 1993). It is also comforting to know that there is no difference in methadone treatment outcomes between Hispanic and African-American men and women. Both of these minorities of both genders achieve similar treatment outcomes after six months of treatment (Mulvaney et al, 1999). While methadone maintenance patients have high rates of alcohol abuse, ranging between 13% to 25%, these rates were not substantially different from the rates of heavy drinking reported in the general population (Ottomanelli, 1999). However, research has found that heavy drinking was not a major factor in treatment retention or outcome (Kreek, 1991).

Keep in mind that simply giving methadone is rarely sufficient to achieve these kinds of outcomes. Programs must also offer supportive services, such as counseling, vocational rehabilitation and social and psychological/psychiatric services in a comprehensive treatment plan. The addition of basic counseling services is associated with major increases in clinical efficacy (McLellan et al, 1993).

Controversies with Methadone Maintenance

Despite its general acceptance in medicine and its effectiveness documented by researchers, a number of controversies continue to be associated with its use. These include methadone diversion, what is the most effective therapeutic dose, the quality of staff in methadone programs, its isolation from other health-care institutions, nonspecific interventions or poorly integrated interventions from other substances of abuse such as alcohol and cocaine, its opposition from abstinence-oriented treatment programs, such as 12-step programs and therapeutic communities. Also, heroin addicts often have high rates of psychiatric co-morbidities, particularly anxiety and affective disorders (Milby et al, 1996) and personality disorders especially antisocial personality disorders (Craig, 2003). Many of these patients are also the very ones who are non-responders to methadone and who continued to be negatively visible around the clinic. Hence, methadone maintenance programs, especially those which are not hospital-based but which are housed in the community, have not achieved full acceptance by their surrounding community.

The Dosage Controversy

Here we will explore one of the more contentious controversies associated with methadone.

Despite the success often achieved with methadone and supportive services, not all patients or programs attain such outcome. The US General Accounting Office (GAO) studied 24 programs comprising 5600 active patients. They found that many patients on methadone continue to use heroin as well as other drugs. In 10 of the clinics over 20% of the patients ere still using heroin after six months of treatment and at two clinics over 50% were using heroin. The dosage levels at 21 of 24 clinics were below 60mg, which many clinicians believe to be the minimally therapeutic maintenance dose (GAO, 1990). Ball and Ross (1991) cited evidence that an adequate dose of methadone should be between 60mg – 100mg daily, since these dosages were associated with the highest rates of treatment retention and the lowest rates of illicit heroin use. Similar findings have been reported by other researchers (D'Aunno & Vaughn, 1992). These findings were included in the position statement of the American Psychiatric Association on methadone maintenance which stipulated that an adequate dose of methadone was between 60mg – 100mg/day (APA, 1994b). (See Figure 1).

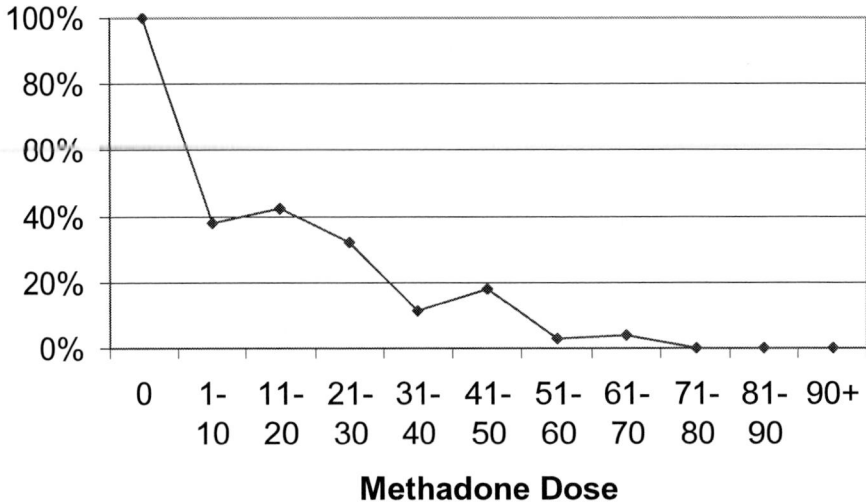

Methadone Dose

From Ball and Ross, 1991, p. 248. In the public domain.

Figure 1. Heroin Use in Past 30 Days (N=407)

While the preponderance of research does show that higher doses are generally associated with better outcomes than are lower doses, there are reports in the literature showing that low dose methadone (averaging 30mg/day) attained "outcome" rates (i.e., illicit heroin use) comparable to rates of high-dose programs, it did so at the expense of lower treatment retention (Craig, 1980). Other researchers found little difference in toxicology screens for heroin use between patients maintained on doses above or below 50mg/day and suggested that other variables may affect heroin use other than dose (Maddux et al, 1991).

In a naturalistic study, high versus low dose methadone maintenance patients (N=265) were compared on the outcome variables of illicit drug use, treatment retention, missed medication days, and ratings of counselors of patient progress. Initial results found no significant differences on any outcome variable associated with methadone dose. However, there were significant differences on these same variables by assigned therapists. Some counselors got better results with their patients than other counselors and these findings were independent of dose (Blaney & Craig, 1999).

Studies show that patients show marked improvement in illicit use of heroin compared to their use prior to admission. These improvements are generally maintained during methadone maintenance treatment. However, success rates are very low after methadone treatment. As many as 90% relapse within one year of discharge and range from 9% to 21% drug-free at following after five years post-treatment (Weddington, 1995).

Harm Reduction vs. Abstinence

Research continues to demonstrate that methadone maintenance treatment is associated with reduced risks of criminality, reduced onset of HIV and TB, and reduction of sexually transmitted disorders. This is referred to as harm reduction. Proponents of harm reduction argue that patients should remain in methadone maintenance, even though they continue to use heroin because studies show that these patients are using less heroin than prior to methadone induction and this reduction of use is associated with reduction in risks of developing the aforementioned diseases.

In contrast to this are proponents of an abstinence model of treatment. There are two forms of this model. First, there are those who argue that being on methadone is not abstinence since they are using a (legal) narcotic. Rather they argue that patients should be off all drugs. Some staff in therapeutic communities (i.e. residential treatment programs), half-way houses and some Narcotics Anonymous chapters want patients to be off methadone and drug free. In other words, they want patients totally abstinent. A second form of this are some methadone maintenance programs, who, while understanding the harm reduction benefits of methadone maintenance, argue that the goal of methadone maintenance is the elimination of illicit heroin, Therefore, the patient must be totally abstinent from heroin or face administrative detoxification and eventual discharge. Proponents of this model differ in the length of time they give a patient before enacting this provision.

There is no immediate way to resolve this controversy, as it is really a matter of the philosophical belief system of program staff. The position statement of the American Psychiatric Association on Methadone Maintenance Treatment (1994) states that many patients need two or more years of methadone maintenance treatment before adequate outcome rates have been attained and some may need this treatment for the rest of their lives.

Diversion

Initially the Food and Drug Administration regulated methadone maintenance treatment programs (MMTPs) and issued rules for the issuance of take-home methadone privileges. These rules stipulate eight conditions before methadone pick-up schedules are reduced. Initially patients must attend the clinic daily and ingest the methadone at the clinic for at least three months before take-home privileges can be considered. (Patients may be given a Sunday take-home dose if the clinic is closed on Sunday). Additional requirements include such things as an absence of criminal activity, adherence to program rules, regular attendance at counseling, an ability to safely store methadone away from children, etc. The Substance Abuse and Mental Health Service Administration (SAMHSA) now has regulatory oversight over MMTPs and has retained these same restrictions. Currently patients may be given up to a one month supply of take-home methadone after meeting clean time requirements and the other stipulations.

All this has meant that methadone has been diverted to the streets where it is sold. This has created an additional public health problem and generated neighborhood complaints about drug selling in and around the clinic and contiguous neighborhoods. Although many programs require methadone ingestion in front of a staff member (patients are then required to say something after swallowing), and test for methadone in toxicology screens to ensure ingestion, this does not impact the problem of methadone diversion. SAMHSA now requires MMTPs to have a Diversion Control Plan as part of their accreditation review. These Diversion Control Plans stipulate the steps program take to minimize methadone diversion. These steps include such things as (a) requiring only one patient at a time in front of the methadone dispensing window with other patients maintaining a stipulated distance between the ingesting patient and the next patient in line, (b) requiring a picture ID before dosing, convex mirrors placed in the dosing area allowing the methadone dispensers (pharmacists, nurses) to view peripheral activity, randomly "calling back" for bottles for patients on reduced pick-ups to verify responsible use, cameras placed within the pharmacy area, and continued monitoring and verification that patients continue to meet the SAMHSA regulations for continuation on reduced pick-up.

Detoxification

Another issue is when and how to detoxify a patient on methadone. The position statement by APA (1994) states that detoxification should not be considered until at least two years of methadone maintenance treatment, assuming that the patient is stable in other areas of their life. Proponents of harm reduction might even argue that the patient shouldn't be detoxed at all, since doing so increases their risk of exposure to HIV, TB and STDs. This is contentious for staff operating from an abstinent oriented model.

While medical ethics gives the right for a patient to know their medication dose at any time, blind dose reductions is far preferable to non-blind detoxification. In blind dose procedures, the patient doesn't know whether or not their dose has been reduced, nor how much of a reduction has occurred. Clinical experience indicates that blind dose reduction tends to be more successful than open dosing.

A far more serious question pertains to the outcome studies of patients who have been detoxed off methadone. These studies show that, on average, most of these patients relapse and return to heroin use within one year of getting off methadone (Ball & Ross, 1991; Hser, Hoffman, Grella, & Anglin, 2001; Sells, Demaree, & Hornick, 1979). Many had died and many others were incarcerated. With this kind of outcome evidence, there is debate as to whether it is even advisable for a patient to be withdrawn from methadone, whether or not they are doing well on this therapy.

LAAM and its Aftermath

Levo-alpha-acetyl-methadol (LAAM) is a synthetic opiate approved by the FDA in 1993 as a Schedule II controlled substance and sold under the name of ORLAAM. It was initially developed in 1948 as an analgesic but was subsequently found to be able to suppress the opiate withdrawal syndrome for more that 72 hours. Subsequently 27 separate studies allegedly established the safety and efficacy of LAAM as a maintenance treatment for opiate addiction. LAAM was dispensed three days a week with an increased dose for the weekend. It was metabolized into two active metabolites, nor-LAAM and dinor-LAAM.

LAAM was similar in action to other narcotics in the same class and hence was cross-reactive and tolerant to these drugs. Its major benefit was a reduced frequency of administration and visits to the clinic, and an alleged easier ability to detoxify a patient from LAAM compared to methadone e (NCADI, 1995)

After several years of use, it was learned that LAAM had an adverse effect on the QT interval in the heart. The medication was withdrawn and is no longer in use. The issue here is whether the early enthusiasm for Buprenorphine (see below) will suffer the same fate?

Buprenorphine

Buprenorphine HCL is a partial opiate agonist developed and approved to treat opiate addicts in a doctor's office, thereby bypassing the extensive federal regulations required for patients enrolled in a methadone maintenance program. However, methadone maintenance programs can also use Buprenorphine but patients must then conform to these federal regulations. The drug purportedly minimizes withdrawal symptoms, decreases cravings, and partially blocks the effects of other opiates.

The drug is available in two forms. Subutex contains only Buprenorphine, while Suboxone contains Buprenorphine HCL/naloxone HCL dehydrate in a ration of 4:1. Both forms come in sublingual tablets. The drug binds to the opiate receptors in the brain thereby satisfying the addict's need for an opiate and also suppressing withdrawal symptoms. However, this drug only partially excites these receptors and so the patient does not get the full agonist effects caused by other opiate drugs. The drug affixes to and occupies these receptors for several days making it more difficult for other opiate drugs to excite these receptors. Buprenorphine is a partial agonist at the mu-opioid receptor and an antagonist at the kappa-opioid receptor; Naloxone is an antagonist at the kappa-opioid receptor. It is a Scheduled III narcotic in the *Controlled Substances Act.* It also has a ceiling effect making it more difficult to overdose on this drug. However, it does have sedating effects that interact with other drugs, such as benzodiazepines making these combinations potentially dangerous. Buprenorphine is metabolized to nonbuprenorphine byCYP3A4.Those wanting detailed information about the drug's pharmacokinetics should consult the package insert.

Generally patients are initially started on methadone maintenance or are transferred to Subutex. After stabilization, they are switched to Suboxone. Buprenorphine is metabolized to nonbuprenorphine by CYP3A4.

Buprenorphine cost more than methadone so one question is whether there is a cost-benefit ratio is favor of this drug. The Health Economics Resource center of the Department of Veterans Affairs developed an economic model comparing the effects of buprenorphine maintenance to methadone maintenance in terms of incremental costs, health care costs, and incremental effectiveness. They determined that the drug was cost effective in terms of its effects at reducing the health care costs associated with HIV infection. However, they also concluded that methadone maintenance was more cost effective than any scenarios developed by the authors. Methadone should remain the treatment of choice for patients addicted to opiates unless methadone maintenance treatment programs are not conveniently available within a community, or not attain the desirable clinical effectiveness, is not tolerated by the patient or when the patient has difficulty meeting the methadone clinic's hours of operation. In such cases, Buprenorphine is another treatment option and it was deemed safer and more effective for certain types of patients (Barnett, Zaric, & Brandeau, 2001). Additionally, it was found to be well tolerated by patients for short-term hospital-based detoxification (DiPaula, Schwartz, R., Montoya, I. D., Barrett, D., & Tang, 2002).

Naltrexone: Theory and Outcome

Naltrexone hydrochloride was the first drug developed by NIDA in the treatment of opiate addiction (Ginzburg, 1984). It is an orally administered narcotic antagonist which blocks the physiological (but not the psychological) effects of opiates from 48 to 72 hours after an oral dose. It works by preferentially occupying the opiate receptor sites (i.e., mu, kappa, delta) in the brain, displacing agonists if present, and blocks the effects of any subsequent use of opiates as long as the drug is present in the body. Displacing agonists will result in a precipitate opiate withdrawal syndrome so that patients would have to be free of opiates for at least 24 hours prior to administration of this drug. It's principal metabolite 6-beta-naltrexol have peak plasma levels within 1 to 4.5 hours. The plasma half-life is about 8 hours.

Trexan or revia (the brand name for Naltrexone) is a near-ideal pharmacological treatment of opiate dependence. It absolutely is effective when taken as prescribed. The patient will not feel the effects of heroin while on naltrexone. In addition to physiological explanations, at the theoretical level, the laws of learning also should explain why naltrexone is effective. When a patient is on naltrexone and uses heroin, the patient does not feel any effects from the heroin. In other words, there is a lack of reward. Upon repeated trials of using heroin and getting no reward, the paradigm of extinction is occurring which would predict that ultimately the patient would eventually stop using heroin.

Guess what? The patient tends to stop using the naltrexone so that they can use and feel the effects of heroin. Hence the drug has a low acceptability within the addict population. It is best used for patients who have a lot to lose if they relapse (i.e., physicians, lawyers, accountants, etc).

ASSESSING CLIENT OUTCOMES

What outcome criteria should we use to measure success. We have all heard the phrase "the operation was a success but the patient died". Historically, total abstinence has been the criteria of treatment success, but many argue that reduction in use is just a valid measure of treatment success. Is reduction in sexually transmitted diseases, TB, and HIV/AIDS a treatment success even though there is no diminution of heroin use? Is employment a valid measure of good outcome? If a patient remains free from illicit drugs but still has problems with the law, is that treatment success? You can see that this is a value judgment of those that define success and policy makers that distribute money to successful programs.

Heroin Maintenance?

Perhaps the most controversial proposal is to give heroin addicts prescribed heroin. Most recently this has been proposed by a few politicians as a way to combat crime in urban areas. Actually, this is an old idea (Drug Abuse Council, 1977). Since the United States policy views heroin as primarily a criminal problem, the idea of heroin maintenance is given little consideration in America. Because The United Kingdom viewed heroin as primarily a medical problem, the idea of heroin maintenance is less controversial and has been tried there. English doctors report that many addicts try to obtain higher doses of heroin and/or supplement their dose with street heroin. Also, the demand for heroin did not abate even with the presence of prescription heroin and the heroin black market continues to flourish in

England. In a more recent study emanating from the United Kingdom, it was found that co-prescription of heroin combined with methadone was more effective than methadone maintenance alone (Metrebian, 2004; Metrebian, Shanahan, & Wells, 1998). To date, with concerns of spreading heroin addiction, the notion of heroin maintenance in America is not presently viable. Furthermore, England is relying more on methadone maintenance as the treatment of choice for heroin addiction.

Heroin addiction has shown some resilience to drug fads and continues despite drug epidemics of psychedelics in the 1960s, cocaine free-basing in the 1980s and is likely to remain when the current methamphetamine epidemic subsides. Therefore we need to continue to develop and research more effective treatments for this disorder and focus less of the controversies.

REFERENCES

Alexander, BK; and Dibb, GS: Opiate addicts and their parents. *Fam. Proc.* 14, 499-514. 1975.

American Psychiatric Association. *Diagnostic and Statistical Manual of Mental Disorders.* 4th ed. Washington, DC: APA, 1994.

American Psychiatric Association. Position statement on methadone maintenance treatment. *American Journal of Psychiatry. 151, 792-793. 1994b.*

Author. *National Survey on Drug Use and Health.* Rockville, MD: National Institute on Drug Abuse, 2003.

Author. *Monitoring the Future.* Rockville, MD: National Institute on Drug Abuse, 2004.

Ball, JC; and Ross, A. *The Effectiveness of Methadone Maintenance Treatment: Patients, Programs, Services, and Outcomes.* New York: Spring-Verlag, 1991.

Barnett, PG; Zaric, GS; and Brandeau, ML. The cost-effectiveness of Buprenorphine maintenance therapy for opiate addiction in the United States. *Addict.* 96: 1267-1278, 2001.

Blaney, T: and Craig, RJ: Methadone maintenance: Does dose determine differences in outcome? *J. Sub. Ab. Treat.* 16, 221-228. 1999

Blatt, SJ; McDonald, C: Sugarman, A; and Wilber, C. Psychodynamic theories of opiate addiction: New directions for research. *Clin. Psychol. Rev.* 4, 159-189. 1984

Craig, RJ: *Counseling the Alcohol and Drug Dependent Client: A Practice Approach.* Boston, Mass: Allyn & Bacon. 2004.

Craig, RJ: Prevalence of personality disorders among cocaine and heroin addicts. *Directions in Addiction Treatment and Prevention.* 7, 33-42. 2003.

Craig, RJ: Effectiveness of low-dose methadone maintenance for the treatment of inner-city heroin addicts. *Int. J. Addict..* 15, 791-710. 1980.

Craig, RJ, and Olson, RE. Predicting methadone maintenance treatment outcomes using the Addiction Severity Index and the MMPI-2 content scales (Negative Treatment Indicators and Cynicism scales). *Am. J. Drug & Alc. Abuse.* 30, 823-839. 2004

Davis, KH; Hawks, RL; and Blanke, RV. Assessment of laboratory quality in urine drug testing: A proficiency testing pilot study. *JAMA*, 260, 1749-1754. 1988

D'Aunno, T: and Vaughn, TE: Variations in methadone treatment practices. *JAMA*. 267, 253-258. 1992.

DiPaula, BA; Schwartz, R; Montoya, ID; Barrett, D; and Tang, C. Heroin detoxification with Buprenorphine on an inpatient psychiatric unit. *J. Sub. Ab. Treat* 23, 163-169.

Dole, VP; Nyswander, M. E.. Heroin addiction – a metabolic disease. *Arch Intern Med* 120: 19-24, 1967

Dole, VP; Nyswander, M. E.; and Kreek, M. J. Narcotic blockade. *Arch. Intern Med* 118: 304-309, 1966

Drug Abuse Council. *What's happening with Heroin maintenance?* Washington, DC. 1977.

General Accounting Office: M*ethadone Maintenance: Some Treatment Programs are Not Effective; Greater Federal Oversight Needed.* Washington, DC: U.S. Government Printing Office. 1990.

Ginzburg, HM. *Naltrexone: Its clinical utility.* Rockville, MD: NIDA Treatment Research Report. 1984

Hansen, HJ; Caudill, SP: and Boone, J. Crisis in drug testing. *JAMA*, 253, 2382 – 2387. 1985

Harbin, HT: and Maziar, HM: The families of drug abusers: A literature review. *Fam. Proc.* 14 411-431. 1975

Hser, Y-I; Hoffman, V: Grella, CE: and Anglin, MD: A 33-year follow-up of narcotic addicts. *Arch. Gen. Psychiat.* 58, 503-508. 2001

Hubbard, RL: and Marsden, ME: Relapse to use of heroin, cocaine and other drugs in the first year of treatment: In *Relapse and Recovery in Drug Abuse*. NIDA Research Monograph 72. Rockvile, MD: U. S. Government Printing Office. 1986

Khantzian, EJ. The self-medication hypothesis of addictive disorders: Focus on heroin and cocaine dependence. *Am. J. Psychiat.* 142, 1259-1264. 1985.

Kreek, MJ: Using methadone effectively: Achieving goals by application of laboratory, clinical, and evaluation research and by development of innovative programs. In R. W. Pickens, C. G. Leukefeld, and C. R. Schuster (Eds). *Improving drug abuse retention.* Research Monograph 106, pp 136-151. Rockville, MD: NIDA

Lerrieri, DJ; Sayers, M; and Pearson, HW: *Theories on Drug Abuse: Selected Contemporary Perspectives.* Rockville, MD: NIDA, 1980.

Maddux, JF: Esquivel, M: Vogtsberger, KN: and Desmond, DP: methadone dose and urine morphine. *J. Sub. Ab. Treat.* 8, 195-201. 1991

McLellan, AT: Arndt, IO: Metzger, DS: woody, GE: and O'Brien, CP. The effects of psychosocial services in substance abuse treatment. *JAMA*. 269, 1953-1959. 1993.

McLellan, AT, Kushner, H., Metzger, DS, Peters, R, Smith, I, Grissom, G, Pettinati, H, Argeriou, M. The fifth edition of the Addiction Severity Index. *J. Subst. Abuse Treat*, 9, 199-213. 1992

Metrebian, N. Supervised co-prescription of heroin to treatment-resistant heroin addicts is more effective than treatment with methadone alone. *Evidence-based Ment. Hlth.* 7m 23, 2004.

Metrebian, N, Shanahan, W., and Wells, B. feasibility of prescribing injectable heroin and methadone to opiate dependent drug users; associated health gains and harm reductions. *Med. J. Aust.* 168, 596-600. 1998.

Metzger, J: HIV seroconversion among in and out of treatment intravenous drug users: An 180month prospective follow-up. *AIDS,* 9, 1049-1056. 1993.

Milby, JB; Sims, MK: Khuder, S; Schumacher, JE; Huggins, N; McLellan, AT; Woody, G and Haas, N. Psychiatric comormidity: Prevalence in methadone maintenance treatment. *Am. J. Drug & Alc. Ab*. 22, 95-107. 1996.

Mulvaney, FD: Brown, LS: Aletrman, AI: Sage, RE: Cnaan, A: Cacciola, J: and Rutherford, M. Methadone-maintenance outcomes for Hispanic and African-American men and women. *Drug and Alc. Depend*. 54, 11-18. 1999.

National Clearinghouse for Alcohol and Drug Information. *LAAM in the Treatment of Opiate Addiction*. Rockville, MD: Substance Abuse and Mental Health Services Administration. 1995

Sells, SB:, Demaree, RG: and Hornick, CW: *Comparative Effectiveness of Drug Abuse Treatment Modalities*. NIDA Services Research Administrative Report. Washington, DC: NIDA. 1979.

Stanton, MD: The role of family and significant others in the engagement and retention of drug-dependent individuals. In LS Onken, JD Blaine, & JJ Boren (Eds). *Beyond the therapeutic alliance: Keeping the Drug-Dependent Individual in Treatment*. NIDA Research Monograph No. 165, pp. 157-180). Rockville, MD: National Institute on Drug Abuse. 1997

Weddington, WW. Methadone maintenance for opioid addiction. In N.S> Miller and M.S. Gold (Eds). *Pharmacological Therapies for Drug and Alcohol Addiction*. New York: Marcell Dekker (pp 411-417). 1995

Wikler, A. Dynamics of drug dependence: Implications of a conditioning theory for research and treatment. *Arch. Gen. Psychiat*. 28: 611-616.

WWW.cleartest.com/products/index.html (2006).

In: Men and Addictions: New Research
Author: Lyman J. Katlin

ISBN 978-1-60692-098-5
© 2009 Nova Science Publishers, Inc.

Chapter 8

NEW RESEARCH ON METHAMPHETAMINE ABUSE (GENDER DIFFERENCES IN METHAMPHETAMINE EFFECTS: REVIEW OF ANIMAL AND HUMAN STUDIES)

Bin Liu and Dean E. Dluzen[*]

Department of Anatomy; Northeastern Ohio Universities
College of Medicine (NEOUCOM), OH, USA

I. INTRODUCTION

Psychostimulants, including amphetamine, cocaine, methylenedioxy-methamphetamine, nicotine, methylphenidate and methamphetamine (MA), represent the most commonly abused drugs *[National Institute on Drug Abuse webpage: Commonly Abused Drugs; http://www.nida.nih.gov/drugpages/drugsofabuse.html]*. In recent years, experimental and clinical studies on MA have experienced resurgence, in part, due to the increased abuse of this psychostimulant and the serious medical and social problems associated with MA abuse. According to the 2004 *National Survey on Drug Use and Health*, nearly 12 million Americans have tried MA *[National Survey on Drug Use and Health - SAMHSA web site; http://oas.samhsa.gov/nsduh.htm]*.

MA use can produce neurochemical changes in abusers as shown by post-mortem (Wilson *et al.*, 1996) and neuroimaging studies (McCann *et al.*, 1998; Sekine *et al.*, 2001; Volkow *et al.*, 2001a;b). This psychostimulant is a well established neurotoxic agent producing degeneration of monoaminergic nerve terminals as well as a diverse array of actions leading to cell death and apoptosis in various brain regions (Cadet *et al.*, 2003; Davidson *et al.*, 2001; Seiden *et al.*, 1993). Depletions of neurochemicals resulting from MA have been demonstrated in non-human primates (McCann *et al.*, 1998; Villemagne *et al.*, 1998; Woolverton *et al.*, 1989) and rats (Cass, 1997; Ricaurte *et al.*, 1980; Wallace *et al.*, 2001). In specific, MA administration produces significant dopamine (DA) and serotonin (5-

HT) depletions in the striatum and nucleus accumbens (Amano *et al.*, 1996; Cass, 1997; Ricaurte *et al.*, 1980; Sabol *et al.*, 2001; Seiden and Ricaurte, 1987; Wallace *et al.*, 2001; Wilson *et al.*, 1996). The increased use and adverse effects exerted by MA indicate the need for a consideration of this psychostimulant within this review.

An important, but often neglected, characteristic of MA use and resultant effects upon behavioral and neurobiological responses are differences which exist between males and females. This represents a critical issue as it can differentially affect approximately half the population. Moreover, the significance for considering the issue of gender in neurobiological research, and, in particular, in response to MA has been emphasized (Bisagno *et al.*, 2003; Cahill, 2006). In this way, uses of, responses to, and treatments for, MA should require gender considerations. In this chapter, we summarized findings on gender differences in MA effects in animals and humans. Since the focus of this review is upon MA, we have limited our review to this specific psychostimulant, however, in certain instances data from other drugs of abuse are included. In this report the terms gender and sex will be used interchangeably, although the former is more often associated with human studies (Dluzen, 2005).

II. ANIMAL MODELS OF METHAMPHETAMINE (MA) TREATMENT

Animal models have, and will continue to, serve as important tools to assess the effects of MA. These models are required to explore a more precise and thorough understanding of the neurobiological mechanisms and behavioral consequences of MA use, however there exist notable limitations in their use and applicability. Accordingly, a brief consideration of the limitations associated with MA-treated animal models is necessary when relating findings from animal and human studies.

1. Dosing Regimens

The two major categories of MA dosing regimens that have been used to study MA-induced neurotoxicity include acute (1 day) and chronic (>1 day). The category of acute can be subdivided into binge and acute bolus. An example of a binge treatment would consist of a 5-20 mg/kg dose administered 4× at 2 hour intervals using either a subcutaneous or intraperitoneal route (Fukumura *et al.*, 1998). Examples of an acute bolus treatment would consist of a single administration of MA in doses ranging from 2.5-40 mg/kg through either a subcutaneous or intraperitoneal route (Fukumura *et al.*, 1998). Such acute dosing regimens are currently the most frequently used modes of administration in animal models. Both regimens are capable of inducing perturbations of the nigrostriatal dopaminergic (NSDA) system with reductions in DA contents of the caudate nucleus and nucleus accumbens as well as in spontaneous and locomotor activities being reported to a binge MA (10 mg/kg×4 at 2 h

* Correspondence: Dean Dluzen; Department of Anatomy; Northeastern Ohio Universities College of Medicine (NEOUCOM); 4209 State Route 44; Post Office Box 95; Rootstown, OH 44272-0095; TEL: 330-325-6300; FAX: 330-325-5913; E-mail: ded@neoucom.edu

intervals) treatment (Wallace *et al.*, 2001) and reductions in caudate-putamen monoamine and tyrosine hydroxylase being reported to an acute bolus MA (40 mg/kg) treatment (Cappon *et al.*, 2000). However, the effectiveness of these two acute MA regimens shows a clear difference. Noteworthy, exposure of mice to a binge of MA at 10 mg/kg×4 at 2 h intervals was approximately four times less effective in inducing apoptotic cell death than a single bolus administration of 30 mg/kg of MA, which suggests that an acute bolus drug administration of MA is more effective in inducing striatal apoptosis in mice (Zhu *et al.*, 2006). While chronic may be defined by > 1 day, such treatments typically involve relatively prolonged administrations which can consist of a twice-daily intraperitoneal 10 mg/kg dose for 30 days or a single daily 2.5 mg/kg dose for 60 days (Gomes-da-Silva *et al.*, 2000; Mattei and Carlini, 1996). The chronic model can be distinguished from the acute model in that the latter results in loss of DA function whereas the chronic model results in apoptosis (Davidson *et al.*, 2001). As is evident from this description of dosing regimens, there exists a notable chasm between these MA administrations in animals and MA use in humans.

2. Pharmacokinetics

Pharmacokinetic experiments have been performed by administering MA in doses of 0.1-3.0 mg/kg via intravenous injection (Milesi-Halle *et al.*, 2005; Riviere *et al.*, 1999). Animals display significant differences in MA pharmacokinetics when compared to humans (Cho *et al.*, 2001; Riviere *et al.*, 1999). Pharmacokinetic parameters in animal models of MA treatment show that MA half-life is much shorter (70 min) in rats (Cho *et al.*, 2001; Melega *et al.*, 1995; Riviere *et al.*, 1999) than that in humans, which is approximately 12 h (Cook *et al.*, 1992; Cook *et al.*, 1993) or 6-34 h (Anggard *et al.*, 1973). Therefore, a chronic dosing regimen, such as 2.5 mg/kg × 60 d (Mattei and Carlini, 1996) would not accurately model human long-term abuse. A more sustained dosing regimen is needed to model the longer half-life and near steady-state plasma levels as well as the potential for increased neurotoxicity in humans. Different protocols have been employed which attempt to achieve this goal of simulating human MA exposure (Cho *et al.*, 2001; Segal and Kuczinski, 2006). However, no study has been performed using this chronic dosing regimen of MA to observe the reactions of this chronic MA treatment in animal models as related to sex differences.

3. Genetics and Environment

A further consideration when relating animal with human studies is that of genetic and environmental factors and their interaction. In the typical laboratory experiment a rat or mouse is randomly selected, treated with MA and returned to its controlled environmental conditions. Such paradigms fail to account for any potential genetic susceptibility or NSDA alteration that makes individuals more vulnerable to the effects of MA. Nor do these paradigms adequately account for the environmental factors that contribute to MA access and acceptability. In this way, the combination of genetic and environmental factors associated with MA use and effects within humans are not adequately modeled in the laboratory experiments. A genetic factor that can be isolated and evaluated in both animal and human studies, and one that serves as the primary emphasis of this chapter is the sex of the subject.

III. Sex Differences in Animal Studies

1. Clearance and Metabolism

Male rats or mice are commonly used as animal models for studying MA effects due to their convenience (Bisagno *et al.*, 2002; Cappon *et al.* 2000; Wallace *et al.*, 2001; Zhu *et al.*, 2006). However, even at the most basic level of MA effects, that of clearance, significant gender differences are present in these rodent models. Determinations of the MA serum condition-time curve (AUC) reveal a higher increase in female versus male rats (Milesi-Halle *et al.*, 2005). The total MA clearance and non-renal clearance were significantly lower, and MA urinary excretion higher, in female than that of male values at the 1.0 and 3.0 mg/kg dose (Milesi-Halle *et al.*, 2005), which is consistent with the findings that females clear most drugs at a slower rate than males (Mugford and Kedderis, 1998). Such findings suggest that females offer some advantages over males for modeling those specific components of MA disposition in humans (Milesi-Halle *et al.*, 2005). These gender differences have not been obtained in all experiments as no marked sex difference in the urinary excretion of MA and metabolites have also been reported (Yamada *et al.*, 1986). In accord with these findings of a lower clearance rate in females are data which suggest that males have a higher metabolic rate of MA. The activity levels of cytochrome P450 in microsomal benzphetamine N-demethylation are about two-fold greater in male Long-Evans rats (Ryan *et al.*, 1993). Since this system has been associated with metabolism of MA (Shiiyama *et al.*, 1997), the basis for the higher metabolic rate of MA within males can be understood.

2. Behavioral Responses

A. Conditioned Place Preference

The conditioned place preference test represents an approach to assess the preference or reinforcing effects of a drug. When tested in this paradigm, female mice showed a more potent MA-induced conditioned place preference response. This sex difference appears to be primarily attributable to a sexually dimorphic action of estrogen, as estrogen treatment of gonadectomized female, but not male, mice increased the ability for MA to facilitate this response (Chen *et al.*, 2004). In the same group of Sprague-Dawley rats that showed a significant gender difference (females>males) in MA-induced locomotor activity (distance traveled), no statistically significant female versus male place preferences were observed. Both females and males demonstrated increasing preference for the drug-paired side as a function of increasing MA dose, but these increases were not different between these females and males (Schindler *et al.*, 2002). In this way, the capacity for a gender-dependent stimulatory effect of MA upon locomotor activity can be distinguished from that of the preference or reinforcing properties of MA which do not appear to differ between female and male rats.

B. Self-Administration/Acquisition and Maintenance

In contrast to the absence of gender differences observed when tested in this conditioned place paradigm, in a test for the acquisition and maintenance of MA self-administration in

Wistar rats, a clear gender difference was obtained. Female rats met the criterion for acquisition of MA self-administration with shorter latencies, administered more MA infusions and did so at lower doses than that of males (Roth and Carroll, 2004). Such results suggest that female rats are more vulnerable to and motivated by the effects of MA (Lynch et al., 2002). While there may exist a number of explanations for these differences in a behavioral response which would appear relatively similar, it might be that these two "MA-use" paradigms (conditioned place preference and acquisition/maintenance) are reflecting slightly different MA-induced neuronal effects which can be discriminated when the variable of gender is isolated in rats. Such behavioral results suggest differences in neurochemical functioning between females and males, which are reviewed below.

C. Activity

It was reported that females are more sensitive to the acute and chronic effects of MA with regard to locomotor activity (Mattei and Carlini, 1996; Schindler *et al.*, 2002). While MA increased the motor activity and stereotyped behavior such as sniffing, continuous licking, and false bites in both female and male rats, females show greater sensitivity both after acute and chronic MA treatment (Mattei and Carlini, 1996). Females travel significantly greater distances than males after MA treatment and display a dramatically different temporal profile of drug-induced locomotor activity along with a tendency for greater rearing frequency when compared to males (Milesi-Halle *et al.*, 2005).

3. Neurochemical Responses

A. Striatal Dopamine (DA) Output

The significantly increased amount of locomotor activity to MA in females as described above would seem to be associated with a correspondingly greater amount of striatal DA release in females. However, this does not necessarily seem to be the case. DA output from superfused striatal tissue of female and male mice in response to a direct infusion of varying doses of MA consistently showed higher levels of DA output from males, with statistically significant differences obtained to a 1 mM dose of MA (Dluzen and Salvaterra, 2005). Interestingly, these gender differences in MA-stimulated DA release were not present when comparing gonadectomized or prepubertal female and male mice, and were reversed (females > males) when striatal tissue was challenged with a depolarizing concentration of potassium chloride.

In other paradigms involved with the study of MA-induced DA output, there are interesting results which support these seemingly paradoxical effects. For example, estrogen can diminish the degree of striatal DA depletion to MA within female, but not male mice (as described below). However, when estrogen is co-infused with MA into superfused striatal tissue, it is equally effective in decreasing the amount of MA-induced DA output in female and male mice (Myers *et al.*, 2003). In addition, the anti-estrogen, tamoxifen, which can also diminish the degree of striatal DA depletion to MA within male (and female) mice (as described below), was shown to increase the amount of MA-induced DA output when co-infused with MA into superfused striatal tissue of male mice (Willett and Dluzen, 2004). These findings indicate a complex relationship between the initial capacity for MA to evoke

DA output from superfused striatal tissue fragments and the subsequent ability for this psychostimulant to result in a depletion of striatal DA concentration (neurotoxicity). When considering the responses observed in the male, the acute changes in striatal DA output induced by MA (greater responsiveness in males versus females, decreased responsiveness in the presence of estrogen, increased responsiveness in the presence of tamoxifen) appear to be essentially opposite from that observed for striatal DA concentrations (decreased levels in males versus females, no protection/preservation with estrogen and protection/preservation with tamoxifen).

B. Striatal DA Concentrations

When tested with equivalent doses of MA, the degree of striatal DA depletion is typically greater in male mice. In these experiments, the binge mode of MA administration, consisting of either 10 or 20 mg/kg × 4 at 2 hour intervals, was used with CD-1, C57/BL, Swiss-Webster as well as heterozygous mutant brain-derived neurotrophic factor mice and striatal DA concentrations were determined at > 2 days post-MA (Dluzen, 2004; Dluzen *et al.*, 2001; Dluzen *et al.*, 2003; Heller *et al.*, 2001; Miller *et al.*, 1998; Wagner *et al.*, 1993; Yu and Liao, 2000b; Yu and Wagner, 1994). In the BALBc mouse strain no gender differences were obtained in striatal DA to MA, however, striatal serotonin levels showed greater reductions within males of this strain (Yu and Liao, 2000b). Such mouse strain differences in response to MA have been reported by others (Kita *et al.*, 1998). Intrastriatal infusion of MA to female and male mice produces a similar gender difference to that observed with systemic treatment (i.e., striatal DA depletions in males > females) suggesting that these gender differences were not due to peripheral metabolism of MA (Yu and Liao, 2000b). Under conditions of comparable MA treatments (10 mg/kg × 4 at 2 hour intervals), no statistically significant gender differences in MA-induced striatal DA depletion were obtained in Sprague-Dawley rats (Fukumura *et al.*, 1998; Gehrke *et al.*, 2003), suggesting an important species difference with regard to sex differences and MA-induced neurotoxicity. While these studies suggest a relatively ubiquitous finding for MA to induce a more severe depletion of striatal DA (and serotonin) within male mice, such findings are mostly confined to one type of MA administration (binge mode) and may be species specific. Accordingly, considering the importance of a gender difference to MA, it is clear that there is a need to test this phenomenon with additional modes of MA administration and other species. The significance for testing other species is highlighted by the presence of gender differences in mice and an absence of gender difference in rats as observed for MA-induced neurotoxicity and MA-induced condition place preference performance.

4. Gonadal Steroid Hormones

A. Estrogen

When comparing MA-induced striatal DA depletion between intact female and male mice with that between gonadectomized female and male mice comparable results were obtained. That is, in both the intact and gonadectomized conditions levels of striatal DA were approximately two-fold greater in females following MA treatment (Yu and Wagner, 1994). One conclusion resulting from this study is that the gender differences in sensitivity to MA would seem to be independent of gonadal steroid hormones. However, subsequent work involving hormonal treatment has indicated that estrogen, progesterone and possibly testosterone exert decided effects upon MA-induced striatal DA depletion which can then contribute to the sex differences observed.

When ovariectomized mice were treated with estrogen prior to MA, the amount of striatal DA depletion was significantly attenuated as compared with non-estrogen treated mice. This effect was observed under conditions of a wide range of estrogen treatment regimens (D'Astous et al., 2004; Dluzen and McDermott, 2002; Gao and Dluzen, 2001a; Mickley and Dluzen, 2004; Yu and Liao, 2000a;). While estrogen can exert this apparent neuroprotective effect when administered prior to MA, no beneficial effect was obtained if the estrogen was administered after MA (Gajjar et al., 2003; Gao and Dluzen, 2001a). Nor does estrogen show any neuroprotectant potential against MA within intact or gonadectomized male mice (Anderson et al., 2005; Dluzen et al., 2001; Gao and Dluzen, 2001b) or within female mice that were gonadectomized prior to puberty (Anderson et al., 2005; Yu et al., 2002). Although the anti-estrogen, tamoxifen, abolishes the capacity for estrogen to function as a neuroprotectant against MA within the ovariectomized mouse (Gao and Dluzen, 2001a), by itself, tamoxifen offers neuroprotection upon striatal DA when administered to intact female and male mice (Dluzen et al., 2001). Combining the active metabolite of tamoxifen, 4-hydroxytamoxifen, with estrogen, however, has been shown to be effective in decreasing striatal DA depletions to MA in both gonadectomized female and male mice (Yu et al., 2002).

B. Progesterone

The gonadal steroid hormone, progesterone, is also effective in diminishing MA-induced striatal DA depletion within gonadectomized female and male mice (Yu and Liao, 2000a; Yu et al., 2002) and progesterone combined with estrogen was effective in ovariectomized mice (Yu and Liao, 2000a). These latter findings are particularly interesting since the neuroprotection observed with the combination of estrogen and progesterone suggests that the interactions of these two gonadal steroids may represent a physiological basis for these gender differences. In fact, the extent of MA-induced striatal DA depletion does vary as a function of the mouse (BALBc) estrous cycle with the greatest amount of MA-induced depletion observed in diestrus, the time when estrogen and progesterone are at their lowest levels (Yu and Liao, 2000b).

C. Testosterone

In contrast to that of estrogen and progesterone, the predominantly male gonadal steroid hormone, testosterone, shows no evidence for neuroprotection against MA in either male or female mice (Gao and Dluzen, 2001b). In fact, there are data which show that testosterone produces further reductions in MA-induced striatal DA concentrations as compared with that obtained from intact or gonadectomized male mice not treated with testosterone (Dluzen et al., 2002; Lewis and Dluzen, 2004), suggesting that this predominantly male gonadal steroid hormone might exacerbate MA-induced neurotoxicity. In this regard, the gender differences in MA-induced neurotoxicity may involve a combination of increased neuroprotection by estrogen within females and increased neurodegeneration by testosterone in males.

5. Developmental Effects

It has been concluded that exposure to MA *in utero* results in long-lasting, gender dependent effects, as evidenced when challenged with MA as adults. This conclusion is based upon the findings that more striatal dopaminergic parameters were altered in male (DA, DOPAC and HVA) versus female (3-MT and HVA) mice exposed to MA *in utero* when subsequently challenged with MA as adults (Heller *et al.*, 2001). However, an inspection of striatal DA concentrations from these mice seems to indicate a basic gender difference with an apparent absence of significant differences between groups treated with saline or MA *in utero*. That is, the amount of striatal DA depletion is overall greater in male mice treated with 15 or 20 mg/kg doses of MA, but there is no significant difference in striatal DA between males treated with MA or saline *in utero*. There is also a sex difference with regard to seizure induction in rats exposed to MA prenatally. The first fasciculation started earlier and the threshold of chronic seizure was lower in MA-exposed male rats (Slamberova, 2005). In addition, female rats subjected to prenatal MA exposure showed differences in seizure induction as a function of their estrous cycle (Slamberova, 2005; Slamberova and Rokyta, 2005), suggesting an interaction between gonadal steroid hormones in the adult and this prenatal MA exposure. Since treatment of pregnant rats with MA produces a number of adverse secondary effects upon the pregnancy and maternal behavior, the exact bases for the effects of *in utero* treatment require careful evaluation. For example, MA treatment of pregnant rats results in a higher incidence of delivery failure and death of the mother (Acuff-Smith *et al.*, 1992) and MA-injected mothers have shorter gestation periods, smaller litters and lower weight gains (Martin, 1975; Martin *et al.*, 1976) as well as negative effects upon maternal behavior (Slamberova *et al.*, 2005).

MA exposure during the first month of life in rats (postnatal days 1-29) has a gender-specific stimulatory effect upon tyrosine hydroxylase activity, the rate-limiting enzyme for DA synthesis. Males, but not females, show increased tyrosine hydroxylase activity and mRNA levels within the caudate-putamen and substantia nigra after MA treatment when assessed at 30 days of age (Gomes-da-Silva *et al.*, 2000). These pre-pubertal sex differences, as observed in the 30-day old rat are particularly intriguing when considering the absence of any male versus female differences in MA-induced striatal DA depletion, within adult rats (Fukumura et al., 1998; Gehrke et al., 2003). If early post-natal (days 2-5) female mouse pups are masculinized, with testosterone treatment or male mouse pups are feminized, with gonadectomy, the capacity for estrogen to function as a neuroprotectant retains its sexually dimorphic difference (Anderson *et al.*, 2005). That is, estrogen was able to decrease the amount of striatal DA depletion to MA within adult females, that were masculinized neonatally, but not within adult males that were feminized neonatally. Although neonatal manipulations failed to alter this gender-dependent neuroprotective effect of estrogen, when female mice were gonadectomized prior to puberty, estrogen was no longer capable of demonstrating a neuroprotective effect, and in males, gonadectomy prior to puberty did not permit the estrogen to function as a neuroprotectant (Anderson *et al.*, 2005; Yu *et al.*, 2002). When taken together, it seems that the pubertal period represents a particularly crucial developmental stage where the potential for a display (in mice) or lack of display (in rats) for MA-induced gender differences may be formulated. It has been reported that a number of hepatic P450 forms show gender differences at the pre-pubertal period (Kato and Yamazoe, 1992). Whether these changes in hepatic P450 observed at this critical developmental period contribute to these sex-specific (and sex-dependent) alterations in response to MA remains to be determined.

6. Hyperthermia

The magnitude of hyperthermia produced by MA is correlated with the severity of striatal DA depletion (Bowyer et al., 1994; Clausing and Bowyer, 1999; Fukumura et al., 1998). Consistent with the persistently greater reductions in striatal DA observed in males, MA increases maximum core temperatures more in male than female mice (Miller and O'Callaghan, 1995). MA also increases maximum core temperatures to a greater degree in male rats (Fukumura et al., 1998). Interestingly, the sex difference which exists in MA-induced hyperthermia as observed in both mice and rats would seem inconsistent with MA-induced striatal DA depletion where sex differences exist only in the mice but not rats (Fukumura et al., 1998; Gehrke et al., 2003). In this way, the greater increases in core temperature observed in response to MA within male versus female rats is not associated with a sex difference to MA-induced striatal DA depletion within this species (Fukumura et al., 1998; Gehrke et al., 2003). It has often been assumed that these changes in temperature represent a critical component for the MA-induced neurotoxicity response. From the present findings, it seems that the variable of temperature may interact with that of species and sex with regard to MA-induced neurotoxicity of the NSDA system. Since brain hyperthermia both proceeds and is greater than that of body hyperthermia in response to MA (Brown et al., 2003), it will be important to establish whether sex/species differences exist in brain hyperthermia.

7. Conclusions – Animal Studies

Definitive conclusions regarding sex differences as related to MA from animal (and human) studies are difficult owing to the myriad of variables involved with these reports. MA regimens administered, species/strain, estrous cycle stage, developmental period and temperature represent a few of the more salient factors which can contribute to, interact with, and/or mitigate against the observation of a sex difference. While remaining cognizant of these qualifying conditions, some notable generalizations do emerge when collating these data.

Female rodents tend to be more sensitive to the reinforcing and activity-enhancing properties of MA. Although more sensitive to these effects of MA, females (mice) show a decidedly diminished sensitivity for the DA releasing and neurotoxic effects of MA. The sex differences in MA clearance and metabolism could be involved with the increased reinforcing and activity responses seen in females, however, it is more difficult to reconcile this with the decreased MA-stimulated DA release observed in females. An alternative or additional component of dopaminergic function which could contribute to these seemingly paradoxical findings is that of the uptake of MA and/or DA evoked by MA through dopamine and vesicular monoamine transporters. Female rodents have a greater density of striatal DA uptake sites (Morissette and Di Paolo, 1993) and show increased activities in both dopamine and vesicular monoamine transport function (Bhatt and Dluzen, 2005; Walker et al., 2000;

2006). Moreover, there are differences in these dopamine transporter densities as a function of the estrous cycle and in response to estrogen (Morissette *et al.*, 1990; Morissette and Di Paolo, 1993) demonstrating that gonadal steroid hormones are involved with this modulation of transporter function. The dopamine and vesicular monoamine transporters represent key elements for modulating MA and DA responses through their capacity for extra-neuronal uptake of MA and DA through the dopamine transporter and intra-neuronal sequestering of MA and DA within vesicles by the vesicular monoamine transporter. Therefore, the sex differences which exist in dopamine and vesicular monoamine transporters can be involved with the complex patterns of MA and DA responses that are observed between male and female rodents. Not only can these dopamine and vesicular monoamine transporters be involved with modulating responses to MA, but in turn, they are affected (decreased) by the MA treatment (Fleckenstein *et al.*, 2000) and their function is modulated by temperature (Xie *et al.*, 2000).

The sex differences observed in response to MA are clearly modulated by gonadal steroid hormones. Within adult mice estrogen can function as a neuroprotectant against MA-induced neurotoxicity in female, but not male, mice. Also there are indications that the predominantly male gonadal steroid hormone, testosterone, can enhance MA-induced neurotoxicity in male mice. In this regard, the sex differences in MA-induced neurotoxicity may involve a combination of positive effects of estrogen in the female along with negative effects of testosterone in the male. In spite of these modulatory effects of gonadal steroids, the differences to MA observed between males and females appear to be "hard-wired" in that sex differences in MA-induced neurotoxicity remain present between gonadectomized male and female mice, as well as in mice where their sexual phenotype was altered as a result of hormonal manipulations within the neonatal period. Interestingly, the pubertal period seems to be a particularly significant stage with regard to the neurotoxic effects of MA within the adult. In mice, ovariectomy prior to puberty abolishes the capacity for estrogen to function as a neuroprotectant against MA within the adult female. In rats, repeated treatments with MA beginning on postnatal day one resulted in increased tyrosine hydroxylase levels in male, but not females as determined on postnatal day 30. This sex difference in tyrosine hydroxlase at 30 days of age can be contrasted with the absence of a sex difference with regard to MA-induced striatal DA depletion when rats are tested as adults.

IV. Gender Differences in Human Studies

Males and females report that their main reason for using MA is availability. They differ with regard to their second most commonly reported reason, with females indicating increased productivity and males curiosity (Cretzmeyer *et al.*, 2003). Similarly, there are a number of circumstances under which males and females differ in regard to the use of, and responses to, MA. In the following section we summarize these dissimilarities.

1. Clearance and Metabolism

The pharmacokinetics of MA have been examined in humans after intravenous injection, inhalation (smoking) and oral doses(Cook *et al.*, 1990; Cook *et al.*, 1992; Cook *et al.*, 1993). In addition to measures of MA itself, the two primary metabolites of MA, amphetamine and 4-hydroxy-MA (Caldwell *et al.*, 1972) can also be monitored in these pharmacokinetic studies. With regard to MA, the plasma half-life in humans is about 12 hours, ranging from 9-13 hours, which can be contrasted with the approximate one-hour half-life reported in rats. There do not appear to be any direct pharmacokinetic tests of MA between males and females, however, gastrointestinal transit time is greater in the luteal phase which would suggest a greater absorption in women (Lynch et al., 2002). Such findings not only suggest a potential basis for gender differences in MA metabolism and clearance, but also potential differences within women as a function of their menstrual cycle. Within the brain, significantly higher metabolism is observed in the parietal cortex and lower metabolism in the thalamus and striatum of detox MA abusers. The fact that similar results were obtained when males and females were analyzed separately (Volkow et al., 2001a), suggests an absence of a gender difference in brain metabolism of these recovering MA abusers.

2. Methamphetamine (MA) Use

A. Age at Onset

Although the gender differences in age at onset for MA use are not always statistically significant, in all reports reviewed females were younger. Brecht *et al.* (2004) reported a non-significant difference in MA initiation in females (18.54 years) versus males (19.34 years). Similarly, when considering the overall age at onset for eight different illegal substances of abuse agents (not including MA), it was found that no significant differences were present, but females (18.52 years) were again younger than males (19.16 years) (Westermeyer and Boedicker, 2000). In a study conducted in Taiwan a statistically significant gender difference was obtained for age at onset with females starting MA use at an earlier age than males (25.3 versus 28.0 years) (Lin *et al.*, 2004). These authors speculated that this difference might be attributable to the mandatory military service policy for men in Taiwan which could have the effect of sheltering and thereby delaying use in males. However, data obtained from programs in California also revealed a statistically significant earlier age for MA use onset in women (19.2 years) as compared with men (20.6 years) (Hser *et al.*, 2005). Taking these data together, it seems that women may be an increased risk for an earlier age of onset for MA use.

B. Dependence

It has been suggested that females are more likely to use MA than males (National Institute of Justice, 1999). Consistently, a 3-year study on females aged 8 to 22 found that girls and young women reported more MA use, became dependent on MA faster and suffered more adverse effects sooner than boys and young men (Rawson *et al.*, 2005). Significantly more adolescent females reported dependence on MA (Kim and Fendrich, 2002) and MA as their primary drug of choice (63.7%) versus males (15%) even after controlling for age; and older teens (17 and 18 years) and adolescent females were more likely than younger teens and adolescent males to use MA (Rawson *et al.*, 2005). Similar findings have been obtained from other investigators. Along with higher rates of dependence on MA (Kim and Fendrich, 2002), females are more motivated to self-administer MA (Lynch *et al.*, 2002). Likewise, a two-fold greater percentage of females report that amphetamine is their drug of choice (Cretzmeyer *et al.*, 2003). Brecht *et al.* (2004) report a non-significant trend for females to transition to regular use from first MA use more quickly than did males (1.60 versus 2.56 years). When considering these findings on age at onset and dependence on MA, it will be interesting to determine the extent to which genetic alterations that have been obtained within female MA users (see Genetics section) may be involved with this potential for increased MA use in women. In contrast to these findings, there is one report based upon a survey of middle school students which suggests that boys are more likely to use club drugs (crystal MA, ecstasy, GHB and ketamine) than girls (Goldsamt *et al.*, 2005). Since the overall use of several drugs was combined in this survey, it is not possible to identify the specific role of MA in this report.

C. Response to Treatment

A consistent finding that emerges from a number of studies is that females are more likely to seek treatment for, and acknowledge dependence upon, MA (Kim and Fendrich, 2002). For example, it has been reported that although 30% of treatment admissions for MA abuse are females, they account for 47% of those in treatment programs (Cretzmeyer *et al.*, 2003). Females also accounted for 54% of MA abusers entering treatment in San Diego County, however, in the San Francisco area admissions for amphetamine-type abuse treatment programs was 73% male (Heischober and Miller, 1991). More females have tried treatment programs (Senjo, 2005), are more likely to seek treatment (Lin *et al.*, 2004) and females have longer initial treatment durations (Brecht *et al.*, 2004). Women also seem to show greater benefits from treatment programs. In the categories of family relationships and medical problems, greater improvements are reported for females (Hser *et al.*, 2005). These authors go on to point out that these improvements are particularly significant when considering that women had been subjected to greater initial stress (unemployment, childcare, life with substance abusers), had been physically or sexually abused and reported more psychiatric problems (depression, cognition). It is interesting to note that individuals who are depressed are more likely to seek treatment (Semple *et al.*, 2005). Since a pervasive characteristic of female MA abusers is depression (see Comorbidity section), it will be of interest to establish whether the greater propensity for female MA abusers to seek treatment is related to, or independent of, the depression that is associated with MA use in women.

D. Comorbidity

A salient comorbidity variable of MA use in women is depression. Female MA users had significantly greater depression scores than males (Semple *et al.*, 2004), show greater percentages of depression versus males (38.8% versus 29.8%) as reported by Hser *et al.* (2005), 68% versus 50% by Zweben *et al.* (2004) and 54% versus 46% for adolescent females as reported by Rawson *et al.* (2005). Moreover, females are more likely to be suicidal (Lin *et al.*, 2004; Zweben *et al.*, 2004). Whether this depression is greater in female MA abusers as compared with females who do not engage in substance abuse and therefore represents a type of self-medication or whether these differences indicate a basic/existing gender difference, remains to be determined. The possibility that females may more likely be using MA as a type of self-medication is suggested by data on gender differences for the reasons of MA use. Females report escape/emotional family problems (Cretzmeyer *et al.*, 2003), coping with mood (Semple *et al.*, 2004), losing weight (Brecht *et al.*, 2004; Cretzmeyer et al., 2003; Semple et al., 2004) and acquisition of more energy (Brecht *et al.*, 2004; Cretzmeyer *et al.*, 2003; Rawson *et al.*, 2002a) as reasons for use of MA. It seems likely that all of these factors can be related to depression. Accordingly, the use of MA can then be seen as an attempt to alleviate these depression-related characteristics.

E. Other Drugs

There does not appear to be any definitive data as to whether male or female MA abusers are more likely to use other drugs of abuse, although it seems that there is a general consensus for this to be a characteristic more related to males. It has been reported that more juvenile females indicate trying other drugs (Kim and Fendrich 2002), but it has also been reported that more males used other drugs (Brecht *et al.*, 2004). Women are less apt to have used hallucinogens or inhalants (Westermeyer and Boedicker, 2000), but used more sedatives (Lin *et al.*, 2004). Men using MA report more alcohol and marijuana use than women (Hser *et al.*, 2005). In addition, more males report using hallucinogens, inhalants, PCP, heroin and downers and are more likely to use another drug in the absence of MA availability (Brecht *et al.*, 2004). From these data, a preliminary conclusion which emerges is that males who use MA may more probably use other drugs of abuse while female retain a preference for MA. Statements regarding MA use in women within these reports support this conclusion. For example, Cretzmeyer *et al.* (2003) note that MA appears to be a drug that is attractive to whites who are most likely female. In addition, the popularity of MA among women has been attributed to its appetite suppressing, mood elevating and energy enhancing qualities, which are of particular significance to women (Strauss and Falkin, 2001). However, this conclusion needs to be qualified since factors other than gender may be related with use of other drugs in these MA abusers. In specific, the degree of MA abuse, comorbidity, and/or the type of alternative drug of abuse can all contribute to the mitigation of gender differences.

3. Behavioral Effects

A. Criminal Records

Based upon arrest records male MA users would clearly be seen as showing more severe pathological behaviors. Males who use MA (or traffic in MA) are arrested more often than females (Brecht *et al.*, 2004; Hser *et al.*, 2005; Senjo, 2005), a greater percentage of males are involved with crime (54.8% versus 25.9%) (Lin *et al.*, 2004) and felony conviction times are longer in males (14.2 versus 6.2 months) (Semple *et al.*, 2004). Only for the arrest category of status offenses (running away, truancy) are females more likely to be arrested (Kim and Fendrich, 2002).

B. Violence

Given the frequency and more serious nature of the arrest records of males using MA, it is somewhat surprising to find that data from two different studies indicate that violent behavior appears more characteristic of female MA abusers. While 10% of male MA users report violent behavior, this level is 13% for females (Hser *et al.*, 2005) and more females report trouble controlling their anger (Zweben *et al.*, 2004). There is also a report of no gender difference in violent behavior (Brecht *et al.*, 2004), however, even this lack of a significant difference is notable when considering the gender differences in arrest records as described above. In this way, no study of which we are aware has reported a greater incidence of violence in males who use MA, although these males have a decided record indicating more severe or pathological behaviors. While violent behavior may be somewhat more characteristic of females, as based upon the reports listed above, females are also subjected to more violence. Sexual abuse and violence were indicated by 57.6% of females versus 15.7% of male MA abusers (Cohen *et al.*, 2003) and more females experienced childhood sexual abuse, 44% versus 24% for males (Brecht *et al.*, 2004).

C. Sex

MA can be used as a means to enhance the sexual experience. The data available from one report indicate no gender difference for this behavioral category in MA users (Rawson *et al.*, 2002b). Females reported as strong an association between substance use and sex as males. Sexual thoughts, behaviors and activities were enhanced with the use of MA, with similar responses from males and females.

D. Activity

While MA increases activity (Batki and Harris, 2004), it seems that females are more likely to use MA to achieve this goal. In general, females report a desire or need for more energy as can be achieved with MA (Brecht *et al.*, 2004). It appears that females feel this increased energy will aid in increasing their productivity (Cretzmeyer *et al.*, 2003). MA is perceived as a treatment to diminish exhaustion and fatigue associated with work, home care, childcare and family responsibilities encountered by women (Rawson *et al.*, 2002a).

E. Learning

When assessed in an auditory verbal learning test a significant MA by sex interaction was obtained. This interaction resulted from a poorer performance by male versus female MA users. No significant differences were obtained between male and female controls (Chang *et al.* 2005).

4. Neuroanatomical and Neurochemical Effects

A. Neuroanatomical Changes

MA users show significantly decreased DA, tyrosine hydroxylase and dopamine transporter levels (Wilson *et al.*, 1996). One approach to evaluate MA effects upon the brain involves volumetric measures of brain areas (Chang *et al.*, 2005). Whole brain areas did not differ between MA and control subjects, however, males showed an overall significantly greater volume for the whole brain as well as for specific areas including cerebellum (vermis), thalamus and caudate. Within the striatal regions (globus pallidus and putamen), significantly increased volumes were obtained with MA abusers, but no significant differences were observed between males and females. Female MA users did show significantly larger volumes of the posterior middle portion of the corpus callosum as compared with females not using MA. No such significant differences were obtained when comparing male MA abusers with controls. In fact, the volumes within this area were non-significantly decreased in males using MA. Female MA users also differed from males with regard to cerebral blood flow. Specifically, male MA users show more hypoperfused regions in the frontal and parietal cortex, while female MA abusers show more hyperperfused regions in the parietal and occipital areas (Chang et al., 2002). These authors have speculated that this capacity for increased perfusion may contribute to a diminution in neuronal injury within female MA abusers.

B. Neurochemical Changes

To our knowledge, there are no specific studies in which neurochemical responses were assessed in response to MA. There is one recent study in which the effect of amphetamine upon DA release was compared between healthy adult men and women (Munro et al., 2006). Although no gender differences were present for basal release of DA, amphetamine stimulated striatal DA release of men was significantly higher than that of women. Statistically significant differences were observed within the anterior putamen, anterior and posterior caudate nucleus and ventral striatum. These higher levels of DA release were associated with greater positive subjective feelings to the amphetamine administration in these males. Within women, no differences in amphetamine stimulated DA release were observed when comparing results obtained at the luteal versus follicular phase of the menstrual cycle. Nor were there any differences in the subjective responses to the amphetamine challenge between these two menstrual cycle changes.

5. Gonadal Steroids

We are unaware of any studies relating gonadal steroids of males or females with MA use or effects of MA. The limited data offered on this topic involves that of amphetamine. There are data from one study in which it was reported that subjective responses to amphetamine vary across the menstrual cycle with more positive feelings being associated with higher estrogen levels (Lynch et al., 2002). In a comprehensive study involving the simultaneous monitoring of DA release combined with reports of subjective feelings in response to amphetamine within healthy volunteer men and women, it was found that males showed significantly greater DA responses along with more positive feelings to the amphetamine treatment. However, these responses did not correlate with testosterone levels in these males. In women, neither DA responses nor subjective feelings to the amphetamine treatment were related to estrogen levels as no changes were obtained between women at the follicular versus luteal phase of their menstrual cycle when estradiol levels were 59.63 versus 118.41 pg/ml, respectively (Munro et al., 2006).

6. Developmental Effects

There is one report in which 65 children who were exposed to amphetamine during fetal life were evaluated when they reached 14 years of age (Cernerud *et al.*, 1996). In general, these children were found to be below that of their classmates with regard to school achievements. The notable observation with regard to gender differences in these children was that the girls were shorter and weighed less while the males were taller and heavier than their respective peer control groups. These results were quite unexpected and therefore a clear explanation is not apparent. The authors have speculated that this fetal amphetamine exposure may have altered the pubertal onset for these children and/or the parental neglect to which these children may be been subjected to could have altered their developmental progression.

7. Genetics

The association among genetic alterations, MA use and gender has received considerably more attention in human as compared with animal studies. Since the data presented in this review does indicate significant gender differences in a number of parameters involved with MA use, an ideal demonstration would be for an association of a genetic alteration that would be unique for either male or female MA abusers. There exist four studies which meet these criteria. Kobayashi *et al.* (2004) report a significant association between three single nucleotide polymorphisms located in the vicinity of α-synuclein T10a7 which were limited to female, but not male, MA abusers. A second gene which has attracted attention as potentially related to MA abuse is that of glutathione S-transferase M1 (GSTM1), since this gene has been associated with the DA-related condition of schizophrenia. The frequency of carrying a deletion of the GSTM1 gene was significantly higher in female versus male MA abusers and a significant difference in genotype distribution was present between females who abuse MA versus female controls. No such statistically significant differences were observed in males (Koizumi *et al.* 2004). Since the angiotensin converting enzyme (ACE) gene has been shown to be involved with DA transmission, potential polymorphisms in this gene have also been investigated as related to MA abuse. Control males showed a significant increase in the frequency (0.57) of the allele I of the I/D ACE polymorphism compared with control females (0.43). However, an opposite, albeit non-significant, trend (Males = 0.48 and Females = 0.56) was observed in MA dependent subjects (Sery *et al.*, 2001). In this way, when comparing the changes between controls and MA abusers within a gender, these data reveal a greater degree of change within females. Finally, the findings of an association between the GABA$_A$ subunit cluster on 5q33 with the development of alcoholism has prompted an analysis of this gene as related to MA abuse. No association between single nucleotide polymorphisms and the GABA$_A$ subunit gene were observed between male control and MA abusers. By contrast, statistically significant differences between female controls and MA abusers were obtained for two of the polymorphisms investigated (Lin *et al.*, 2003). It is interesting to note that in each of these studies the genetic alteration obtained seems to be characteristic of the female. From the data reviewed in the MA Use section, it also seems to be the female who is more vulnerable to, and dependent upon MA. While it is clear that more work needs to be done in this area these initial relationships offer a potential means for understanding the differences between men and women in the progression to dependence and abuse of MA.

8. Conclusions – Human Studies

The overall nature of substance abuse is typically considered to be more prominent in males. However, when focusing upon MA, the picture that emerges is one where women tend to start MA use at an earlier age, are more dependent upon MA, find MA more appealing and are decidedly committed to this psychostimulant. Related to this apparently increased vulnerability in women was the identification of specific genetic alterations and neuroanatomical changes obtained in female MA abusers. Such findings highlight a particular need for considering gender when evaluating the use, effects and treatments involving MA.

An additional characteristic which emerged was the relatively consistent comorbidity of depression and/or depression-related characteristics in females using MA. The fact that females are more likely to seek treatment for MA abuse may be related to this depression, which is a condition often associated with treatment. The pervasiveness of this particular trait suggests the possibility that one of the appealing features of MA use within women may enable a alleviation of this depression. The use of MA could then serve as a type of self-medication for this condition.

Like that observed within animal studies, there seems to be an apparent paradox with regard to data indicating that females are more responsive or vulnerable to MA, but may show a diminished striatal DA response as seen when assessed for amphetamine-stimulated release of DA from the striatal area. Three studies using three different radioligands showed that women have more dopamine transporters than men in the striatum (Lavalaye *et al.*, 2000; Mozley *et al.*, 2001; Staley *et al.*, 2001). As described previously for the animal studies, dopamine transporters play a critical role with regard to MA and DA responses and therefore may be associated with these complex responses. In further support of the significance of the dopamine transporter as related to MA are data which show that dopamine transporter density in the caudate and putamen is reduced in persons using MA (McCann *et al.*, 1998; Sekine *et al.*, 2001; Volkow *et al.*, 2001b) and this reduction was associated with motor slowing, memory impairment (Volkow *et al.*, 2001b) and other psychotic symptoms (Sekine *et al.*, 2001). In addition, vesicular monoamine transporters in the caudate nucleus, anterior putamen, and striatum show lower levels of binding sites in abstinent MA users, indicating its role and the possibility of nerve terminal degeneration (Johanson *et al.*, 2006).

V. COMPARISON OF ANIMAL AND HUMAN STUDIES

A primary reason for conducting research using animal models is to glean some information or insights into the basic mechanisms and effects of treatments for eventual application within man. To this end, where possible, it is important to assess whether and/or the degree to which these data from animal experiments might be analogous and applicable to conditions in man. In at least four aspects, there appear to be clear similarities between analogous animal and human studies as identified in this review.

First, at the very fundamental issue regarding the use or appeal of MA, there exists a noteworthy similarity between animal and human studies. It seems that females, both rodent and human, show a greater potential for MA use. This basic finding is particularly significant as it suggests an elemental biochemical resemblance shared by females across these species that may render them more susceptible to the effects of MA. Accordingly, while social or environmental factors can affect MA use in humans, an inherent biochemical perturbation may be at the foundation of the gender differences to MA. A comparison of the genetic alterations present within women MA abusers with that of animal models, in particular, those which display an increased sensitivity or susceptibility for MA may serve as an approach to address this issue. Such animal models exist (e.g. Rubenstein et al., 1997) but have not been evaluated with regard to the variable of sex. Second, as to the nature of change in NSDA function resulting from this basic biochemical difference, one possible candidate could involve DA release. For this parameter, MA-stimulated DA release from mice and amphetamine-stimulated DA release from humans are significantly greater in males. When inquiring as to the reason(s) for this gender difference in stimulated DA release, the third similarity and possible explanation could be dissimilarities present in metabolism/clearance between males and females. However, a perhaps more likely scenario may involve the gender differences in dopamine (and vesicular monoamine) transporters, which represents the fourth salient similarity present between animal and human studies. This parameter would more likely be closely allied with changes in DA release as related to MA. In this way, there are clear similarities in prominent behavioral and neurochemical effects of MA between animal and human studies. Such similarities permit a means for understanding the bases for these gender differences and will enable us to identify avenues for future research.

REFERENCES

Acuff-Smith K.D., George M., Lorens S.A. and Vorhees C.V. (1992) Preliminary evidence for methamphetamine-induced behavioral and ocular effects in rat offspring following exposure during early organogenesis. *Psychopharmacology (Berl) 109*, 255-263.

Amano T., Matsubayashi H. and Sasa M. (1996) Hypersensitivity of nucleus accumbens neurons to methamphetamine and dopamine following repeated administrations of methamphetamine. *Ann.N.Y.Acad.Sci. 801*, 136-147.

Anderson L.I., Leipheimer R.E. and Dluzen D.E. (2005) Effects of neonatal and prepubertal hormonal manipulations upon estrogen neuroprotection of the nigrostriatal dopaminergic system within female and male mice. *Neuroscience 130*, 369-382.

Anggard E., Jonsson L.E., Hogmark A.L. and Gunne L.M. (1973) Amphetamine metabolism in amphetamine psychosis. *Clin.Pharmacol.Ther. 14*, 870-880.

Batki S.L. and Harris D. S. (2004) Quantitative drug levels in stimulant psychosis: relationship to symptom severity, catecholamines and hyperkinesia. *Am. J. Addict.* 13, 461-470.

Bhatt S.D. and Dluzen D. E. (2005) Dopamine transporter function differences between male and female CD-1 mice. *Brain Res.* 1035, 188-195.

Bisagno V., Bowman R. E. and Luine V.N. (2003) Functional aspects of estrogen neuroprotection. *Endocrine* 21, 33-41.

Bisagno V., Ferguson D. and Luine V.N. (2002) Short toxic methamphetamine schedule impairs object recognition task in male rats. *Brain Res. 940*, 95-101.

Bowyer J.F., Davies D.L., Schmued L., Broening H.W., Newport G.D., Slikker W., Jr. and Holson R.R. (1994) Further studies of the role of hyperthermia in methamphetamine neurotoxicity. *J.Pharmacol.Exp.Ther. 268*, 1571-1580.

Brecht M.L., O'Brien A., von Mayrhauser C. and Anglin M.D. (2004) Methamphetamine use behaviors and gender differences. *Addict.Behav. 29*, 89-106.

Brown P.L., Wise R. A. and Kitatkin E. A. (2003) Brain hyperthermia is induced by methamphetamine and exacerbated by social interaction. *J. Neurosci.* 23, 3924-3929.

Cadet J.L., Jayanthi S. and Deng X. (2003) Speed kills: cellular and molecular bases for methamphetamine-induced nerve terminal degeneration and neuronal apoptosis. *FASEB J.* 17, 1775-1778.

Cahill L. (2006) Why sex matters for neuroscience. *Nat.Rev.Neurosci. 7*, 477-484.

Caldwell J., Dring L.G. and Williams R.T. (1972) Metabolism of (14 C)methamphetamine in man, the guinea pig and the rat. *Biochem. .J. 129*, 11-22.

Cappon G.D., Pu C. and Vorhees C.V. (2000) Time-course of methamphetamine-induced neurotoxicity in rat caudate-putamen after single-dose treatment. *Brain Res. 863*, 106-111.

Cass W.A. (1997) Decreases in evoked overflow of dopamine in rat striatum after neurotoxic doses of methamphetamine. *J.Pharmacol.Exp.Ther. 280*, 105-113.

Cernerud L., Eriksson M., Jonsson B., Steneroth G. and Zetterstrom R. (1996) Amphetamine addiction during pregnancy: 14-year follow-up of growth and school performance. *Acta Pediatr.* 85, 204-208.

Chang L., Cloak G., Patterson K., Grob C., Miller E. N., and Ernst T. (2005) Enlarged striatum in abstinent methamphetamine abusers: a possible compensatory response. *Biol. Psychiat.* 57, 967-974.

Chang L., Ernst T., Speck O., Patel H., DeSilva M., Leonido-Yee M. and Miller E. N. (2002) Perfusion MRI and computerized cognitive test abnormalities in abstinent methamphetamine users. *Psychiat. Res. Neuroimag.* 114, 65-79.

Chen H.H., Yang Y.K.., Yeh T.L., Cherng C.F., Hsu H.C., Hsiao S. Y. and Yu L. (2003) Methamphetamine-induced conditioned place preference is facilitated by estradiol pretreatment in female mice. *Clin. J. Physiol.* 46, 169-174.

Cho A.K., Melega W.P., Kuczenski R. and Segal D.S. (2001) Relevance of pharmacokinetic parameters in animal models of methamphetamine abuse. *Synapse 39*, 161-166.

Clausing P. and Bowyer J.F. (1999) Time course of brain temperature and caudate/putamen microdialysate levels of amphetamine and dopamine in rats after multiple doses of d-amphetamine. *Ann.N.Y.Acad.Sci. 890*, 495-504.

Cohen J.B., Dickow A., Horner K., Zweben J. E., Balabis J., Vandersloot D., Reibber C. and The Methamphetamine Treatment Project (2003) Abuse and violence history of men and women in treatment for methamphetamine dependence. *Am. J. Addict.* 12, 377-385.

Cook C.E., Jeffcoat A.R., Hill J.M., Pugh D.E., Patetta P.K., Sadler B.M., White W.R. and Perez-Reyes M. (1993) Pharmacokinetics of methamphetamine self-administered to human subjects by smoking S-(+)-methamphetamine hydrochloride. *Drug Metab Dispos. 21*, 717-723.

Cook C.E., Jeffcoat A.R., Perez-Reyes M., Sadler B.M., Hill J.M., White W.R. and McDonald S. (1990) Plasma levels of methamphetamine after smoking of methamphetamine hydrochloride. *NIDA Res.Monogr 105*, 578-579.

Cook C.E., Jeffcoat A.R., Sadler B.M., Hill J.M., Voyksner R.D., Pugh D.E., White W.R. and Perez-Reyes M. (1992) Pharmacokinetics of oral methamphetamine and effects of repeated daily dosing in humans. *Drug Metab Dispos. 20*, 856-862.

Cretzmeyer M., Sarrazin M.V., Huber D.L., Block R.I. and Hall J.A. (2003) Treatment of methamphetamine abuse: research findings and clinical directions. *J.Subst.Abuse Treat. 24*, 267-277.

D'Astous M., Gajjar T.M., Dluzen D.E. and Di Paolo T. (2004) Dopamine transporter as a marker of neuroprotection in methamphetamine-lesioned mice treated acutely with estradiol. *Neuroendocrinology 79*, 296-304.

Davidson C., Gow A.J., Lee T.H. and Ellinwood E.H. (2001) Methamphetamine neurotoxicity: necrotic and apoptotic mechanisms and relevance to human abuse and treatment. *Brain Res.Rev. 36*, 1-22.

Dluzen D.E. (2004) The effect of gender and the neurotrophin, BDNF, upon methamphetamine-induced neurotoxicity of the nigrostriatal dopaminergic system in mice. *Neurosci.Lett. 359*, 135-138.

Dluzen D. E. (2005) Estrogen, testosterone and gender differences. *Endocrine 27*, 259-267.

Dluzen D.E., Anderson L.I. and Pilati C.F. (2002) Methamphetamine-gonadal steroid hormonal interactions: effects upon acute toxicity and striatal dopamine concentrations. *Neurotoxicol.Teratol. 24*, 267-273.

Dluzen D.E. and McDermott J.L. (2002) Estrogen, anti-estrogen, and gender: differences in methamphetamine neurotoxicity. *Ann.N.Y.Acad.Sci. 965*, 136-156.

Dluzen D.E., McDermott J.L. and Anderson L.I. (2001) Tamoxifen diminishes methamphetamine-induced striatal dopamine depletion in intact female and male mice. *J.Neuroendocrinol. 13*, 618-624.

Dluzen D.E. and Salvaterra T.J. (2005) Sex Differences in Methamphetamine-Evoked Striatal Dopamine Output Are Abolished following Gonadectomy: Comparisons with Potassium-Evoked Output and Responses in Prepubertal Mice. *Neuroendocrinology 82*, 78-86.

Dluzen D.E., Tweed C., Anderson L.I. and Laping N.J. (2003) Gender differences in methamphetamine-induced mRNA associated with neurodegeneration in the mouse nigrostriatal dopaminergic system. *Neuroendocrinology 77*, 232-238.

Fleckenstein A.E., Gibb J. W. and Hanson G. R. (2000) Differential effects of stimulants on monoaminergic transporters: pharmacological consequences and implications for neurotoxicity. *Eur. J. Pharmacol. 406*, 1-13.

Fukumura M., Cappon G.D., Broening H.W. and Vorhees C.V. (1998) Methamphetamine-induced dopamine and serotonin reductions in neostriatum are not gender specific in rats with comparable hyperthermic responses. *Neurotoxicol.Teratol. 20*, 441-448.

Gajjar T.M., Anderson L.I. and Dluzen D.E. (2003) Acute effects of estrogen upon methamphetamine induced neurotoxicity of the nigrostriatal dopaminergic system. *J.Neural Transm. 110*, 1215-1224.

Gao X. and Dluzen D.E. (2001a) Tamoxifen abolishes estrogen's neuroprotective effect upon methamphetamine neurotoxicity of the nigrostriatal dopaminergic system. *Neuroscience 103*, 385-394.

Gao X. and Dluzen D.E. (2001b) The effect of testosterone upon methamphetamine neurotoxicity of the nigrostriatal dopaminergic system. *Brain Res. 892*, 63-69.

Gehrke B.J., Harrod S.B., Cass W.A. and Bardo M.T. (2003) The effect of neurotoxic doses of methamphetamine on methamphetamine-conditioned place preference in rats. *Psychopharmacology (Berl) 166*, 249-257.

Goldsamt L.A., O'Brien J., Clatts M.C. and McGuire L. S. (2005) The relationship between club drug use and other drug use: a survey of New York city middle school students. Subst. Use Misuse 40, 1539-1555.

Gomes-da-Silva J., Perez-Rosado A., de Miguel R., Fernandez-Ruiz J., Silva M.C. and Tavares M.A. (2000) Neonatal methamphetamine in the rat: evidence for gender-specific differences upon tyrosine hydroxylase enzyme in the dopaminergic nigrostriatal system. *Ann.N.Y.Acad.Sci. 914*, 431-438.

Heischober B. and Miller M.A. Methamphetamine abuse in California. In: Miller M.A., Kozel N.J., editors. Methamphetamine abuse: epidemiologic issues and implications. Washington, D.C.:NIDA, 1991; 60-71.

Heller A., Bubula N., Lew R., Heller B. and Won L. (2001) Gender-dependent enhanced adult neurotoxic response to methamphetamine following fetal exposure to the drug. *J.Pharmacol.Exp.Ther. 298*, 769-779.

Hser Y.I., Evans E. and Huang Y.C. (2005) Treatment outcomes among women and men methamphetamine abusers in California. *J.Subst.Abuse Treat. 28*, 77-85.

Johanson C.E., Frey K.A., Lundahl L.H., Keenan P., Lockhart N., Roll J., Galloway G.P., Koeppe R.A., Kilbourn M.R., Robbins T. and Schuster C.R. (2006) Cognitive function and nigrostriatal markers in abstinent methamphetamine abusers. *Psychopharmacology (Berl) 185*, 327-338.

Kato R. and Yamazoe Y. (1992) Sex-specific cytochrome P450 as a cause of sex- and species-related differences in drug toxicity. *Toxicol. Lett.* 64/65, 661-667.

Kim J.Y.S. and Fendrich M. (2002) Gender differences in juvenile arestees' drug use, self-reported dependence and perceived need for treatment. *Psychiat. Serv.* 53, 70-75.

Kita T., Paku S., Takahashi M., Kubo K., Wagner G.C. and Nakashima T. (1998) Methamphetamine-induced neurotoxicity in BALB/c, DBA/2N and C57BL/6N mice. *Neuropharmacology 37*, 1177-1184.

Kobayashi H., Ide S., Hasegawa J,, Ujike H., Sekine Y., Ozaki N., Inada T., Harano M., Komiyama T., Yamada M., Iyo M., Shen H-W., Ikeda K. and Sora I. (2004) Study of association between *a*-synuclein gene polymorphism and methamphetamine psychosis/dependence. *Ann. NY Acad. Sci.* 1025, 325-334.

Koizumi H., Hashimoto K., Kumakiri C., Shimizu E., Sekine Y., Ozaki N., Inada T., Harano M., Komiyama T., Yamada M., Sora I., Ujike H., Takei N. and Iyo M. (2004) Association between the glutathione s-transferase M1 gene deletion and female methamphetamine abusers. *Am. J. Med. Genet. Part B (Neuropsychiat. Genet.)* 126B, 43-45.

Lavalaye J., Booij J., Reneman L., Habraken J.B. and van Royen E.A. (2000) Effect of age and gender on dopamine transporter imaging with [123I]FP-CIT SPET in healthy volunteers. *Eur.J.Nucl.Med. 27*, 867-869.

Lewis C.M. and Dluzen D.E. (2004) Effect of testosterone upon methamphetamine-induced neurotoxicity of striatal dopamine within male and female mice. *Society for Neuroscience 34th Annual Meeting* Abstract, # 345.4.

Lin S.K., Ball D., Hsiao C.C., Chiang Y.L., Ree S.C. and Chen C.K. (2004) Psychiatric comorbidity and gender differences of persons incarcerated for methamphetamine abuse in Taiwan. *Psychiatry Clin.Neurosci. 58*, 206-212.

Lin S.K., Chen C.K., Ball D., Liu H.C. and Loh E.W. (2003) Gender-specific contribution of the GABA(A) subunit genes on 5q33 in methamphetamine use disorder. *Pharmacogenomics.J. 3*, 349-355.

Lynch W.J., Roth M.E. and Carroll M. E. (2002) Biological basis of sex differences in drug abuse: preclinical and clinical studies. *Psychopharmacology 164*, 121-137.

Martin J.C. (1975) Effects on offspring of chronic maternal methamphetamine exposure. *Dev.Psychobiol. 8*, 397-404.

Martin J.C., Martin D.C., Radow B. and Sigman G. (1976) Growth, development and activity in rat offspring following maternal drug exposure. *Exp.Aging Res. 2*, 235-251.

Mattei R. and Carlini E.A. (1996) A comparative study of the anorectic and behavioral effects of fenproporex on male and female rats. *Braz.J.Med.Biol.Res. 29*, 1025-1030.

McCann U.D., Wong D.F., Yokoi F., Villemagne V., Dannals R.F. and Ricaurte G.A. (1998) Reduced striatal dopamine transporter density in abstinent methamphetamine and methcathinone users: evidence from positron emission tomography studies with [11C]WIN-35,428. *J.Neurosci. 18*, 8417-8422.

Melega W.P., Williams A.E., Schmitz D.A., DiStefano E.W. and Cho A.K. (1995) Pharmacokinetic and pharmacodynamic analysis of the actions of D-amphetamine and D-methamphetamine on the dopamine terminal. *J.Pharmacol.Exp.Ther. 274*, 90-96.

Mickley K.R. and Dluzen D.E. (2004) Dose-response effects of estrogen and tamoxifen upon methamphetamine-induced behavioral responses and neurotoxicity of the nigrostriatal dopaminergic system in female mice. *Neuroendocrinology 79*, 305-316.

Milesi-Halle A., Hendrickson H.P., Laurenzana E.M., Gentry W.B. and Owens S.M. (2005) Sex- and dose-dependency in the pharmacokinetics and pharmacodynamics of (+)-methamphetamine and its metabolite (+)-amphetamine in rats. *Toxicol.Appl.Pharmacol. 209*, 203-213.

Miller D.B., Ali S.F., O'Callaghan J.P. and Laws S.C. (1998) The impact of gender and estrogen on striatal dopaminergic neurotoxicity. *Ann.N.Y.Acad.Sci. 844*, 153-165.

Miller D.B. and O'Callaghan J.P. (1995) The role of temperature, stress, and other factors in the neurotoxicity of the substituted amphetamines 3,4-methylenedioxymethamphetamine and fenfluramine. *Mol.Neurobiol. 11*, 177-192.

Morissette M., Biron D. and Di Paolo T. (1990) Effect of estradiol and progesterone on striatal dopamine uptake sites. *Brain Res. Bull.* 25, 419-422.

Morissette M. and Di Paolo T. (1993) Sex and estrous cycle variations of rat striatal dopamine uptake sites. *Neuroendocrinology 58*, 16-22.

Mozley L.H., Gur R.C., Mozley P.D. and Gur R.E. (2001) Striatal dopamine transporters and cognitive functioning in healthy men and women. *Am.J.Psychiatry 158*, 1492-1499.

Mugford C.A. and Kedderis G.L. (1998) Sex-dependent metabolism of xenobiotics. *Drug Metab Rev. 30*, 441-498.

Munro C.A., McCaul M.E., Wong D.F., Oswald L.M., Zhou Y., Brasic J., Kuwabara H., Kumar A., Alexander M., Ye W. and Wand G.S. (2006) Sex differences in striatal dopamine release in healthy adults. *Biol.Psychiatry 59*, 966-974.

Myers R.E., Anderson L.I. and Dluzen D.E. (2003) Estrogen, but not testosterone, attenuates methamphetamine-evoked dopamine output from superfused striatal tissue of female and male mice. *Neuropharmacology 44*, 624-632.

National Institute of Justice (1999) Report on methamphetamine uses in five western cities. US Department of Justice, National Institute of Justice, Washington, DC.

Rawson R.A., Gonzales R. and Brethen P. (2002a) Treatment of methamphetamine use disorders: an update. *J.Subst.Abuse Treat. 23*, 145-150.

Rawson R.A., Gonzales R., Obert J.L., McCann M.J. and Brethen P. (2005) Methamphetamine use among treatment-seeking adolescents in Southern California: participant characteristics and treatment response. *J.Subst.Abuse Treat. 29*, 67-74.

Rawson R.A., Washton A., Domier C.P. and Reiber C. (2002b) Drugs and sexual effects: role of drug type and gender. *J.Subst.Abuse Treat. 22*, 103-108.

Ricaurte G.A., Schuster C.R. and Seiden L.S. (1980) Long-term effects of repeated methylamphetamine administration on dopamine and serotonin neurons in the rat brain: a regional study. *Brain Res. 193*, 153-163.

Riviere G.J., Byrnes K.A., Gentry W.B. and Owens S.M. (1999) Spontaneous locomotor activity and pharmacokinetics of intravenous methamphetamine and its metabolite amphetamine in the rat. *J.Pharmacol.Exp.Ther. 291*, 1220-1226.

Roth M.E. and Carroll M.E. (2004) Sex differences in the acquisition of IV methamphetamine self-administration and subsequent maintenance under a progressive ratio schedule in rats. *Psychopharmacology (Berl) 172*, 443-449.

Rubinstein M., Phillips T.J., Bunzow J.R., Falzone T.L., Dziewczapolski G., Zhang G., Fang Y., Larson J.L., McDougall J.A., Chester J.A., Saez C., Pugsley T.A., Gershanik O., Low M.J. and Grandy D.K. (1997) Mice lacking dopamine D4 receptors are supersensitive to ethanol, cocaine, and methamphetamine. *Cell 90*, 991-1001.

Ryan D.E., Thomas P.E., Levin W., Maines S.L., Bandiera S. and Reik L.M. (1993) Monoclonal antibodies of differentiating specificities as probes of cytochrome P450h (2C11). *Arch.Biochem.Biophys. 301*, 282-293.

Sabol K.E., Roach J.T., Broom S.L., Ferreira C. and Preau M.M. (2001) Long-term effects of a high-dose methamphetamine regimen on subsequent methamphetamine-induced dopamine release in vivo. *Brain Res. 892*, 122-129.

Schindler C.W., Bross J.G. and Thorndike E.B. (2002) Gender differences in the behavioral effects of methamphetamine. *Eur.J.Pharmacol. 442*, 231-235.

Segal D. S. and Kuczenski R. (2006) Human methamphetamine pharmacokinetics simulated in the rat: single daily intravenous administration reveals elements of sensitization and tolerance. *Neuropsychopharmacology* 31, 941-955.

Seiden L.S. and Ricaurte G.A. (1987) Neurotoxicity of MA and related drugs. In Psychopharmacology: the third generation of progress. Herbert Y. Meltzer, Ed.: 356-366. Raven Press. New York.

Seiden L.S., Sabol K.E. and Ricaurte G.A. (1993) Amphetamine: effects on catecholamine systems and behavior. *Annu.Rev.Pharmacol.Toxicol. 33*, 639-677.

Sekine Y., Iyo M., Ouchi Y., Matsunaga T., Tsukada H., Okada H., Yoshikawa E., Futatsubashi M., Takei N. and Mori N. (2001) Methamphetamine-related psychiatric symptoms and reduced brain dopamine transporters studied with PET. *Am.J.Psychiatry 158*, 1206-1214.

Semple S.J., Grant I. and Patterson T.L. (2004) Female methamphetamine users: social characteristics and sexual risk behavior. *Wom. Hlth.* 40, 35-50.

Semple S.J., Grant I. and Patterson T.L. (2005) Utilization of drug treatment programs by methamphetamine users: the role f social stigma. *Am. J. Addict.* 14, 367-380.

Senjo S. R. (2005) Trafficking in meth: an analysis of the difference between male and female dealers. J. Drug Educ. 35, 59-77.

Sery O., Vojtova V. and Zvolsky P. (2001) The association study of DRD2, ACE and AGT gene polymorphisms and methamphetamine dependence. *Physiol Res. 50,* 43-50.

Shiiyama S., Soejima-Ohkuma T., Honda S., Kumagai Y., Cho A.K., Yamada H., Oguri K. and Yoshimura H. (1997) Major role of the CYP2C isozymes in deamination of amphetamine and benzphetamine: evidence for the quinidine-specific inhibition of the reactions catalysed by rabbit enzyme. *Xenobiotica 27*, 379-387.

Slamberova R. (2005) Flurothyl seizure susceptibility is increased in prenatally methamphetamine exposed adult male and female rats. *Epilep. Res.* 65, 121-124.

Slamberova R., Charousova P. and Pometlova M. (2005) Maternal behavior is impaired by methamphetamine administered during pre-mating, gestation and lactation. *Reprod.Toxicol. 20*, 103-110.

Slamberova R. and Rokyyta R. (2005) Seizure susceptibility in prenatally methamphetamine-exposed adult female rats. *Brain Res.* 1060, 193-197.

Staley J.K., Krishnan-Sarin S., Zoghbi S., Tamagnan G., Fujita M., Seibyl J.P., Maciejewski P.K., O'Malley S. and Innis R.B. (2001) Sex differences in [123I]beta-CIT SPECT measures of dopamine and serotonin transporter availability in healthy smokers and nonsmokers. *Synapse 41*, 275-284.

Strauss S. and Falkin G. P. (2001) Women offenders who use and deal methamphetamine: implications for mandated drug treatment. *Wom. Crim. Just.* 12: 77-97.

Villemagne V., Yuan J., Wong D.F., Dannals R.F., Hatzidimitriou G., Mathews W.B., Ravert H.T., Musachio J., McCann U.D. and Ricaurte G.A. (1998) Brain dopamine neurotoxicity in baboons treated with doses of methamphetamine comparable to those recreationally abused by humans: evidence from [11C]WIN-35,428 positron emission tomography studies and direct in vitro determinations. *J.Neurosci. 18*, 419-427.

Volkow N.D., Chang L., Wang G.J., Fowler J.S., Franceschi D., Sedler M.J., Gatley S.J., Hitzemann R., Ding Y.S., Wong C. and Logan J. (2001a) Higher cortical and lower subcortical metabolism in detoxified methamphetamine abusers. *Am.J.Psychiatry 158*, 383-389.

Volkow N.D., Chang L., Wang G.J., Fowler J.S., Leonido-Yee M., Franceschi D., Sedler M.J., Gatley S.J., Hitzemann R., Ding Y.S., Logan J., Wong C. and Miller E.N. (2001b) Association of dopamine transporter reduction with psychomotor impairment in methamphetamine abusers. *Am.J.Psychiatry 158*, 377-382.

Wagner G.C., Tekirian T.L. and Cheo C.T. (1993) Sexual differences in sensitivity to methamphetamine toxicity. *J.Neural Transm.Gen.Sect. 93*, 67-70.

Walker Q.D., Ray R. and Kuhn C.M. (2006) Sex differences in neurochemical effects of dopaminergic drugs in rat striatum. *Neuropsychopharmacology 31*, 1193-1202.

Walker Q.D., Rooney M.B., Wightman R.M. and Kuhn C.M. (2000) Dopamine release and uptake are greater in female than male rat striatum as measured by fast cyclic voltammetry. *Neuroscience 95*, 1061-1070.

Wallace T.L., Gudelsky G.A. and Vorhees C.V. (2001) Neurotoxic regimen of methamphetamine produces evidence of behavioral sensitization in the rat. *Synapse 39*, 1-7.

Westermeyer J. and Boedicker A. E. (2000) Course, severity and treatment of substance abuse among women versus men. *Am. J. Drug Alcohol Abuse* 26, 523-535.

Willett M.C. and Dluzen D.E. (2004) Tamoxifen increases methamphetamine-evoked dopamine output from superfused striatal tissue fragments of male mice. *Brain Res. 1029*, 186-194.

Wilson J.M., Kalasinsky K.S., Levey A.I., Bergeron C., Reiber G., Anthony R.M., Schmunk G.A., Shannak K., Haycock J.W. and Kish S.J. (1996) Striatal dopamine nerve terminal markers in human, chronic methamphetamine users. *Nat.Med.* 2, 699-703.

Woolverton W.L., Ricaurte G.A., Forno L.S. and Seiden L.S. (1989) Long-term effects of chronic methamphetamine administration in rhesus monkeys. *Brain Res. 486*, 73-78.

Xie T., McCann U.D., Kim S., Yuan J. and Ricaurte G.A. (2000) Effect of temperature on dopamine transporter function and intracellular accumulation of methamphetamine: implications for methamphetamine-induced dopaminergic neurotoxicity. *J.Neurosci. 20*, 7838-7845.

Yamada H., Oguri K. and Yoshimura H. (1986) Effects of several factors on urinary excretion of methamphetamine and its metabolites in rats. *Xenobiotica 16*, 137-141.

Yu L., Kuo Y., Cherng C.G., Chen H.H. and Hsu C.H. (2002) Ovarian hormones do not attenuate methamphetamine-induced dopaminergic neurotoxicity in mice gonadectomized at 4 weeks postpartum. *Neuroendocrinology 75*, 282-287.

Yu L. and Liao P.C. (2000a) Estrogen and progesterone distinctively modulate methamphetamine-induced dopamine and serotonin depletions in C57BL/6J mice. *J.Neural Transm. 107*, 1139-1147.

Yu L. and Liao P.C. (2000b) Sexual differences and estrous cycle in methamphetamine-induced dopamine and serotonin depletions in the striatum of mice. *J.Neural Transm. 107*, 419-427.

Yu Y.L. and Wagner G.C. (1994) Influence of gonadal hormones on sexual differences in sensitivity to methamphetamine-induced neurotoxicity. *J.Neural Transm.Park Dis.Dement.Sect. 8*, 215-221.

Zhu J.P., Xu W., Angulo N. and Angulo J.A. (2006) Methamphetamine-induced striatal apoptosis in the mouse brain: comparison of a binge to an acute bolus drug administration. *Neurotoxicology 27*, 131-136.

Zweben J. E., Cohen J.B., Christian D., Galloway G.P., Salinardi M., Parent D., Iguchi M. and The Methamphetamine Treatment Program (2004) Psychiatric symptoms in methamphetamine users. *Am. J. Addict.* 13, 181-190.

SHORT COMMENTARY

In: Men and Addictions: New Research
Author: Lyman J. Katlin

ISBN 978-1-60692-098-5
© 2009 Nova Science Publishers, Inc.

Short Commentary A

SOCIAL NORMS AND ARECA QUID CHEWING IN TAIWANESE ADOLESCENTS - A PRELIMINARY STUDY

Shih-Ming Li[1,2] and Jehn-Shyun Huang[1]*

1. Department of Dentistry, National Cheng Kung University, Tainan, Taiwan
2. Institute of Counseling Psychology, Toko University, Chia-Yi, Taiwan

ABSTRACT

Introduction: Social norms and personality play important roles in the initiation and maintenance of addictive behaviors. The aim of this preliminary study was to explore how social norms and personality influence areca quid chewing in adolescents. *Materials and Methods:* A total of 179 students from a junior high school in Chia-Yi city (Taiwan) participated in the study in 2003. Areca quid-chewing behavior and intention scales were used to determine attitude to, and usage of, areca quid. Social norm and conscientiousness scales were denoted as factors for perceived social environment and personality factors. *Results:* Forty of the sample (22.5%) has been areca-quid users. The mean scores for the subjective and behavioral social norms were 7.7 ± 3.75 (range 4-20) and 11.8 ± 3.26 (range 4-19). Statistical significance was demonstrated for the relationships between behavioral and subjective social-norm scores and intention to chew for the high-conscientiousness group ($r=.27$, $p=.008$; $r=.416$, $p<.001$), but not for the low-conscientiousness analog. *Conclusions:* The intention to chew areca quid was enhanced by the perceived social norms in highly conscientious Taiwanese adolescents.

Keywords: areca –quid, chewing, behavior, social norms, personality.

∗ Corresponding Author: Shih-Ming Li, Address: No.51, Sec 2,University Rd, Pu-tzu City,Chia-Yi County 613 Taiwan, Institute of Counseling Psychology, Toko University, Chia-Yi, Taiwan. E-mail address: shiming@mail2000.com.tw.

INTRODUCTION

Areca quid chewing is a popular habit common to about 10-20% of the world's population (i.e., 600-1200 million). Most of these consumers live in Asia, especially India, Sri Lanka, Southeast Asia, the Pacific Islands, China and Taiwan (Gupta and Warnakulasuriya, 2002). In Taiwan, estimates of the number of people succumbing to the areca quid-chewing habit are as high as two million, or approximately 10% of the total population especially high prevalence in male (Ko, Chiang and Chang, 1992). There is a long history of areca-quid chewing in Taiwan, with strong traditions supporting its social use. Offering cigarettes and areca-quid has long been accepted as a social greeting (Lu et al., 1993). Furthermore, there are plenty of evidences suggested that areca quid chewing is associated with habit or, addictive behavior (Chu, 2001).

Typically, this habit is acquired in junior high school, somewhere between the ages of 12 and 15 years old(Ko, Chiang and Chang, 1992; Wang et al., 2004). In 2000, Liou and Chou estimated the prevalence of areca quid chewing to be approximately 11.5% of adolescent students in Taiwan. Surveying the reasons for adolescents' areca quid mastication, three of the five main reasons (ex. influence of senior peers, observed behavior of adults, and popularity) are related to social norms (Wang et al., 2004).

In our serial studies, we found the social norm played the important role in the areca quid chewing and the areca quid was a kind of social drug which had the social benefit (Li et al. 2003; Li, Huang and Wu, 2007). In our previous study, the Attitudes-Social influence-Self-efficacy (ASE) model as a theoretical framework was used to investigate the factors associated with areca quid-chewing behavior among the Taiwanese adolescents. For the social influence component of the ASE, the subject social norm (r=0.53) was significantly correlated with participants' intentions to chew areca quid (Li et al. 2003). For the basic positive and negative expectancies of areca-quid chewing, the positive expectancies can be divided into physical/emotional reward and social benefit. Beyond the basic pharmacological effect of the area quid, the social benefit of areca quid chewing activity was proved to be an independent factor in the following study (Li, Huang and Wu, 2007). Then we go further to explore how social norms and personality influence areca quid chewing in adolescents.

The social norms approach is one of the fastest growing, scientifically validated methodologies for addressing health problems and risk behaviors, especially in the addictive behavior like drinking (Broadwater, Curtin, Martiz, and Zrull,2006) and smoking (Chen, Stanton, Fang, Li, Lin, Zhang, Liu, and Yang, 2006). It has been successfully applied to reduce alcohol use/abuse and smoking on college and university campuses (Oostwee, Knibbe and de Vries, 1996). The social norms theory states that peer influence plays an important role in the lives of young adults, and proposes that student behavior is often greatly influenced by peer perceptions (often referred to as perceived peer norms).

Social-personality psychology has been used to explore self concept and individual variations in personality with respect to behaviors. Conscientiousness refers to the propensity to follow social norms, and individual differences play an important role in determining substance-use/abuse behavior (Roberts and Bogg, 2004).

In Taiwan, the areca chewing behavior was a symbolic of " Taiwan Style Man " which was a subculture in male adolescent (Li, Lin, Ho, et al.,2006).How the chewing behavior will be an index of the group and how the social norm influence adolescents' behavior? The determinants of social norm and personality in adolescent areca-quid chewing behavior have not been fully explored in the literatures. Following the social-personality trait, we will explore the novel relationship between conscientiousness, perceived social norms and the behavioral intention of areca-quid chewing behavior in Taiwanese adolescents.

METHODS

Subjects and Procedure

The students enrolled in the study were selected using random sampling of classes from a senior high school in Chia-Yi City. Situated in southern Taiwan, Chia-Yi is the nation's seventh largest city with a population of 265,000 (2000 census). Its eight junior high schools have a total of 13,961 students who are required to enroll in senior high between 15 and 19 years of age. The questionnaires were administered in a classroom setting to small, randomly selected groups of schoolchildren from each class level (Li, Huang and Wu, 2007).

A total of 179 students from the selected high school in Chia-Yi (n = 179; 109 male, 70 female) participated in this study. The mean age of the sample was 16.4±0.9 years, with 138 of the students (77.5%) reporting that they had never tried areca quid.

Measures

Areca quid-chewing behaviour: Participants were placed into one of five chewing-status categories based on self-reported areca quid use, as assessed from their specific response to the question, "Do you currently or have you ever chewed areca quid?" The response categories were: "never tried", "tried", "chewed every day", "chewed occasionally" and "chewed previously, but had quit". The effective use of similar clustering procedures has been reported in previous related studies (Li et al., 2003).

Areca quid-chewing intention: In this study, the five-point Likert scale was used to measure chewing intention, with the response options ranging from "*strong desire*" to "*strong aversion*" tested across a range of different intra- and inter-personal situations. The Cronbach alpha was 0.90

Perceived social norms: The subjective perception of social norms was assessed by asking the participants to rate the degree of acceptability of areca quid chewing, as might be judged by various individuals (e.g., parents, friends, teachers, and the general public). Participants were asked to assess how they felt that their parents or friends (including other students and roommates) might view areca quid chewing on a five-point semantic-differential scale scored between one and five indicating not at all and well accepted, respectively. The responses to this question were individually averaged in order to construct a social norms scale, with higher overall score, which was a composite of the cumulative scores for each item, reflecting *a perception of* more-tolerant social norms (Li et al., 2003).

Behavioral norms: Questions about perceived prevalence of smoking and frequency of teen smoking were adapted from Eisenberg and Forster's (2003) social norms investigation of smoking-related behavior.

Conscientiousness: Big-Five personality model is the popular personality theory and include 5 personality traits: neuroticism, extraversion, openness, agreeableness, and conscientiousness (Zillig, Hemenover and Dienstbier, 2002) and the model were related to the health related behavior (Korotkov and Hannah, 2004). The conscientiousness in the Big-Five personality model influent the health protective behavior intention and more related to the health-related behavior than other personality traits (Conner and Abraham, 2001). The 10-item measure of the Big-Five dimensions (extraversion, agreeableness, conscientiousness, emotional stability and openness to experience) used by Gosling et al., (2003) was adopted for this study to evaluate the role of personality played in this chewing behavior. The good reliability and construct validity has been demonstrated by these researchers (Gosling et al., 2003).

Data analysis

The relationships between the intention to chew areca quid and social norms were assessed using Pearson's correlation coefficient. The following regression models were used to test the moderator hypotheses (Bovier Chamot and Perneger, 2004): Intention = β_0 + (β_1 * Social Norms) + (β_2 * Conscientiousness) + (β_2 * social norms * Conscientiousness);

For further analysis, the sample population was divided according to high or low mean conscientiousness score, and Pearson's correlation coefficient was used to explore the relationship between the *perceived* social norms and intention to chew areca quid.

RESULTS

From the individual self reports, 77.5% of the student had never tried areca quid, 17.2% had experimented a few times but not persisted, and 1.1% had chewed regularly but quit, with no regular chewers. The score range for chewing intention was 0-27. The means for subjective and behavioral social norms were 7.7 ± 3.75 (range 4-20) and 11.8 ± 3.26 (range 4-19), respectively.

The respective correlation coefficients for the relationship between chewing intention and perceived social norms were r= .22 and r= .29 for the behavioral and subjective social norms. For the behavioral social norm, the frequency of noticing peer chewing was strongly related to chewing intention (r = .335 p<.01), but not to the behavioral analog. For the perceived social norm, a stronger relationship was demonstrated between peer acceptance and chewing intention compared to the other parameters (r=.428 p<.01).

To test the moderator hypotheses, the scores for the perceived and behavioral social norms were combined to create a social norm index. Using the complete regression model above [Intension = β_0 + (β_1 * social norms) + (β_2 * Conscientiousness) + (β_2 * social norms * Conscientiousness)], R^2 = .321, with the moderator hypotheses explaining 32.1% of the intention variation.

To further test the moderator role of conscientiousness, the high (n=95) and low-conscientiousness groups (n=74) were distinguished using mean conscientiousness score. The behavioral and subjective social-norms scores were significantly associated with chewing intention for the high-conscientiousness group (r=.27 p=.008; r=.416 p<.001), but not for the low conscientiousness analog (r=.159 p=.178; r=.154 p=.191).

DISCUSSION

In this study, we found that social norms, which consisted of subjective and behavioral components, were related to areca quid-chewing intention, and that conscientiousness played the moderator role in the relationship. For the high-conscientiousness group, the perceived social norms were strongly related to the chewing intention, however, this relationship was not significant for the low-conscientiousness analog.

In line with previous studies of cigarette smoking (Eisenberg et al., 2003; Kobus, 2003), there appears to be an association between social norms and areca quid-chewing behavior. In their study, Kobus (2003) found that peers play an important role in determining adolescent smoking behavior. This finding was confirmed in the present investigation. The behavior and attitudes of peers was the most important determinants of chewing intention by comparison to the analogous influence of other relevant groups such as parents and adults. Determination of the positive factors that provide a measure of protection from the strong negative influence of peer pressure remains lacking, however. Elaboration of these relationships is very important and worth further investigation.

Conner and Abraham (2001) have found that conscientiousness plays an important role in determining behavioral intention. In this study, however, it only served the moderator role. Conscientiousness is one of the five dimensions that make up the basic Big-Five personality model (Zillig, Hemenover and Dienstbier, 2002), and it appears reasonable to suggest that highly conscientious individuals are more influenced by social rules. The results of this study supported this proposition, with a significant correlation demonstrated between perceived social and behavioral intention for the high-conscientiousness group, but not for the low-conscientiousness analog.

The theory of planned behavior (TPB) is a popular construct for exploration of the relationship between social norms and behavior (Conner and Abraham, 2001; Fekadu and Kraft, 2002). In this theory, intentions are determined by three variables: attitudes, subjective norms, and perceived behavioral control (Conner and Abraham, 2001). It has also been shown that adolescent intention is influenced more by social norms than personal considerations like attitudes (Fekadu and Kraft, 2002). Further, Conner and Abraham (2001) have found that personality plays an important role in planned behavior. In this study, we advanced and improved the role of personality in the TPB and find the moderator role about the personality.

Most of our subjects reported that they had never tried areca quid, and the behavioral intention was represented rather than the behavior itself. Although it has been demonstrated that intention is highly related to *subsequent* behavior, mediator and moderator variables have been identified in the relationship between them (Sheeran and Abraham, 2002). In future studies, a more sophisticated model should be constructed to better account for the areca quid-chewing behavior.

In the present investigation, we found that personality plays the moderator role in relationship between social norms and chewing intention. The highly conscientious adolescents were more influenced by social norms. It seems reasonable to suggest, therefore, that adolescent self-efficacy training is needed in any abuse-prevention program in order to enhance the capacity to counter social pressures and refuse peer pressure driving initiation of areca-quid chewing.

REFERENCES

Broadwater K, Curtin L, Martz D, et al(2006). College student drinking: perception of the norm and behavioral intentions. *Addictive Behaviors*, 31, 632-640.

Bovier PA, Chamot E, and Perneger TV. (2004).Perceived stress, internal resources, and social support as determinants of mental health among young adults. *Quality of Life Research,*13, 161-170.

Chen X, Stanton B, Fang X, et al.(2006). Perceived smoking norms, socioenvironmental factors, personal attitudes and adolescent smoking in China: a mediation analysis with longitudinal data. *Journal of Adolescent Health,*38, 359-368.

Conner M. and Abraham C. (2001).Conscientiousness and the theory of planned behavior: toward a more complete model of the antecedents of intentions and behavior. *Personality and Social Psychology Bulletin,*27, 1547-1561.

Chu NS.(2001). Effects of betel chewing on the central and autonomic nervous systems. *Journal of Biomedical Science*, 8, 229–236.

Eisenberg ME, and Forster JL.(2003). Adolescent smoking behavior: measures of social norms. *American Journal of Preventive Medicine*, 25, 122-128.

Fekadu Z and Kraft P.(2002). Expanding the theory of planned behaviour: the role of social norms and group identification. *Journal of Health Psychology*, 7, 33-43.

Gosling SD, Rentfrow PJ, and Swann WB. (2003). A very brief measure of the Big-Five personality domains. *Journal of Research in Personality,*37, 504-528.

Gupta PC. and Warnakulasuriya S. (2002).Global epidemiology of areca nut usage. *Addiction Biology,*7, 77–83.

Ko YC, Chiang TA, Chang SJ et al. (1992). Prevalence of areca quid chewing habit in Taiwan and related sociodemographic factors. *Journal of Oral Pathological Medicine,* 21, 261–264.

Kobus K. (2003). Peers and adolescent smoking. *Addiction*, 98, 37-55.

Korotkov D. and Hannah TE.(2004). The five-factor model of personality: strengths and limitations in predicting health status, sick-role and illness behaviour. *Personality and Individual Differences,*36, 187-199.

Li S. M., Yu R. L., Hu H. C. et al.(2003). Areca quid chewing by Taiwanese adolescents: application of the attitudes social influence self-efficacy (ASE) model. *Addiction*, 98, 1723-1729.

Li, S. M., Lin, W. S., Ho, C. C., Lou, Y. J.(2006) The stereotype of the " Taiwanese Style. Taiwan Psychology Association 45th. Taiwan Taipei.

Li S.M., Huang JS, and Wu SC. (2007).The outcome expectancy model for areca-quid chewing behavior. *Addictive Behavior,*32,628-633

Liou M. Y., and Chou P.(2000). Epidemiology of areca nut chewing among adolescent students in Taiwan. *Chinese Journal of Public Health*, 19, 42–49.

Lu CT, Lan SJ, Hsieh CC, et al.(1993). Prevalence and characteristics of areca nut chewers among junior high school students in Changhua county, *Taiwan. Community Dental and Oral Epidemiology*, 21, 370–373.

Oostwee T, Knibbe R and de Vries H.(1996). Social influences on young adults' alcohol consumption: norms, modeling, pressure, socializing, and conformity. *Addictive Behavior*, 21, 187-197.

Roberts BW. and Bogg T. (2004).A longitudinal study of the relationships between conscientiousness and the social-environmental factors and substance-use behaviors that influence health. *Journal of Personality,* 72, 325-332.

Sheeran P and Abraham C.(2002). Mediator of moderators: temporal stability of intention and the intention-behavior relation. *Journal of Personality and Social Psychology,* 29, 205-215.

Wang SC, Tsai CC, Huang ST et al.(2004). Betel nut chewing: the prevalence and the intergenerational effect of parental behavior on adolescent students. *Journal of Adolescent Health,* 34, 244-249.

Zillig LMP, Hemenover SH and Dienstbier RA.(2002). What do we assess when we assess a big 5 trait? A content analysis of the affective, behavioral and cognitive processes represented in big 5 personality inventories. *Journal of Personality and Social Psychology,* 28, 847-858.

In: Men and Addictions: New Research
Author: Lyman J. Katlin

ISBN 978-1-60692-098-5
© 2009 Nova Science Publishers, Inc.

Short Commentary B

MANAGEMENT OF HUMAN IMMUNODEFICIENCY VIRUS AND HEPATITIS C VIRUS CO-INFECTIONS IN DRUG ABUSERS

Jag H. Khalsa and Frank Vocci

National Institute on Drug Abuse, NIH
Bethesda, MD, USA

INTRODUCTION

Substance abuse disorders and consequent infections are among the most significant problems in the world today. This chapter will briefly review the health problems of substance abuse and co-occurring infections such as those caused by the human immunodeficiency virus (HIV) and the hepatitis C virus (HCV) and related issues of clinical management.

Millions of people are addicted to licit and illicit drugs of abuse leading to multiple medical and psychiatric consequences. Worldwide, 135 countries and territories now report injection drug use, with 110 countries reporting HIV and acquired immune deficiency syndrome (AIDS) in drug-using populations [116]. In the United States alone, according to the 2005 National Survey on Drug Use and Health, there are an estimated 110 million Americans 12 years of age and older (46%) who have used at least one illicit drug (e.g., cocaine, heroin, amphetamines, etc.) in their lifetime. Approximately 19 million people used an illicit drug in the month prior to the survey (known as current users) [109]. In addition to the problem of drug addiction, the world also faces the significant problem of infections, including those of HIV, HCV, tuberculosis (TB), sexually transmitted infections (STIs), and others. For example, an estimated 500 million persons in the world are infected with various chronic infections; 170 million of these are infected with HCV and approximately 40 million with HIV. Of the estimated 40 million HIV-infected individuals, 5 million were infected during 2003. An estimated 1 million persons infected with HIV live in the United States. Since 1981, when AIDS was first identified, approximately 1 million Americans have become infected with HIV [115]; about 40,000 new cases of HIV are reported each year in the United States. According to the U.S. Centers for Disease Control and Prevention [33, 34], drug use remains the second most common mode of exposure to HIV among AIDS cases in the US. Through June 1997, AIDS cases related to illicit drug injection represented 32% of total HIV diagnoses. In addition to injection drug use as a factor in initial exposure to HIV, ongoing drug use, correlates of the lifestyle associated with drug abuse, and issues of access and adherence to treatment for drug abuse and its associated medical consequences are other drug-related factors that interact with the onset and course of HIV disease. On the basis of an earlier survey, Sullivan and Fiellin [110] noted that between 1966 and 2003, of the estimated 15 million users of illicit drugs in the United States, approximately 1.0 to 1.5 million of them injected drugs and that injection drug users (IDUs) were at significant risk of contracting HCV and HIV, with IDUs accounting for 60% of new HCV cases and 25% of new HIV infections. They also noted that injecting illicit drugs was a major risk factor for HCV/HIV coinfection, which significantly impacts each disorder's progression. Sexual transmission of HCV is low [44], but HCV and HIV have common routes of transmission and common risk factors. Approximately 4 million persons (1.8% of the U.S. population) are infected with HCV. An estimated 80 to 90% of HIV-infected IDUs are also coinfected with HCV. HCV is one of the most important causes of chronic liver disease, which may result in liver cancer and death. Worldwide, about 1 million individuals die each year from liver disease and/or liver cancer. In the United States alone, an estimated 2% of persons with chronic HCV infection (8,000-10,000) may die from liver cancer annually [41].

In terms of other infections, Western industrialized countries are considered to be relatively free from the endemic foci of hepatitis E virus (HEV) infections. HEV infection is seen in northeast Italy and is more frequent among persons at risk for blood-borne viral infections (5.4% among IDUs and 9.3% among chronic hemodialysis patients) [36].

HIV/AIDS, DRUG ABUSE, MEDICAL CONSEQUENCES, AND INTERVENTIONS

HIV, first identified in 1981, is a blood-borne retrovirus that infects CD4 T-cell lymphocytes and macrophages, causing profound immunosuppression that eventually may develop into full-blown AIDS. The course of HIV infection and the development of AIDS may be further complicated by a variety of metabolic and endocrine abnormalities secondary to the direct toxic effects of HIV, other opportunistic infections (OIs) such as hepatic viral infections, TB, STIs, neoplasms, and complications of drugs used during treatment. HIV/AIDS is diagnosed by laboratory tests such as enzyme-linked immunosorbent assay (ELISA), immunoglobulin G to HIV type 1 (HIV-1), HIV ribonucleic acid (RNA), p24 antigen, and HIV culture assays. In the case of acute HIV infection, 40 to 90% of patients with acute HIV infection or acute retroviral syndrome exhibit symptoms [50]. The time from exposure to symptoms, such as a flu-like syndrome consisting of fever, fatigue, and pharyngitis, is about 2 to 4 weeks, with acute illness lasting for 1 to 2 weeks [88].

The most sensitive test for acute infection is the measure of HIV RNA in serum. Greater than 95% of patients seroconvert in less than six months. Seroconversion may be further accelerated by the genotype present, risky sexual behaviors, illicit drug use, and the presence of other OIs. Other clinical features of acute infection may include decreased CD4 T-cell lymphocytes, increased viral load, and progression to AIDS. In the case of chronic HIV infection, the rate of progression to AIDS is variable and depends on factors such as the use of illicit drugs, OI prophylaxis, and antiretroviral therapy. Without treatment, the median time from initial infection to AIDS is about 8 to 10 years [120]. Both viral load and CD4 cell count are used to assess stage of disease progression and treatment strategy [71]. For approximately 5% of individuals, the disease does not progress to AIDS (known as long-term nonprogressors) [12]; these individuals have a low viral load burden, strong virus-specific immune responses, and moderate viral attenuation [13].

The use of illicit drugs is associated with serious adverse medical and health consequences affecting almost every physiological or biochemical system, ranging from immunologic to cardiovascular to metabolic (nutritional) to hormonal consequences. Similarly, viral infections such as HIV and HCV are also associated with serious adverse medical consequences. The combination of both drug abuse and infection(s) is therefore associated with much more serious adverse health consequences than a single agent alone— be it illicit drug use or an infection. Therefore, the interventions, including prevention as well as clinical management of drug-addicted patients coinfected with HIV and/or HCV must be innovative and effective. For example, since the 1960s, methadone has been very effectively used for the treatment of opiate addiction alone or among HIV-infected heroin/opiate addicts following the emergence of the HIV pandemic in the 1980s. Methadone treatment clearly showed its effectiveness in decreasing opiate use and needle sharing among opiate addicts. Furthermore, methadone use also helped decrease the number of multiple sex partners and the practice of exchanging sex for drugs or money [70, 106] and lowered the incidence and prevalence of HIV infection among opiate injectors [72, 74, 104].

INTERVENTIONS/PHARMACOTHERAPEUTIC MANAGEMENT OF HIV/AIDS

Interventions for HIV/AIDS consist of preventive as well as treatment modalities, including lifestyle and behavioral changes and the use of pharmacotherapies. Prevention needs to be targeted to slow the spread of infection by promoting the use of sterile injection equipment and safer sexual practices (e.g., use of condoms) and discouraging the use of illicit drugs. Treatment of HIV/AIDS may consist of postexposure prophylaxis of acute infection [52]. This has been proven safe and effective for IDUs, especially for drug addicts enrolled in methadone maintenance treatment (MMT) programs [78], and to further prevent the spread of infection. Treatment for drug addiction further improves adherence to antiretroviral therapy and prevention of drug resistance.

Treatment during the acute phase of HIV infection produces a strong HIV-specific response of CD4 cells and undetectable RNA [92]. These patients have fewer OIs and reduced disease progression to AIDS [5]. Pharmacologic treatment of chronic HIV infection in the past consisted of monotherapy with the first antiretroviral drug, zidovudine (AZT). Since then, however, many new pharmacologic agents have become available that have proven very effective. These are known collectively as highly active antiretroviral therapy (HAART) and are summarized in table 1. Briefly, HAART consists of two nucleoside reverse transcriptase inhibitors (NRTIs) combined with a non-nucleoside reverse transcriptase inhibitor (NNRTI) or a protease inhibitor (PI) [118]. In addition, a newer mechanism drug, known as Fusion, is now available to treat HIV/AIDS. It is a novel agent that binds selectively and inhibits fusion of HIV to the CD4 cell [60]. HAART has had a profound impact on the morbidity and mortality of HIV/AIDS [82, 19], decreasing mortality from 29.4 per 100 person-years (PYs) in 1995 to 8.8 per 100 PYs in 1997 [82]. Similarly, the incidence of AIDS-defining illnesses has decreased from 50 per 100 PYs before HAART to 13.3 per 100 PYs after HAART. The effectiveness of therapy is impacted by a number of factors, such as adherence, safe sexual practices, injection of illicit drugs, and side effects (e.g., hypersensitivity, mitochondrial toxicity [hepatic steatosis, lactic acidosis, neuropsychiatric symptoms, metabolic abnormalities]) [118], and drug-drug interactions.

The goals of HAART include longstanding viral suppression, restoration and preservation of immunological function, improved quality of life, and decreased HIV-related morbidity and mortality. The RNA level gauges the success of therapy, with the expectation of a one-log decrease at eight weeks and an undetectable viral load (< 50 copies/uL) at four to six months following initiation of treatment [118]. The best virological response is seen when three or more drugs are used [4]. The risk for OIs such as *Pneumocystis carinii*, *Toxoplasmosis gondii*, or *Mycobacterium avium complex* increases as the CD4 count declines below $200/mm^3$, $100/mm^3$, or $50/mm^3$, respectively, the levels at which primary and secondary prophylaxes should be instituted.

Treatment of HIV infection among IDUs poses a great challenge to clinicians due to reported poor adherence to treatment regimens, engaging in risky and unsafe sexual behaviors, and continuation of injection drug use. However, studies show that HAART is effective among drug abusers who are successfully enrolled in drug treatment programs; thus, substance abuse treatment must become an integral part of HIV management [80, 79], for which compliance to treatment is also significant. One of the complications that can occur in this population is pharmacokinetic drug-drug interactions between antiretroviral medications and opioid agonists such as methadone [54]. Methadone increases the blood levels of oral and intravenous (IV) AZT and decreases its clearance [69] but decreases the blood levels of another NRTI, didanosine (ddl), and stavudine (D4T), suggesting that higher doses of these medications might be necessary in patients on methadone. NRTIs themselves do not alter the levels of methadone [89, 90]. On the other hand, NNRTIs, which induce the cytochrome P450 enzyme, significantly decrease blood levels of methadone, requiring increased methadone doses to prevent opiate withdrawal [18, 17]. The co-administration of methadone, a PI, and two other NRTI antiretrovirals leads to increased metabolism of methadone, requiring methadone dose adjustment [1]. On the other hand, co-administration of the recently approved drug addiction treatment medication buprenorphine and AZT had no significant effect on any medication, viral load, or CD4 count in HIV/AIDS patients.

Table 1. Drugs Used in the Treatment of HIV Infection

Multi-class Combination Products		
Brand Name	Generic Names	Manufacturer Name
Atripla	efavirenz, emtricitabine and tenofovir disoproxil fumarate	Bristol-Myers Squibb and Gilead Sciences
Nucleoside Reverse Transcriptase Inhibitors (NRTIs)		
Brand Name	Generic Name(s)	Manufacturer Name
Combivir	lamivudine and zidovudine	GlaxoSmithKline
Emtriva	emtricitabine, FTC	Gilead Sciences

Epivir	lamivudine, 3TC	GlaxoSmithKline
Epzicom	abacavir and lamivudine	GlaxoSmithKline
Hivid	zalcitabine, dideoxycytidine, ddC	Hoffmann-La Roche
Multi-class Combination Products		
Brand Name	Generic Names	Manufacturer Name
Retrovir	zidovudine, azidothymidine, AZT, ZDV	GlaxoSmithKline
Trizivir	abacavir, zidovudine, and lamivudine	GlaxoSmithKline
Truvada	tenofovir disoproxil fumarate and emtricitabine	Gilead Sciences, Inc.
Videx EC	Enteric coated didanosine, ddI EC	Bristol Myers-Squibb
Videx	didanosine, dideoxyinosine, ddI	Bristol Myers-Squibb
Viread	tenofovir disoproxil fumarate, TDF	Gilead
Zerit	stavudine, d4T	Bristol Myers-Squibb
Ziagen	abacavir sulfate, ABC	GlaxoSmithKline
Nonnucleoside Reverse Transcriptase Inhibitors (NNRTIs)		
Brand Name	Generic Name	Manufacturer Name
Rescriptor	delavirdine, DLV	Pfizer
Sustiva	efavirenz, EFV	Bristol Myers-Squibb
Viramune	nevirapine, NVP	Boehringer Ingelheim
Protease Inhibitors (PIs)		
Brand Name	Generic Name(s)	Manufacturer Name
Agenerase	amprenavir, APV	GlaxoSmithKline
Aptivus	tipranavir, TPV	Boehringer Ingelheim
Crixivan	Indinavir, IDV,	Merck
Fortovase	saquinavir (no longer marketed)	Hoffmann-La Roche
Invirase	saquinavir mesylate, SQV	Hoffmann-La Roche
Kaletra	lopinavir and ritonavir, LPV/RTV	Abbott Laboratories
Lexiva	Fosamprenavir Calcium, FOS-APV	GlaxoSmithKline
Norvir	ritonavir, RTV	Abbott Laboratories
Prezista	darunavir	Tibotec, Inc.
Reyataz	atazanavir sulfate, ATV	Bristol-Myers Squibb
Viracept	nelfinavir mesylate, NFV	Agouron Pharmaceuticals
Fusion Inhibitors		
Brand Name	Generic Name	Manufacturer Name
Fuzeon	enfuvirtide, T-20	Hoffmann-La Roche & Trimeris

In evaluating supervised HAART in late-stage HIV among drug users, Greenberg et al. [40] found that response to HAART was quite impressive among a sample of treatment-experienced patients in the late stage of HIV infection in residential health care facilities (RHCFs) in New York City. The patients were 42 years old; 58% male; 60% African-American and 31% Hispanic; 57% IDUs; 23% with a history of dementia; 52% HCV antibody seropositive; and 80% on HAART, of whom 18% had lipodystrophy. Of 88 patients on HAART, 52% had a decreased viral load (> ½ log) vs. 13% of 23 not on HAART); a > ½-log viral load increase was seen in 8% and 35%, respectively. IDUs had higher viral loads of HIV and HCV. In a predominantly minority IDU population who were treatment experienced, 50% successfully responded to treatment with supervised therapy. The RHCFs in New York City provide a unique opportunity to examine further factors associated with response to HAART in an environment in which medication administration and adherence are maximized and monitored carefully [40].

HEPATITIS C INFECTION AND DRUG ABUSE

HCV infection is the most common chronic blood-borne infection, affecting approximately 1,8% of the U,S, population. Of the 3.9 million people in the United States who are antibody positive, 2.7 million are chronically infected with detectable RNA. Approximately 40% of chronic liver disease is related to HCV infection, making it the most common cause of chronic liver disease and the major reason for liver transplantation (LT) performed in the United States. An estimated 8,000 to 10,000 persons with HCV-related liver cancer may die each year. A number of clinical and laboratory tests are used for the diagnosis of liver disease, including levels of alanine transaminase (ALT), aspartate aminotransferase (AST), total protein, albumin, and prothrombin time to evaluate hepatic status and ELISA to determine antibody status. ALT levels are also used to select HCV-infected patients for treatment and liver biopsy. But because serum ALT levels have high visit-to-visit variability, multiple assessments must be used to manage HCV-infected individuals [49]. Reverse transcriptase polymerase chain reaction (RT-PCR) test may be used to detect the presence of HCV RNA within one or two weeks of exposure; the less sensitive quantitative tests measure the viral burden in RNA/uL. Later screening for alpha-fetoprotein levels, liver ultrasonography, and liver biopsy may be performed to assess the stage of liver disease. Acute HCV infection is difficult to diagnose since most patients are asymptomatic. During the acute phase of HCV infection, which may last about six weeks, symptoms may include malaise, nausea, right upper quadrant pain, and jaundice; moreover, 75 to 85% of these patients may become chronically infected. During the chronic phase of HCV infection, which may last several decades, symptoms may include nausea, anorexia, myalgia, and arthralgia, with fatigue being the most common complaint. Alcohol use and advanced age accelerate the disease progression of HCV infection, especially among men. Approximately 20% of these chronic patients will develop liver cirrhosis within 20 years, and 1 to 5% of them will die from HCV-related liver cancer. HCV infection is also associated with the development of diabetes mellitus among IDUs [46].

Besides systemic transmission, other routes by which HCV can be transmitted include sexual transmission [45], although rarely [98]; mother-infant (vertical, < 5%) prepartum or postpartum transmission at the age of 1 year; breast feeding; and probably nosocomial transmission [98]. Maternal infection is a prominent source of pediatric HCV infection in Italy. The facts that most mothers (46%) had a history of covert exposure to HCV, probably through percutaneous routes that are no longer operating, and that the number of those with HIV coinfection has decreased suggest that the frequency of pediatric HCV infection could decrease in the future [8]. HCV infection also occurs in children via prenatal transmission [51]. Although HCV infection was largely an asymptomatic condition, more than half of one group of patients had biochemical evidence of ongoing liver damage. Given the chronicity of this infection in the majority of patients and the long-term risks of cirrhosis and hepatocellular carcinoma, children with HCV infection represent a high-risk group worthy of regular followup.

Rapid progress in the treatment of HCV infection has led to highly successful therapies, resulting in viral eradication and sustained viral response (SVR, defined as absence of the viral RNA at the end of treatment and 24 weeks posttreatment) in more than 50% of patients. Despite these advances, subpopulations such as HIV/HCV-coinfected patients, alcohol abusers, and HCV-infected African Americans have reduced rates of treatment response. Use of pegylated interferon (PEG-IFN) with ribavirin improves the response rates in these groups but does not fully ameliorate the response deficit relative to patients enrolled in typical drug registration clinical trials [101].

In general, adequate management of HCV-infected patients has failed primarily because these patients fear liver biopsy and/or IFN therapy and are challenged as a difficult-to-treat population (i.e., HIV/HCV coinfection, drug abuse or chronic alcoholism). A better collaboration between general practitioners and specialists could help improve the management of these patients [81]. The prevalence of dual infections among mentally ill drug users is also quite significant. Among homeless and mentally ill patients in one study, 6.2% of participants (11/172) were found to be HIV positive; 33% (37/114) had evidence of prior exposure to the hepatitis B virus (HBV) and 30% (34/114) to HCV; 44% (50/114) had a positive reaction to either HBV or HCV (strongly associated with injection drug use). Thus, it is important to note that mental health providers should play a proactive role in the identification of health-related needs and assist with access to general health services for persons with severe mental illness [57].

The prevalences of other infections among drug abusers have been reported as follows: herpes simplex virus type 2 (HSV-2), 44.4%; HCV, 35.1%; HBV, 29.5%; HIV, 2.7%; syphilis, 3.4%; chlamydia, 3.7%; and gonorrhea, 1.7%. In one study [48], of the 407 subjects, 62% had markers for one of the sexually transmitted diseases (STDs). HIV infection was associated with African American race, crack cocaine use, and a history of STDs. HBV infection was associated with age > 30 years, injection drug use, needle sharing, history of treatment for drug use, and African American race; HCV infection was associated with age > 30 years, injection drug use, and needle sharing; HSV-2 infection was associated with age > 30 years, female sex, and African American race; and infection with syphilis was associated with a history of STDs. Among a group of U.S. veterans, between January 1992 and May 1997, the prevalence of HCV infection among 350 HIV-infected patients was 33%. HCV-positive patients were older African American IVDUs with HBV infection and abnormal AST levels. Injection drug use and abnormal AST levels were associated with HCV positivity. Length of survival was similar for HCV-positive and HCV-negative patients when analyzed for three different end points: (1) time from diagnosis of HIV to diagnosis of AIDS, (2) time from diagnosis of HIV to death, and (3) time from diagnosis of AIDS to death. Although the prevalence of HCV infection in this population was high, it did not affect HIV progression or survival [105]. Elevated AST levels associated with HCV infection are also found in other populations that are dually infected. HCV prevalence of 54% has been reported among methamphetamine users in Japan, probably because of a high rate of needle and/or syringe sharing. Although the incidence or prevalence of HIV infection was negligible, Wada et al (1999) suggested that the very high rate of needle and syringe sharing could give rise to a significant increase in the HIV rate among drug users in the future [122].

Spontaneous clearance of hepatitis C virus occurs at a higher frequency than previously reported. HCV genotypes 1 and 3 were the most common genotypes in one patient cohort [29]. Keating et al. [53] determined the rate of spontaneous HCV clearance and genotype in an Irish IDU cohort of 496 patients attending five drug treatment clinics from January 1997 to June 2001 in Dublin. All were HIV and HBV negative; 68.8% were male. HCV RNA negativity (viral clearance) was seen in 38% of patients (IDUs), in 47.4% of females and 34.5% of males. Clearance was independent of age or duration of IV drug use. Viral clearance, as defined as two negative consecutive HCV RNA tests performed a minimum of one year apart, was sustained in 82.2% at two-year followup, giving an overall viral clearance of 31.1%. HCV genotypes 1 and 3 were most commonly identified at 48.8% and 48.5%, respectively, in those with chronic HCV infection. From 2001 to 2003, 44% of 404 observed patients had a coinfection; 90% were drug addicts, and most (90.2%) were on HAART, with prevalent HCV genotypes type 1 (44.6%) and type 3 (36.4%). Treatment with PEG-IFN and ribavirin resulted in SVR in 55% of 9 treated patients [29]. The infection may resolve (viral clearance), persist without complications, or cause end-stage liver disease (ESLD). Viral clearance occurs more often in whites and those not infected with HIV. The risk of ESLD is higher for persons 38 years or older at enrollment (3.67%) and who consume more than 260 g of alcohol per week. Although HCV infection could be self-limiting or associated with ESLD, the majority of adults have persistent viremia without clinically demonstrable liver disease [113]. Incidentally, the predictive factors of HCV seroconversion among IDUs are the exchange of syringes and cotton sharing [63]. Raising the dose of IFN from 3 million units (MU) three times a week (tiw) to 6 MU tiw) does not eradicate HCV (stages A thru C) in most HIV-infected patients, even when HIV is well controlled by treatment. HCV viremia and necroinflammation are temporarily suppressed by IFN, but the relevance of these surrogate end points to progression of liver disease and to survival cannot be assessed [84].

HCV subtype distribution may vary among IDUs. In a study by Garcia et al. [30], most IDUs (48%) had HCV subtype 1a, and 16% had HCV subtype 1b, with no difference in HIV subtypes. However, according to a study by Cilla et al. [16], HCV genotype 3a was prevalent in 65% of IVDUs in Spain, whereas genotype 1b was predominant among patients who had received blood transfusions. Patients with genotype 1b were older than those with genotypes 1a or 3a. HCV infection may resolve (viral clearance), persist without complications, or cause end-stage liver disease (ESLD). Viral clearance occurs more often in whites and in those not infected with HIV. The risk of ESLD is higher for persons who are age 38 years or older at enrollment (3.67%) and who consume more than 260 g of alcohol per week. Although HCV infection could be self-limiting or associated with ESLD, the majority of HCV-infected adults have persistent viremia without clinically demonstrable liver disease [113].

COSTS OF HCV INFECTION

Infection-related costs to society could be enormous. For example, in 1995 HCV-associated social and medical costs to included 26,700 hospitalizations and 2,600 deaths in acute, non-Federal hospitals in the United States for liver diseases caused by HCV. The total charges for these hospitalizations were $514 million. In comparison, alcohol-related liver disease (ALD) was associated with 101,200 hospitalizations and 13,400 deaths, at a cost of $1.8 billion. Simultaneous HCV infection and alcohol abuse were associated with younger ages at the time of hospitalization and death compared with HCV or ALD alone. Alcohol abuse (odds ratio [OR], 1.4; 95% confidence interval [CI], 1.2-1.5) and HIV infection (OR, 4.5; 95% CI, 4.0-4.9) were associated with an increased risk of death among those with HCV. Liver transplantation and patient death were associated with the largest increase in hospitalization charges. Major complications of cirrhosis, such as variceal bleeding, encephalopathy, and hepatorenal syndrome, and sociodemographic factors, such as race and lack of health insurance, were also significantly associated with the risk of death and hospitalization charges, which were similar for HCV and ALD. This study provided new estimates regarding the public health impact of HCV for use in health policy decisions and cost-effectiveness analyses of preventive and therapeutic interventions [55]. In an Australian study, the health care costs of HCV infection among IDUs were estimated at $4 billion for 10,000 new HCV infections in IDUs over a period of 60 years, suggesting that there is a pressing need to halt or slow the current epidemic of HCV infection among IDUs on fiscal grounds alone [10]. In a prospective cohort study of 3,730 HIV-infected patients who were longitudinally followed between 1995 and 2000, it was found that nearly half (42.8%) of the cohort was infected with HCV. Between 1995 and 2000, hospitalization rates for HCV-negative patients decreased from 61.9 to 33.9 per 100 person-years (PYs) of followup. For HCV-positive patients, hospitalization rates decreased between 1995 and 1997 from 55.4 to 43.5 per 100 PYs but increased between 1997 and 2000 from 43.5 to 62.9 per 100 PYs. When stratified by diagnostic category, IDU-related complications increased from 13.6 to 18.4 admissions per 100 PYs, and liver-related complications increased from 5.4 to 26.7 admissions per 100 PYs between 1995 and 2000 in HCV-positive patients (p<.001). However, rates for other OIs remained relatively unchanged, with 14.6 to 13.0 hospitalizations per 100 PYs. HCV infection, female gender, African American ethnicity, and CD4 cell count < 50 cells/mm^3 were predictive of hospitalization. In summary, hospitalization rates decreased significantly for HCV-negative patients but increased significantly for HCV-positive patients. Hospitalization rates for IDU- and liver-related complications increased during this time interval in coinfected patients. In the era of HAART, HIV/HCV-coinfected patients are more likely to suffer from higher hospitalization rates, which will require more health care resources [35].

INTERVENTIONS FOR HCV INFECTION

Since there is no vaccine and no postexposure prophylaxis for HCV infection, its management must focus on providing primary prevention efforts such as a safer blood supply in the developing world, encouraging safe injection practices in health care and other settings, and decreasing the number of people who initiate injection drug use [100]. Furthermore, management of HCV infection may consist of lifestyle changes, pretreatment management, and treatment during the acute and chronic stages of infection. Lifestyle changes may include avoiding alcohol, hepatotoxic medications, high-risk sexual practices, and injection of drugs of abuse, most of which may also increase the risk for contracting other OIs such as HBV and HIV, which are known to accelerate the progression of HCV disease. Both injection-related risk factors (e.g., years of injecting drugs, type of drug injected, direct and indirect sharing of injection paraphernalia) and sex-related risk factors (e.g., lack of condom use, multiple sexual partners, surviving gender) are conducive to the spread of HIV, HCV, and HBV. Therefore, programs must be developed to halt the spread of HIV, HBV, and HCV infections. These programs could include referring participants to drug treatment programs and facilitating access to health and social services with culturally appropriate behavioral interventions that target risky behaviors among ethnic and racial minorities, especially women [25].

During the acute phase of HCV infection, which is most often missed, patients may be successfully treated with a combination of PEG-IFN and ribavirin, with undetectable RNA levels at the end of 24 weeks of treatment. During the chronic phase, when the patient has persistently detectable RNA and elevated ALT levels (> 6 months), moderate inflammation, and fibrosis or necrosis on biopsy (necrosis being the gold standard for staging liver disease), pharmacotherapy consists of PEG-IFN alone or, most often, in combination with ribavirin with an SVR. In chronic HCV infection, coinfection with HIV shows a tendency toward a lower, but not significant, response to IFN [6]. On the other hand, viral genotype may have a significant impact on response to therapy. There are at least 6 genotypes and more than 90 subtypes, with 70% of HCV-infected patients in the United States having genotype 1 and the remainder with genotypes 2, 3, and 4. Genotype 1 has a less favorable prognosis and response to treatment. SVR rates have ranged between 42 and 33% with PEG-IFN plus ribavirin against genotype 1, whereas SVR rates against genotypes 2 and 3 have ranged between 79 and 82%. On the other hand, viral loads (RNA levels) of >2 million copies/ml are not responsive to treatment with PEG-IFN and ribavirin. Incidentally, one must be aware of the side effects of therapy, some of which may be quite serious. Although it has been postulated that failure of IDUs to respond to IFN therapy may be related to different genotypes, Soriano et al. [104] analyzed blood samples from 203 coinfected IDUs who did not respond to at least 24 weeks of IFN-based therapies and found that, at baseline, 131 patients had HCV genotype 1, 4 had HCV genotype 2, 52 had HCV genotype 3, and 16 had HCV genotype 4. Changes in HCV genotype were not found in any patient when samples obtained before and after HCV therapy were compared. HCV therapy did not appear to select for IFN-resistant HCV genotypes that might have been present at baseline. Soriano et al [104] concluded that coinfection with distinct HCV genotypes was unlikely in former IDUs coinfected with HIV and did not explain the lower efficacy of HCV therapy in this population. HCV genotype 1 and multiple HCV genotype infections are associated with faster immunological and clinical progression. HIV disease progression differs by HCV genotype and is faster in individuals whose HCV infection involves more than one HCV genotype. The effect of HCV genotype on HIV progression was greater in the pre-HAART era, suggesting that the effectiveness of HAART may diminish the effect of HCV genotype on HIV disease progression [119]. Other factors such as frequent injection drug use, other opportunistic infections, and risky behaviors could further have negative impact on the disease progression and effectiveness of treatment modality. Side effects of treatment may include fatigue, headache, fever, myalgia, bone marrow suppression with pancytopenia, hemolytic anemia, depression, and suicidal ideation and suicide. About 10 to 40% of patients on IFN develop significant adverse neuropsychiatric complications serious enough to discontinue therapy in 5 to 15% of patients. These neuropsychiatric complications can be further exacerbated by injection drug use. Therefore, patients on IFN alone or in combination with ribavirin should be monitored regularly.

DRUG ABUSE AND HIV/HCV CO-INFECTION

How do HIV/HCV-coinfected patients differ from HIV-infected inpatients in the HAART era? HIV/HCV coinfected patients are less likely to be on HAART and are frequently hospitalized with higher CD4 counts for non-HIV-related medical problems, including complications of liver disease [26]. On the other hand, HAART reduces the incidence of death in HIV-infected patients but with variable rates of survival due to HCV infection and drug use. Management of HCV/HIV co-infected patients with HAART needs to be optimized to achieve similar benefits that have been observed among other individuals on HAART [121].

HIV/HCV coinfection is an important and frequent scenario, especially among IDUs. The prevalence rate of both HIV and HCV infections may range from 30 to 90% and the incidence rate from 10 to 30% per year. Higher levels of infections may be associated with longer duration and higher frequency of injecting drugs of abuse such as cocaine, heroin, or both; incarceration; sharing of drug injection equipment; and lack of access to needle exchange programs. Risk of infection is high in the early years of injection drug use, with prevalence levels often 30 to 50% among IDUs who have been injecting for less than 3 years. Although HCV prevalence is high among IDUs in almost all settings, HIV prevalence rates among IDUs vary widely, between 1% among IDUs in some parts of Europe to more than 20% in some cities in the United States [66]. Both injection-related risk factors (e.g., years of injecting drugs, type of drug injected, direct and indirect sharing of injection paraphernalia) and sex-related risk factors (e.g., lack of condom use, multiple sexual partners, survival sex) are conducive to the spread of multiple infections such as those caused by HIV, HCV, and HBV [25]. Since both HIV and HCV have common transmission pathways, HIV/HCV coinfection is quite frequent, with prevalences as high as 90% of HIV-infected IDUs also infected with HCV in some countries in Central, South, and Southeast Asia and Eastern Europe [31, 86, 67]; 50 to 75% in countries in Southeast Asia [114]; 33% in St. Petersburg, Russia [61]; and 50 to 55% in Australia [22]. Recent reports from India show that there are an estimated 5 million people living with HIV infection [116]. HIV/HCV coinfection also is associated with increased incidence of liver disease and mortality [68]. IDUs coinfected with HIV and HCV may also be coinfected with hepatitis GB virus C (GBV-C), although coinfection with GBV-C does not significantly alter clinical presentation, severity of liver disease, HCV viremia, or response to IFN treatment [38]. In addition, HIV/HCV-coinfected IDUs with a homosexual lifestyle may also be coinfected with GBV-C [7]. Coinfection with chronic HBV may also increase the severity of HCV liver disease [126].

In drug abuse treatment programs such as MMT programs, overall HCV prevalence may be as high as 67%, 29% for HIV-1, and a coinfection rate of 26%. The high prevalences of HCV and HIV-1 infections in MMT patients vary by both current age and age at admission to the MMT program. The prevalence of HCV may run as high as 45% in 35- to 39-year-olds to 92% in 45- to 49-year-olds, with a linear relationship between infection seroprevalence and age at admission into MMT programs [83]. This population needs risk reduction education and treatment for HCV and HIV- 1.

The clinical course of HIV and HCV infections may include a number of adverse health effects. Based on analyses of a large cohort of 18,349 veterans, Backus et al. [3] found that HIV/HCV-coinfected patients had very high rates of comorbid conditions that complicate both the pharmacotherapy and clinical course of both infections. About 37% were HIV positive. Compared with patients infected with HIV-alone, HIV/HCV-coinfected patients were older men; were either African American or Hispanic; reported IV drug use as a risk factor for HIV acquisition; and had diagnoses of mental health illness, depression, alcohol abuse, substance abuse, and hard drug abuse compared with patients infected with HIV alone. The authors suggest that optimal models of integrated care should be developed for populations with HIV, HCV, and HIV/HCV coinfection that also need substance abuse treatment or mental health care [3]. Neuropsychiatric consequences of multiple infections among the IDUs may also include: emotional stress, psychological and coping problems (obsessive-compulsive, phobic anxiety, paranoid ideation, psychoticism) and less fighting spirit, hopelessness and anxious preoccupation towards illness. Routine assessment of psychosocial variables and coping mechanisms should be integrated into all HCV and HIV services, especially those dedicated to treatment of patients with substance abuse, as a vulnerable segment of the population at risk for life-threatening physical illness such as HCV and HIV infections [39]. In addition, these HIV+/HCV+ co-infected patients are significantly more likely to have had past opiate or cocaine or stimulant dependence; have significantly greater rates of past substance-induced major depression; are impaired neurocognitively, have impaired executive functioning, and higher perseveration. Impaired cognitive function appears to be associated with serology (HCV viral load) rather than liver disease severity. The HCV+ patients also have higher degree of HIV-associated dementia. Overall, neuropsychiatric impact of HCV is significant among those who also have advanced HIV/AIDS disease [95]. Prevalence of HIV, HCV, and hepatitis B infections among the mentally ill patients may be as high as 8 times the estimated US population, and that of HIV and HCV may be as high as 11 times the US population [93]. In a small sample of mentally ill homeless patients (n=114), Klinkenberg et al. [57] found 6.2% of the patients had HIV, 33% had HBV, 30% had HCV, and 44% had dual infections of HIV and HCV and injection drug use.

Morbidity and mortality associated with HIV and HCV infections are significant. Based on data available on 864 of 964 registered deaths in France in the year 2000, the underlying causes of death were non-AIDS-defining malignancies (36 cases, 24%), mainly due to lung cancer (16 cases); hepatocarcinoma (7 cases); anorectal carcinoma (3 cases); AIDS-defining malignancies (22 cases, 15%), mainly due to non-Hodgkins lymphoma (10 cases) and uterine cancer (3 cases); cardiovascular diseases (22 cases, 15%); post-HCV hepatic failure (16 cases, 11%); suicide (16 cases, 11%); and bacterial infections (14 cases, 9%). When comparing characteristics of death in the 149 responders vs. the 715 other patients, treatment responders were significantly more frequently coinfected with HCV (45 vs. 33%) and injection drug addicts (40 vs. 27%), alcoholics (38 vs. 28 %), and dyslipidemics (19 vs. 11%). In 2000 approximately 20% of registered deaths of HIV patients in France occurred among immunovirologic responders. It was suggested that, to further reduce mortality among such efficiently treated patients, attention should be focused on treatable conditions such as HCV infection and dyslipidemia and on the prevention of malignancies such as lung cancer and cervical or anorectal carcinoma [65]. Salmon-Ceron et al. [96] also analyzed data from 185 French hospital departments involved in HIV/AIDS management and found that, among 822 HIV-infected patients, 29% were infected by HCV alone, 8% by HBV alone, and 4% by both HCV and HBV. The most frequent causes of death were liver disease (31% of cases) and AIDS (29%) among HIV/HCV-coinfected patients and AIDS (38%) and liver disease (22%) among HIV/HBV-coinfected patients. Liver disease was a more frequent cause of death among patients coinfected by both HCV and HBV (44% of cases). Hepatocellular carcinoma was present in 15% of patients who died from liver disease and was associated with HBV coinfection. Nearly half of the patients who died from liver disease had CD4 levels of more than 200 mm^3. The risk of death from liver disease was the highest in patients coinfected by both HCV and HBV. Other complications may include cutaneous condition such as porphyria cutanea tarda [23].

HIV/HCV COINFECTION PROGRESSION

HIV/HCV coinfection worsens the outcome of chronic HCV infection, increasing both the serum HCV RNA level and liver damage and decreasing the SVR to IFN therapy. Age and alcohol use appear to be the cofactors associated with cirrhosis and mortality. Alcohol consumption of > 50 g/day (four or five drinks) is also a risk factor for liver disease progression among patients with HIV/HCV coinfection. In addition, alcohol-induced cirrhosis can result in changes in drug metabolism in the liver through compromised liver function [58]. IFN therapy has a protective effect against HCV-related cirrhosis regardless of a patient's HIV status [20]. HIV infection that is not treated early is associated with higher HCV viremia and more severe liver injury in IVDUs with chronic hepatitis C [99]. However, HIV/HCV coinfection does not compromise liver histological response to IFN therapy in patients with chronic HCV infection. The rate of histological response between HIV-positive and HIV-negative patients remains in the range of 36 to 40% and at 25% among IFN nonresponders, regardless of their HIV status. In HIV-positive patients, the CD4 cell count did not influence the histological response. In HIV/HCV-coinfected patients treated with IFN, liver histological improvement is frequently observed, similar to that observed in HIV-negative patients. Such beneficial effect of IFN therapy supports early treatment of chronic HCV infection in HIV-infected patients [21].

Although there is evidence of an accelerated progression of hepatic fibrosis in HIV-positive patients with chronic HCV infection, it is not clear whether HCV influences HIV-1 disease progression. HCV does not influence HIV RNA but may be associated with a poor immunologic outcome in HIV-infected persons and may act as a direct cofactor for HIV disease progression. If so, treatment of chronic HCV infection might indirectly benefit HIV disease [15]. Chronic HCV infection also accelerates the course of liver disease in HIV-infected IDUs, leading to cirrhosis and liver failure in a short period of time. Decompensated liver disease (encephalopathy, ascites, jaundice), or complications directly related to it (gastrointestinal bleeding, hepatorenal syndrome, peritonitis) were seen in 8.6% of 1670 hospital admissions. About 25% of the patients had two or more re-admissions. According to Soriano et al. [103], HCV alone or in combination with other hepatotropic viruses was involved in 93 (88.6%) patients admitted for chronic virus-related liver disease (CVLD), which also represents an important cause of hospital admission and death in HIV-infected drug users [103]. Furthermore, HCV-positive patients remain at increased risk for death and hospitalization post-HAART even after additional adjustment for antiretroviral use and time-updated CD4 cell and viral load measures. Deaths and hospitalizations in HCV-positive patients are primarily for non-AIDS-defining infections and complications of injection drug use. It seems that HIV/HCV coinfection and comorbidity associated with injection drug use reduces the realization of substantial health benefits associated with HAART [56].

TREATMENT OF IDUs COINFECTED WITH HCV

Clinical management of a single infection is relatively simple, with a multitude of anti-infective agents (antibiotics against bacterial infections or antiviral agents against viral infections) available in the drug armamentarium. However, clinical management of multiple infections such as HIV, HCV, and others poses a major problem when patients are also addicted to multiple drugs of abuse. For example, how does one treat a patient who is infected with multiple infections such as HIV, HCV, TB, and STDs; is addicted to opiates, cocaine, amphetamines, tobacco, and alcohol; is homeless; and possibly has other comorbid psychiatric complications? In 1997 a National Institutes of Health (NIH) consensus statement on management of HCV recommended that IDUs should have a period of abstinence from illicit drug use for 6 to 12 months prior to HCV treatment [76]. By 2002 NIH consensus panel recommendations shifted, stating that individuals with active injection drug use *could* be considered for HCV treatment [75, 97]. These recommendations were further reinforced through recently released American Association for the Study of Liver Disease practice guidelines for the diagnosis, management, and treatment of HCV [107], which state that treatment of HCV infection *should not be withheld* from IDUs or those who are on an MMT program regimen, provided they wish to take HCV treatment, are able to maintain close monitoring, and practice contraception. In addition to these guidelines, recent studies by Edlin et al. [24], Sylvestre [111] and others presented at a NIH workshop on hepatitis C and substance abuse held in Washington, D.C., in October 2003 [59] further show that drug addicts infected with multiple infections can be successfully treated. In addition, HCV treatment is rare in HIV/HCV-coinfected patients, especially in nonwhite urban poor individuals who are less likely to receive HCV testing and subspecialty referral than their white counterparts. Antibody-negative infection may complicate screening and diagnosis in HIV-infected persons [43].

In general, drug abusers face many challenges in gaining access to health care, including distrust of the health care system, cost of therapy, poor adherence to therapy, physician prejudice, and potential for reinfection from injection drug use. IDUs or HIV-infected patients are less likely to receive pretherapeutic evaluation as well as appropriate antiviral therapy, even after evaluation, compared with others [14]. Adherence is important, but drug use itself does not necessarily predict lack of adherence. HCV-infected IDUs can be stabilized with methadone (or buprenorphine) and treated successfully with PEG-IFN alone or in combination with ribavirin and with adjunct drug addiction services such as behavioral therapy. Taylor et al. [112] describe a typical case that could serve as a model of successful therapy. A 42-year-old man, who entered treatment care, had a CD4 cell count of 78/mL but was reluctant to take many of the available antiretroviral agents. For many years, his periods of sobriety and good adherence to antiretroviral medications were interspersed with relapses to heroin, cocaine, and alcohol use as well as episodes of overdose, major depression with psychiatric hospitalization, incarceration, and discontinuation of antiretroviral medications. After four years of HIV primary care, the patient was stabilized to begin therapy for HCV with PEG-IFN and ribavirin with the support of a multidisciplinary team. After starting treatment for HCV infection, the patient achieved an early virologic response and continues to have an undetectable HCV RNA level by PCR testing and 100% adherence to onsite PEG-IFN injections, with no adverse events related to his addiction or psychiatric symptoms. This case suggests that HIV/HCV-coinfected persons with the common comorbidities of polysubstance dependence and psychiatric illness may effectively and safely undergo pharmacotherapy for HCV infection with the appropriate support. A number of substance abuse treatment programs are available in the United States. Brown et al. [10] showed that these treatment programs present a major intervention point in stemming these epidemics. Currently, these programs vary in corporate structure, source of revenue, patient census, and medical and nonmedical staffing; medical services, counseling services, and staff education target HIV/AIDS more often than HCV infection or STIs. HCV-infected drug addicts in an MMT program can be successfully treated with methadone or naltrexone without any adverse impact on levels of serum transaminases [62].

Many IV opiate users are infected with HCV, but few are treated. Although this complies with various guidelines, virtually no published evidence supports such a recommendation. In a multicenter study, HCV-infected patients in opiate maintenance treatment programs received IFN plus high- or low-dose ribavirin (1,000/1,200 mg or 600 mg). Of the 420 HCV-positive patients, 27 (6%) were enrolled; 393 (94%) either failed to meet the inclusion criteria or refused treatment. Virologic end-of-treatment response was achieved in 12/27 (44%) patients and SVR in 13/27 (48%). Response depends on viral genotype, not ribavirin dose and the two doses of ribavirin do not differ in their side effects. In a small fraction of HCV-infected IVDUs in an opiate maintenance treatment program, antiviral therapy was found to be feasible, safe, and effective. The success rate was comparable to that achieved in controlled studies that excluded drug users [47]. IDUs or those receiving drug dependency treatment can be successfully treated for chronic HCV infection. In other words, HCV-infected drug addicts in an MMT program can be successfully treated with methadone or naltrexone without any adverse impact on levels of serum transaminases [62]. Strategies to improve access to HCV treatment for current and recovering IDUs include the following: drug dependency treatment education and training for hepatologists and other HCV treatment physicians, HCV treatment education and training for addiction medicine physicians, development of multidisciplinary clinics, and peer-based education and support for individuals considering and receiving HCV treatment [22a]. Furthermore, treatment of HIV infection with a combination of two nucleoside analogs alone or with an additional PI significantly increases CD4 cell counts and decreases HIV viral load with no impact on HCV viremia and ALT and AST levels [32].

Despite expedited referrals for HCV care, only a few participants receive an evaluation, and far fewer are treated. Furthermore, gender (male sex), poor immune system (lowest level of CD4+ lymphocytes), and highest viral load are significantly correlated with liver disease progression [94]. In addition, high HCV RNA levels are associated with a poor response to treatment of chronic HCV infection, but a substantial reduction in HCV RNA level results in a favorable treatment response. Older age, alcohol use, and coinfection with HIV are predictors of higher HCV RNA levels among drug users [27]. Because increasingly effective treatment is available, better methods must be developed to improve the evaluation and treatment of HCV-infected drug users, including those coinfected with HIV [28]. In an Italian study, Rezza et al. [91] showed that among IDUs attending one of three drug treatment centers in Naples, none of the initially noninfected participants seroconverted for HIV, whereas the HCV infection rate was approximately 29 per 100 PYs. Age (being older than 28 years) and injecting cocaine were associated with HCV seroconversion. The protective role of methadone treatment was marginally significant.

In addition to pharmacologic treatment for HCV-related liver disease, LT is being evaluated as a therapeutic option for HIV-infected patients with end-stage liver disease (ESLD), but experience is still scarce. Orthotopic LT is a safe therapeutic option in the short term for HIV-infected persons with ESLD, including patients with a history of drug abuse. An antiretroviral regimen consisting of three nucleosides could be used to avoid interactions with immunosuppressive drugs [73]. Although LT is still an experimental therapy with limited worldwide experience and little long-term survival data, it is an acceptable therapeutic option in selected patients such as HIV-infected patients also infected with HBV or other causes of chronic liver disease. Longer followup in large series is needed before a conclusive directive could be provided for HIV/HCV-coinfected patients requiring LT [77].

Unfortunately, vaccination is not available for HIV or HCV infection. However, HBV vaccination of IDUs can be strongly recommended since it shows good adherence in a population that is difficult to treat and can have a leading role in reducing HBV infection among IDUs and their contacts [64]. Vaccinating heroin users against HBV may help to create a stronger prohealth attitude among heroin users, leading to a reduction in HCV risk behavior [85].

Despite drug users being at high risk for HCV infection, many are uninformed or misinformed about the virus and its associated consequences. Based on an evaluation of 246 drug treatment programs nationwide that provide HCV education, Strauss et al. [108] found that, compared with drug-free programs, MMT programs cover a significantly greater number of HCV-related and other specific topics (e.g., how to avoid transmitting HCV, the importance of testing for HCV, treatment options if HCV positive). However, fewer than three-quarters of drug-free programs address what to do if one is coinfected with HIV and HCV and how to maintain health if one is HCV positive, and only about half of the drug-free and MMT programs educate HCV-positive patients about the importance of obtaining vaccinations against the hepatitis A virus and HBV. Drug treatment programs need to educate patients about the proactive steps these individuals can take to deal with HCV, provide critically needed HCV services, and encourage patients to make full use of these services [108]. Astone et al. [2] reported that some programs that are about 4.5 times more likely to provide HCV education to all patients if they dispense methadone; almost 4 times more likely to provide this service if they educate most of their staff about HCV; 2 times more likely if they are residential programs; and almost 2 times more likely if they conduct HIV testing onsite, suggesting a need to increase HCV educational services in drug treatment programs [2]. Although only 34% of 110 opiate-dependent patients being treated in an opiate dependence program in San Francisco knew about HCV treatment, 54% of the sample became "definitely interested" in HCV treatment after hearing about the risks and benefits. Men were five times more likely than women to know of some HCV treatment. Whites were seven times and Latinos were about six times more likely than African Americans to know about HCV treatment. In general, MMT programs could play an important role in increasing access to HCV treatment through educating patients about treatment options [123]. This suggests that education programs need to be established to educate the patients about the dangers of substance abuse and co-occurring infections and health care providers, infectious disease specialists and hepatologists about the knowledge of drug addiction, and psychiatrists and others about the knowledge of infections.

CONCLUSIONS

The literature reviewed in this chapter suggests that there are millions of people who use drugs of abuse and who are coinfected with multiple infections having significant and serious morbidity and mortality and immunologic, neuropsychiatric, and hepatic complications, including death from liver cancer. There was an earlier perception among infectious disease clinicians and/or hepatologists that drug addicts with infections, including HIV and HCV, are difficult to treat. Significant barriers to treatment exist at the level of the treatment system, the treating physician, and the infected patient. However, research shows that drug addicts who are enrolled in drug treatment programs using methadone maintenance and buprenorphine, if closely monitored for adherence and compliance to treatment regimens, can be successfully treated with expensive but effective antiretroviral therapies.

REFERENCES

[1]   Akerele E.O.; Levin F.; Nunes E.; Brady R.; Kleber H. (2002). Effects of HIV triple therapy on methadone levels. *Am. J. Addict,* 11, 308-314.

[2]   Astone J.; Strauss S.M.; Vassilev Z.P.; Des Jarlais D.C. (2003). Provision of hepatitis C education in a nationwide sample of drug treatment programs. *J. Drug Educ,* 33(1), 107-17.

[3]   Backus L.I.; Boothroyd D.; Deyton L.R. (2005). HIV, hepatitis C and HIV/hepatitis C virus co-infection in vulnerable populations. *AIDS,* Oct;19 Suppl 3, S13-9.

[4]   Baxter J.D.; Mayers D.L.; Wentworth D.N.; et al. (2000). A randomized study of antiretroviral management based on plasma genotype antiretroviral resistance testing in patients failing therapy. CPCRA 046 Study team for the Terry Beirn Community Programs for Clinical Research on AIDS. *AIDS,* 14, f83-93.

[5]   Berrey M.M., Schacker T.; Collier A.C.; et al. (2001). Treatment of primary human immunodeficien;y virus type 1 infection with potent antiretroviral therapy reduces frequency of rapid progression to AIDS. *J. Infec. Dis,* 183, 1466-1475.

[6]   Boldorini R.; Vigano P.; Monga G.; Nebuloni M.; Cargnel A.; Gubertini G.; Migliaretti G.; Costanzi G. (1997). Hepatic histology of patients with HIV infection and chronic hepatitis C treated with interferon. *J. Clin. Pathol,* 50(9), 735-40.

[7]   Bonacini M.; Qian D.; Govindarajan S.; Valinluck B. (1998). Prevalence of hepatitis G virus RNA in the sera of patients with HIV infection. *J. Acquir. Immune Defic. Syndr. Hum. Retrovirol.,* 19(1), 40-3.

[8]   Bortolotti F.; Iorio R.; Resti M.; Verucchi G.; Giacchino R.; Vegnente A.; Vajro P.; Marazzi M.G.; Marcellini M.; Barbera C.; Zuin G.; Zancan L.; Maggiore G. (2001). An epidemiological survey of hepatitis C virus infection in Italian children in the decade 1990-1999. *J. Pediatr. Gastroenterol. Nutr,* 32(5), 562-6.

[9]   Broers B.; Junet C.; Bourquin M.; Deglon J.J.; Perrin L.; Hirschel B. (1998). Prevalence and incidence rate of HIV, hepatitis B and C among drug users on methadone maintenance treatment in Geneva between 1988 and 1995. *AIDS,* 12(15), 2059-66.

[10] Brown K.; Crofts N. (1998). Health care costs of a continuing epidemic of hepatitis C virus infection among injecting drug users. *Aust. N. Z. J. Public Health*, 22(3 Suppl), 384-8.

[11] Brown L.S. Jr.; Kritz S.A.; Goldsmith R.J.; Bini E.J.; Rotrosen J.; Baker S.; Robinson J.; McAuliffe P. (2006). Characteristics of substance abuse treatment programs providing services for HIV/AIDS, hepatitis C virus infection, and sexually transmitted infections: The National Drug Abuse Treatment Clinical Trials Network. *J. Subst. Abuse Treat*, 30(4), 315-21.

[12] Buchbinder S.P.; Katz M.H.; Hessol N.A.; O'malley P.M.; Holmberg S.D. (1994). Long-term HIV-1 infection without immunologic progression. *AIDS*, 8, 1123-1128.

[13] Cao Y.; Qin L.; Zhang L.; Safrit J.; Ho D.D. (1995). Virologic and immunologic characterization of long-term survivors of human immunodeficiency virus type 1 infection. *New Engl. J. Medicine*, 332, 201-208.

[14] Cacoub P.; Goderel I.; Morlat P.; Sene D.; Myers R.P.; Alric L.; Loustaud-Ratti V.; Melin P.; Limal N.; Ouzan D.; Perronne C.; Carrat F. (2005). The GERMIVIC Group. Management of chronic hepatitis C in French departments of internal medicine and infectious diseases. *Epidemiol. Infect*, 133(2), 305-14.

[15] Carlos Martin J.; Castilla J.; Lopez M.; Arranz R.; Gonzalez-Lahoz J.; Soriano V. (2004). Impact of chronic hepatitis C on HIV-1 disease progression. *HIV Clin. Trials*, 5(3), 125-31.

[16] Cilla G.; Garcia-Bengoechea M.; Perez-Trallero E.; Montalvo I.; Vicente D.; Arenas J.I. (1996). Genotyping of hepatitis C virus isolates from Basque Country, Spain. *Epidemiol. Infect*, 117(3), 533-6.

[17] Clarke S.M.; Mulcahy F.M.; Tija J.; et al. (2001). The pharmacokinetics of methadone in HIV-positive patients receiving the non-nucleoside reverse transcriptase inhibitor efavirenz. *Br. J. Clin. Pharmacol*, 51, 213-217.

[18] Clarke S.M.; Mulcahy F.M..; Tija J.; et al. (2001). The pharmacokinetic interactions of nevirapine and methadone and guidelines for the use of Nevirapine to treat injection drug users. *Clin. Infect. Dis*, 33, 1595-1597.

[19] Detels R.; Munoz A.; McFarlane G.; et al. (1998). Effectiveness of potent antiretroviral therapy on time to AIDS and death in men with known HIV infection duration. Multicenter AIDS Cohort Study Investigators. *JAMA*, 280, 1497-1503.

[20] Di Martino V.; Rufat P.; Boyer N.; Renard P.; Degos F.; Martinot-Peignoux M.; Matheron S.; Le Moing V.; Vachon F.; Degott C.; Valla D.; Marcellin P. (2001). The influence of human immunodeficiency virus coinfection on chronic hepatitis C in injection drug users: a long-term retrospective cohort study. *Hepatology*, 34(6), 1193-9.

[21] Di Martino V.; Thevenot T.; Boyer N.; Cazals-Hatem D.; Degott C.; Valla D.; Marcellin P. (2002). HIV coinfection does not compromise liver histological response to interferon therapy in patients with chronic hepatitis C. *AIDS*, 16(3), 441-5.

[22] Dore G.J.; Law M.; MacDonald M.; Kaldor J.M. (2003). Epidemiology of hepatitis C virus infection in Australia. J Clin Virol, 26(2), 171-84. [22.a.] Dore G.J.; Thomas D.L. (2005). Management and treatment of injection drug users with hepatitis C virus (HCV) infection and HCV/human immunodeficiency virus coinfection. *Semin. Liver Dis*, 25(1), 18-32.

[23] Drobacheff C.; Derancourt C.; Van Landuyt H.; Devred D.; de Wazieres B.; Cribier B.; Rey D.; Lang J.M.; Grosieux C.; Kalis B.; Laurent R. (1998). Porphyria cutanea tarda

associated with human immunodeficiency virus infection, *Eur. J. Dermatol,* 8(7), 492-6.

[24] Edlin B.R.; Kresina T.F.; Raymond D.B.; Carden M.R.; Gourevitch M.N.; Rich J.D.; Cheever L.W.; Cargill V.A. (2005). Overcoming barriers to prevention, care, and treatment of hepatitis C in illicit drug users, *Clin. Infect. Dis,* 40 (suppl 5), s276-s285)

[25] Estrada A.L. (2002). Epidemiology of HIV/AIDS, hepatitis B, hepatitis C, and tuberculosis among minority injection drug users, *Public Health Rep,* 117 Suppl 1, S126-34.

[26] Falusi O.M.; Pulvirenti J.; Sarazine J.; Shastri P.; Gail C.; Glowacki R. (2003). HIV-infected inpatients in the HAART era: how do hepatitis C virus coinfected patients differ? *AIDS Patient Care STDS,* 17(1), 13-6.

[27] Fishbein D.A.; Lo Y.; Netski D.; Thomas D.L.; Klein R.S. (2006). Predictors of hepatitis C virus RNA levels in a prospective cohort study of drug users, *J. Acquir. Immune Defic. Syndr,* 41(4):471-6.

[28] Fishbein D.A.; Lo Y.; Reinus J.F.; Gourevitch M.N.; Klein R.S. (2004). Factors associated with successful referral for clinical care of drug users with chronic hepatitis C who have or are at risk for HIV infection, *J. Acquir. Immune Defic. Syndr,* 37(3), 1367-75.

[29] Francisci D.; Valente M.; Di Candilo F.; Sfara C.; Conte M.E.; Canovari B.; Baldelli F.; Stagni G. Epidemiological, clinical and therapeutical aspects of HIV/HCV coinfection in a series of HIV seropositive Umbrian patients, *Recenti. Prog. Med,* 95(11), 521-4.

[30] Garcia F.; Roldan C.; Garcia F. Jr.; Hernandez J.; Garcia-Valdecasas J.; Bernal M.C.; Piedrola G.; Maroto M.C. (1998). Subtype distribution among intravenous drug users with chronic type C hepatitis in southern Spain, *Microbios,* 95(380), 15-24.

[31] Garfein R.S.; Doherty M.C.; Monterroso E.R.; Thomas D.L.; Nelson K.E.; Vlahov D. (1998). Prevalence and incidence of hepatitis C virus infection among young adult injection drug users, *J. Acquir. Immune Defic. Syndr. Hum. Retrovirol,* 18(suppl 1), 11-19.

[32] Gayle H. (2000). An overview of the global HIV/AIDS epidemic, with a focus on the United States, *AIDS.* 14(supplement 2), S8-S17.

[33] Gavazzi G.; Richallet G.; Morand P.; Bouchard O.; Bosseray A.; Leclercq P.; Micoud M. (1998). Effects of double and triple antiretroviral agents on the HCV viral load in patients coinfected with HIV and HCV, *Pathol. Biol.* (Paris). 46(6), 412-5.

[34] Gayle H.D.; Hill G.L. (2001). Global impact of human immunodeficiency virus and AIDS. *Clin. Microbiol. Rev,* 14(2), 327-335.

[35] Gebo K.A.; Diener-West M.; Moore R.D. (2003). Hospitalization rates differ by hepatitis C satus in an urban HIV cohort, *J. Acquir. Immune Defic. Syndr,* 34(2), 165-73.

[36] Gessoni G.; Manoni F. (1996). Hepatitis E virus infection in north-east Italy: serological study in the open population and groups at risk, *J. Viral Hepat,* 3(4), 197-202.

[37] Gjeruldsen S.R.; Myrvang B.; Opjordsmoen S. (2003). A 25-year follow-up study of drug addicts hospitalised for acute hepatitis: present and past morbidity, *Eur. Addict. Res,* 9(2), 80-6.

[38] Goeser T.; Seipp S.; Wahl R.; Muller H.M.; Stremmel W.; Theilmann L. (1997). Clinical presentation of GB-C virus infection in drug abusers with chronic hepatitis C, *J. Hepatol,* 26(3), 498-502.

[39] Grassi L.; Satriano J.; Serra A.; Biancosino B.; Zotos S.; Sighinolfi L.; Ghinelli F. (2002). Emotional stress, psychosocial variables and coping associated with hepatitis C virus and human immunodeficiency virus infections in intravenous drug users, *Psychother Psychosom,* 71(6), 342-9.

[40] Greenberg B.; Berkman A.; Thomas R.; Hoos D.; Finkelstein R.; Astemborski J.; Vlahov D. (1999). Evaluating supervised HAART in late-stage HIV among drug users: a preliminary report, *J. Urban Health,* 76(4), 468-80.

[41] Gunn R.A.; Murray P.J.; Ackers M.L.; Hardison W.G.; Margolis H.S. (2001). Screening for chronic hepatitis B and C virus infections in an urban sexually transmitted disease clinic: rationale for integrating services, *Sex Transm. Dis,* 28(3), 166-70.

[42] Hagan H.; Des Jarlais D.C. (2000). HIV and HCV infection among injecting drug users. *Mt. Sinai. J. Med,* 67(5-6), 423-8.

[43] Hall C.S.; Charlebois E.D.; Hahn J.A.; Moss A.R.; Bangsberg D.R. (2004). Hepatitis C virus infection in San Francisco's HIV-infected urban poor, *J. Gen. Intern. Med,* 19(4), 357-65.

[44] Hammer G.P.; Kellogg T.A.; McFarland W.C.; Wong E.; Louie B.; Williams I.; Dilley J.; Page-Shafer K.; Klausner J.D. (2003). Low incidence and prevalence of hepatitis C virus infection among sexually active non-intravenous drug-using adults, San Francisco, 1997-2000, *Sex Transm. Dis,* 30(12), 919-24.

[45] Hershow R.C.; Kalish L.A.; Sha B.; Till M.; Cohen M. (1998). Hepatitis C virus infection in Chicago women with or at risk for HIV infection: evidence for sexual transmission, *Sex Transm. Dis,* 25(10), 527-32.

[46] Howard A.A.; Klein R.S.; Schoenbaum E.E. (2003). Association of hepatitis C infection and antiretroviral use with diabetes mellitus in drug users, *Clin. Infect. Dis,* 36(10), 1318-23.

[47] Huber M.; Weber R.; Oppliger R.; Vernazza P.; Schmid P.; Schonbucher P.; Bertisch B.; Meili D.; Renner E.L. (2005). Interferon alpha-2a plus ribavirin 1,000/1,200 mg versus interferon alpha-2a plus ribavirin 600 mg for chronic hepatitis C infection in patients on opiate maintenance treatment: an open-label randomized multicenter trial, *Infection,* 33(1), 25-9.

[48] Hwang L.Y.; Ross M.W.; Zack C.; Bull L.; Rickman K.; Holleman M. (2000). Prevalence of sexually transmitted infections and associated risk factors among populations of drug abusers, *Clin. Infect. Dis,* 31(4), 920-6.

[49] Inglesby T.V.; Rai R.; Astemborski J.; Gruskin L.; Nelson K.E.; Vlahov D.; Thomas D.L. (1999). A prospective, community-based evaluation of liver enzymes in individuals with hepatitis C after drug use, *Hepatology,* 29(2), 590-6.

[50] Kahn J.O.; Walker B.D. (1998). Acute human immunodeficiency virus type 1 infection. *N. Engl. J. Med,* 339, 33-39.

[51] Karim B.; Alex G.; Smith A.L.; Hardikar W. (2000). Hepatitis C infection in children: a Melbourne perspective, *J. Paediatr. Child Health,* 36(4), 385-8.

[52] Katz M.H.; Gerberding J.L. (1997). Postexposure treatment of people exposed to the human immunodeficiency virus through sexual contact or injection-drug use, *N. Engl. J. Medicine,* 336, 1097-1100.

[53] Keating S.; Coughlan S.; Connell J.; Sweeney B.; Keenan E. (2005). Hepatitis C viral clearance in an intravenous drug-using cohort in the Dublin area, *Ir. J. Med. Sci,* 174(1), 37-41.

[54] Khalsa J.H.; Genser S.; Vocci F.; Francis H.; Bean, P. (2002). The challenging interactions between antiretroviral agents and addiction drugs, *Am. Clin. Lab,* 21(3), 10-13.

[55] Kim W.R.; Gross J.B.Jr.; Poterucha J.J.; Locke G.R. 3rd.; Dickson E.R. (2001). Outcome of hospital care of liver disease associated with hepatitis C in the United States, *Hepatology,* 33(1), 201-6.

[56] Klein M.B.; Lalonde R.G.; Suissa S. (2003). The impact of hepatitis C virus coinfection on HIV progression before and after highly active antiretroviral therapy, *J. Acquir. Immune Defic. Syndr,* 33(3), 365-72.

[57] Klinkenberg W.D.; Caslyn R.J.; Morse G.A.; Yonker R.D.; McCudden S.; Ketema F.; Constantine N.T. (2003). Prevalence of human immunodeficiency virus, hepatitis B, and hepatitis C among homeless persons with co-occurring severe mental illness and substance use disorders, *Compr. Psychiatry,* 44(4), 293-302.

[58] Kresina T.F.; Flexner C.W.; Sinclair J.; Correia M.A.; Stapleton J.T.; Adeniyi-Jones S.; Cargill V.; Cheever L.W. (2002). Alcohol use and HIV pharmacotherapy, *AIDS Res. Hum. Retroviruses,* 18(11), 757-70.

[59] Kresina T.F.; Khalsa J.; Cesari H.; Francis H. (2005). Hepatitis C infection and substance abuse: medical management and developing models of integration, *Clin. Infect. Dis,* 40(5), s259-s262.

[60] Lallezari J.P.; Henry K.; O'Hearn M.; et al. (2003). Enfuvirtide, an HIV-1 fusion inhibitor, for drug-resistant HIV infection in North and South America [comment], *N. Engl. J. Med,* 348, 2175-2185.

[61] Law M.G. (1999). Modelling the hepatitis C virus epidemic in Australia. Hepatitis C Virus Projections Working Group, *J. Gastroenterol. Hepatol,* 14, 1100-1107

[62] Lozano Polo J.L.; Gutierrez Mora E.; Martinez Perez V.; Santamaria Gutierrez J.; Vada S.J.; Vallejo Correas J.A. (1997). Effect of methadone or naltrexone on the course of transaminases in parenteral drug users with hepatitis C virus infection, *Rev. Clin. Esp,* 197(7), 479-83.

[63] Lucidarme D.; Bruandet A.; Ilef D.; Harbonnier J.; Jacob C.; Decoster A.; Delamare C.; Cyran C.; Van Hoenacker A.F.; Fremaux D.; Josse P.; Emmanuelli J.; Le Strat Y.; Desenclos J.C.; Filoche B. (2004). Incidence and risk factors of HCV and HIV infections in a cohort of intravenous drug users in the North and East of France, *Epidemiol. Infect,* 132(4), 699-708.

[64] Lugoboni F.; Migliozzi S.; Mezzelani P.; Pajusco B.; Ceravolo R.; Quaglio G. (2004). Progressive decrease of hepatitis B in a cohort of drug users followed over a period of 15 years: the impact of anti-HBV vaccination, *Scand. J. Infect. Dis,* 36(2), 131-3.

[65] May T.; Lewden C.; Bonnet F.; Heripret L.; Bevilacqua S.; Jougla E.; Costagliola D.; Morlat P.; Salmon D.; Chene G; Groupe d'Etude Mortalite 2000. (2004). Causes and characteristics of death among HIV-1 infected patients with immunovirologic response to antiretroviral treatment, *Presse Med,* 33(21), 1487-92.

[66]   MacDonald M.; Law M.; Kaldor J.M.; Hales J.; Dore G.J. (2003). Effectiveness of needle and syringe programmes for preventing HIV transmission, *Int. J. Drug Policy,* 14: 353-357.

[67]   MacDonald M.A.; Wodak A.D.; Dolan K.A.; van Beek I.; Cunningham P.H.; Kaldor J.M. (2000). Hepatitis C virus antibody prevalence among injecting drug users at selected needle and syringe programs in Australia, 1995-1997. Collaboration of Australian NSPs, *Med. J. Aust,* 172, 57-61

[68]   Mayor A.M.; Gomez M.A.; Fernandez D.M.; Rios-Olivares E.; Thomas J.C.; Hunter R.F. (2006). Morbidity and mortality profile of human immunodeficiency virus-infected patients with and without hepatitis C co-infection, *Am. J. Trop. Med. Hyg,* 74(2), 239-45.

[69]   McCance-Katz E.F.; Rainey P.M.; Jatlow P.; Friedland G. (1998). Methadone effects on Zidovudine disposition, AIDS Clinical Trials Group 262, *J. Acquir. Immune Defic. Syndr,* 18, 435-443.

[70]   Meandzija B.; O'Connor P.G.; Fitzgerald B.; Rounsaville B.J.; Kosten T.R. (1994). HIV infection and cocaine use in methadone maintained and untreated intravenous drug users, *Drug Alcohol. Dependence,* 36, 109-13

[71]   Mellors J.W.; Munoz A.; Giorgi J.V; et al. (1997). Plasma viral load and CD4+ lymphocytesas prognostic markers of HIV-1 infection, *Ann. Intern. Med,* 126, 946-954.

[72]   Metzger D.S.; Woody G.E.; McLellan A.T.; et al. (1993). Human immunodeficiency virus seroconversion among intravenous drug users in- and out-of-treatment: an 18-month prospective follow-up, *J. Acquir. Immune Defic. Syndr,* 6, 1049-56.

[73]   Moreno S.; Fortun J.; Quereda C.; Moreno A.; Perez-Elias M.J.; Martin-Davila P.; de Vicente E.; Barcena R.; Quijano Y.; Garcia M.; Nuno J.; Martinez A. (2005). Liver transplantation in HIV-infected recipients, *Liver Transpl,* 11(1), 76-81.

[74]   Moss A.R.; Vranizan K.; Gorter R.; Bachetti P.; Watters J.; Osmond D. (1994). HIV seroconversion in intravenous drug users in San Francisco, 1985-1990, *AIDS,* 8, 223-31.

[75]   NIH. (2002). National Institutes of Health Consensus Development Conference Statement, Management of Hepatitis C. *Hepatology,* 36 (suppl 1), s3-s20.

[76]   NIH. (1997). National Institutes of Health. Management of hepatitis C. NIH Consensus Statement, available at http://odp.odo.nih.gov/consensus/cons/105/105_intro.htm).

[77]   Norris S.; Taylor C.; Muiesan P.; Portmann B.C.; Knisely A.S.; Bowles M.; Rela M.; Heaton N.; O'Grady J.G. (2004). Outcomes of liver transplantation in HIV-infected individuals: the impact of HCV and HBV infection, *Liver Transpl,* 10(10), 1271-8.

[78]   O'Connor P.G. (2000). HIV post-exposure therapy for drug users in treatment. *J. Subst. Abuse Treat,* 18, 17-21.

[79]   O'Connor P.G.; Molde S.; Henry S.; Shockcor W.T.; Schottenfeld R.S. (1992). Human immunodeficiency virus infection in intravenous drug users: a model for primary care, *Am. J. Med,* 93, 382-386.

[80]   O'Connor P.G.; Selwyn P.A.; Schottenfeld R.S. (1994). Medical care for injection-drug users with human immunodeficiency virus infection, *N. Engl. J. Med.,* 331, 450-459.

[81]   Ouzan D, Cavailler P, Hofliger P, Mamino C, Joly H, Tran A. [Modalities of care in anti HCV positive patients identified in General Medicine in the Alpes-Maritimes district], *Gastroenterol Clin. Biol.* 2003 Apr;27(4):376-80.

[82] Pallela, F.J.; Delaney K.M.; Moorman A.C. et al. (1998). Declining morbidity and mortality among patients with advanced human immunodeficiency virus infection, HIV Outpatient Study Investigators, *N. Engl. J. Med.*, 338, 853-860

[83] Piccolo P.; Borg L.; Lin A.; Melia D.; Ho A.; Kreek M.J. (2002). Hepatitis C virus and human immunodeficiency virus-1 co-infection in former heroin addicts in methadone maintenance treatment, *J. Addict. Dis*, 21(4), 55-66.

[84] Prestileo T.; Mazzola G.; Di Lorenzo F.; Colletti P.; Vitale F.; Ferraro D.; DiStefano R.; Camma C.; Craxi A. (2000). Response-adjusted alpha-interferon therapy for chronic hepatitis C in HIV-infected patients, *Int. J. Antimicrob. Agents*, 16(3), 373-8.

[85] Quaglio G.L.; Lugoboni F.; Pajusco B.; Sarti M.; Talamini G.; Mezzelani P.; Des Jarlais D.C, GICS. (2003). Hepatitis C virus infection: prevalence, predictor variables and prevention opportunities among drug users in Italy, *J. Viral Hepat*, 10(5), 394-400.

[86] Quaglio G.; Lugoboni F.; Pajusco B. (2003). Factors associated with hepatitis C virus infection in injection and noninjection drug users in Italy, *Clin. Infect. Dis*, 37, 33-40

[87] Quaglio G.; Talamini G.; Lechi A.; Venturini L.; Lugoboni F.; Mezzelani P.; Gruppo Intersert di Collaborazione Scientifica (GICS). (2001). Study of 2708 heroin-related deaths in north-eastern Italy 1985-98 to establish the main causes of death, *Addiction*, 96(8), 1127-37.

[88] Quinn, T.C. (1997). Acute primary HIV infection, *JAMA*, 278, 58-62.

[89] Rainey P.M.; Friedland G.; McCance-Katz E.F.; et al. (2000). Interaction of methadone with Didanosine and Stavudine, *J. Acquir. Immun. Defic. Syndr, JAIDS*, 24, 241-248.

[90] Rainey P.M.; Friedland G.; Snidow J.W.; et al. (2002). The pharmacokinetics of methadone following co-administration with a Lamivudine/Zidovudine combination tablet in opiate-dependent subjects, *Am. J. Addict*, 11, 66-74.

[91] Rezza G.; Sagliocca L.; Zaccarelli M.; Nespoli M.; Siconolfi M.; Baldassarre C. (1996). Incidence rate and risk factors for HCV seroconversion among injecting drug users in an area with low HIV seroprevalence, *Scand. J. Infect. Dis*, 28(1), 27-9.

[92] Rosenberg E.S.; Altfeld M.; Poon S.H.; et al. (2000). Immune control of HIV-1 after early treatment of acute infection, *Nature*, 407, 523-526.

[93] Rosenberg S.D.; Goodman L.A.; Osher F.C.; Swartz M.S.; Essock S.M.; Butterfield M.I.; Constantine N.T.; Wolford G.L.; Salyers M.P. (2001). Prevalence of HIV, hepatitis B, and hepatitis C in people with severe mental illness, *Am. J. Public Health*, 91(1), 31-7.

[94] Rubio Caballero M.; Rubio Rivas C.; Egido Garcia R.; Nogues Biau A. (2004). Chronic hepatitis C in HIV co-infected patients. Study of 55 cases with liver biopsy, Med Clin (Barc). 2004 Oct 9;123(12):441-4. Comment in: *Med. Clin. (Barc).* 123(12), 460-2.

[95] Ryan E.L.; Morgello S.; Isaacs K.; Naseer M.; Gerits P. (2004). The Manhattan HIV Brain Bank, Neuropsychiatric impact of hepatitis C on advanced HIV, *Neurology*, 62(6), 957-62.

[96] Salmon-Ceron D.; Lewden C.; Morlat P.; Bevilacqua S.; Jougla E.; Bonnet F.; Heripret L.; Costagliola D.; May T.; Chene G. (2005). Liver disease as a major cause of death among HIV infected patients: role of hepatitis C and B viruses and alcohol, J Hepatol, 42(6), 799-805. Comment in: *J. Hepatol.* 2005 Nov;43(5):911-2; author reply 912.

[97] Seeff L.B.; Hoofnagle J.H. (2003). The National Institutes of Health Consensus Development Conference Management of Hepatitis C 2002, *Clin. Liver Dis*, 7(1), 261-87.

[98] Serfaty L. (1999). Non-transfusional and non-intravenous drug addiction related transmission of hepatitis C virus, *Presse Med,* 28(21), 1135-40.

[99] Serfaty L.; Costagliola D.; Wendum D.; Picard O.; Meyohas M.C.; Girard P.M.; Lebas J.; Delamare C.; Poupon R.; Housset C. (2001). Impact of early-untreated HIV infection on chronic hepatitis C in intravenous drug users: a case-control study, *AIDS,* 15(15), 2011-6.

[100] Shepard C.W.; Finelli L.; Alter M.J. (2005). Global epidemiology of hepatitis C virus infection, *Lancet Infect. Dis,* 5(9), 558-67.

[101] Sherman K.E. (2003). Implications of peginterferon use in special populations infected with HCV, *Semin Liver Dis,* 23 Suppl 1, 47-52.

[102] Smyth B.P.; Keenan E.; O'Connor J.J. (1998). Bloodborne viral infection in Irish injecting drug users, *Addiction,* 93(11), 1649-56.

[103] Soriano V.; Garcia-Samaniego J.; Valencia E.; Rodriguez-Rosado R.; Munoz F.; Gonzalez-Lahoz J. (1999). Impact of chronic liver disease due to hepatitis viruses as cause of hospital admission and death in HIV-infected drug users, *Eur. J. Epidemiol,* 15(1), 1-4.

[104] Soriano V.; Ramos B.; Nunez M.; Barreiro P.; Maida I.; Garcia-Samaniego J.; Gonzalez-Lahoz J. (2005). Failure of hepatitis C therapy in HIV-coinfected drug users is not due to a shift in hepatitis C virus genotype, *J. Infect. Dis,* 192(7), 1245-8.

[105] Staples C.T. Jr.; Rimland D.; Dudas D. (2000). Hepatitis C in the HIV (human immunodeficiency virus) Atlanta V.A. (Veterans Affairs Medical Center) Cohort Study (HAVACS): the effect of coinfection on survival, *Clin. Infect. Dis,* 29(1), 150-4. *Comment in: Clin. Infect. Dis,* 2000 Feb;30(2):409-10.

[106] Stark K.; Muller R.; Bienzle U.; Guggenmoos-Holsmann I. (1996). Methadone maintenance treatment and HIV risk-taking behavior among injecting drug users in Berlin, *J. Epidemiol. Community Health,* 50, 534-7.

[107] Strader D.B.; Wright T.; Thomas D.L.; Seef L.B. (2004). Diagnosis, management, and treatment of hepatitis C, *Hepatology,* 39, 1147-1171.

[108] Strauss S.M., Astone J.M.; Hagan H.; Des Jarlais D.C. (2004). The content and comprehensiveness of hepatitis C education in methadone maintenance and drug-free treatment units, *J. Urban Health,* 81(1), 38-47.

[109] Substance Abuse and Mental Health Services Administration (SAMHSA). (2006). Overview of Findings from the 2005 National Survey on Drug Abuse and Health, Office of Applied Studies, NSDUH Series H-24, DHHS Publications, Rockville, MD.

[110] Sullivan L.E.; Fiellin D.A. (2004). Hepatitis C and HIV infections: implications for clinical care in injection drug users, *Am. J. Addict,* 13(1), 1-20.

[111] Sylvestre, D.L. (2005). Treatment for hepatitis C virus infection among current injection drug users, *Clin. Infect. Dis,* 40 (suppl 5): s321-s324)

[112] Taylor L.E.; Gholam P.M.; Schwartzapfel B.; Rich J.D. (2005). Hepatitis C treatment in an HIV-HCV-coinfected patient with drug addiction and psychiatric illness: a case report, *AIDS Read,* 15(11), 629-31, 634-6, 638.

[113] Thomas D.L.; Astemborski J.; Rai R.M.; Anania F.A.; Schaeffer M.; Galai N.; Nolt K.; Nelson K.E.; Strathdee S.A.; Johnson L.; Laeyendecker O.; Boitnott J.; Wilson L.E.; Vlahov D. (2000). The natural history of hepatitis C virus infection: host, viral, and environmental factors, *JAMA,* 284(4), 450-6; Comment in: *JAMA.* 2000 Nov 22-29;284(20):2592-3.

[114] Thomas D.L.; Vlahov D.; Solomon L. (1995). Correlates of hepatitis C virus infections among injection drug users, *Medicine* (Baltimore), 74, 212-220

[115] United Nations AIDS (UNAIDS). 2003 Report on the global epidemic of AIDS: Executive Summary; UNAIDS/03-20E, English, ISBN 929-1735-116, Joint United Nations Programme on HIV/AIDS/WHO.

[116] United Nations AIDS (UNAIDS). 2006 Report on the global epidemic of AIDS: Executive Summary; UNAIDS/06-20E, English, ISBN 929-1735-116, Joint United Nations Programme on HIV/AIDS/WHO.

[117] United Nations Office on Drugs and Crime. (2002). Global illicit drug trends 2002, New York, NY. United Nations Office on Drugs and Crime.

[118] USPHS/Kaiser. (2003). Guidelines for the use of antiretroviral agents in HIV-infected adults and adolescents. November 10, 2003. Available at http://www.aidsinfo.nih.gov/gudelines/adult/AA_1.11003.pdf

[119] van Asten L.; Prins M. (2004). Infection with concurrent multiple hepatitis C virus genotypes is associated with faster HIV disease progression, AIDS, 18(17), 2319-24.

[120] Vergis, E.N.; Mellors J.W. (2000). Natural history of HIV-1 infection, *Infect. Dis. Clin. North Am,* 14, v-vi, 809-825

[121] Voirin N.; Trepo C.; Miailhes P.; Touraine J.L.; Chidiac C.; Peyramond D.; Livrozet J.M.; Ritter J.; Chevallier P.; Fabry J.; Allard R.; Vanhems P. (2004). Survival in HIV-infected patients is associated with hepatitis C virus infection and injecting drug use since the use of highly active antiretroviral therapy in the Lyon observational database, *J. Viral Hepat,* 11(6), 559-62.

[122] Wada K.; Greberman S.B.; Konuma K.; Hirai S. (1999). HIV and HCV infection among drug users in Japan, *Addiction,* 94(7), 1063-9.

[123] Walley A.Y.; White M.C.; Kushel M.B.; Song Y.S.; Tulsky J. P. (2005). Knowledge of and interest in hepatitis C treatment at a methadone clinic, *J. Subst. Abuse Treat,* 28(2), 181-7.

[124] Williams A.B.; McNelly E.A.; Williams A.E.; D'Aquila R. T. (1992). Methadone maintenance treatment and HIV type 1 seroconversion among injecting drug users, *AIDS Care,* 4, 35-41.

[125] WHO. (2004). World Health Organization Report: Neuroscience of Psychoactive Substance Use and Dependence: Summary, 2004, 1211 Geneva 27, Switzerland; telephone: 41-22-7912470; ISBN # 92-4-159124-2, NLM-WM270.

[126] Zarski J.P.; Bohn B.; Bastie A.; Pawlotsky J.M.; Baud M.; Bost-Bezeaux F.; Tran van Nhieu J.; Seigneurin J.M.; Buffet C.; Dhumeaux D. (1998). Characteristics of patients with dual infection by hepatitis B and C viruses, *J. Hepatol,* 28(1), 27-33.

INDEX

D

I

J

K

L

M

N

O

P

T

U

V